D0881148

Training Needs Assessment

Techniques in
Training and Performance Development
Series

Training Needs Assessment

Allison Rossett
San Diego State University

Joseph W. Arwady
Series Developer and Editor

Educational Technology Publications
Englewood Cliffs, New Jersey 07632

Library of Congress Cataloging-in-Publication Data

Rossett, Allison.
    Training needs assessment.

    (Techniques in training and performance development
series)
    Bibliography: p.
    Includes index.
    1. Training needs. 2. Employees, Training of.
I. Title. II. Series.
HF5549.5.T7R65   1987   658.3'124   87-9070
ISBN 0-87778-195-8

Printed in the United States of America.

Library of Congress Catalog Card Number:
87-9070.

International Standard Book Number:
0-87778-195-8.

First Printing: June, 1987.
Second Printing: December, 1989.
Third Printing: September, 1990.
Fourth Printing: October, 1991.
Fifth Printing: October, 1992.
Sixth Printing: March, 1994.
Seventh Printing: February, 1996.
Eighth Printing: September, 1998.
Ninth Printing: January, 2002.

This book is dedicated, quite simply, to my parents with appreciation for their support.

ACKNOWLEDGMENTS

This book is chock full of people, their stories and their ideas. Some are former and current clients who invited me into their companies. They gave me a chance to learn about training related to fast foods, telephony, shortage control, gas and oil and computerized sales. Others are professional colleagues and friends who knew of my fascination with needs assessment and whispered tales in my ears. All deserve acknowledgment for telling me about their experiences and allowing me to use them here.

I want to express appreciation to Joe Harless, Roger Kaufman, Tom Gilbert, Ron Zemke and Bob Mager. Their work has carved out the area called needs assessment or analysis or front end analysis, creating my desire to work within it as well as a market for my thinking and writing.

I'd like to say thank you to my colleagues and students at San Diego State University. My colleagues in Educational Technology contributed to an environment where I felt personal obligation to develop our profession. I don't think the book would have happened if I hadn't been fortunate enough to come and work in a place with such smart and productive faculty and students.

Generations of students and alumni have endured drafts of these chapters during the years it has taken me to get the book completed. Their comments were useful and pointed. Jan Garbosky often put aside her own work to read chapters and sections. Joe Williams read a final draft of the book. Jan and Joe made wonderful suggestions.

Finally, I'm grateful to a patient editor and cheerleading friends. Nobody hassled me too much when I let priorities other than this book prevail. They had faith that it would get written. And, in fact, the delay is probably for the best. I looked at some notes and materials from 1984, the year I should have completed this book.

The conceptualization in the current book is much, much beyond where I was then. I've learned from the people with whom I've worked in seminars, classes and consultancies. I've profited from the opportunity to do additional research and development. I hope you'll think it was worth the wait.

EDITOR'S PREFACE

If I weren't writing about a book and its author, I'd tell you about Allison Rossett, the person I've come to know over the past four years. Starting with a telephone call to solicit a total stranger's interest in authoring the book, and developing to where I am writing this preface, ours has been one of my most rewarding work partnerships. I think Allison Rossett has the talent and insight to cut across disciplines and become one of a handful of people whose work earns the respect of *separate professional audiences*. She is that good.

To begin with, she knows her subject as well as anyone. Only Zemke and Kramlinger (in *Figuring Things Out: A Trainer's Guide to Needs and Task Analysis*) have accompanied her in the journey from academic blueprint to practitioner's operating table. And no one has dissected the body from so many angles and with such extensive documentation of its many parts.

Training Needs Assessment is a complete book. It frames the subject, fits it snugly in context, and embarks on an intricate description of needs assessment procedures, tools, and techniques. Reading the chapters on extant data analysis, subject matter analysis, and needs assessment, it is difficult to imagine treatments any more stylized, useful, or informative. And one could hardly expect to find a better discussion of observing, interviewing, or questionnaires and surveys in a book *specifically about* data collection. Throughout, an abundance of illustrations and examples parlay the book's conceptual order into an engaging description of how it really happens "out there" in the workplace.

Rossett calls her approach *purpose-based training needs assessment*, perhaps to distinguish it from other approaches that never quite come face-to-face with real performance problems. In *Train-*

ing Needs Assessment, the purpose is clear: work with the "hard core employed" until they confirm that your procedures, tools, and techniques make sense. Then, once you understand their problems, needs, and opportunities, work back through the analysis to structure the solution. Sound simple? It is until you try it in actual operating environments with time constraints and financial targets. Fortunately, that's precisely where Allison Rossett honed her approach.

She is an "insider" who works hard to retain an "outsider's" perspective. Despite fifteen years of work on front-end analysis, she disciplines herself to approach each new project as a curious observer. *Training Needs Assessment* is a testament to both "Rossett the insider," who is intimate with the complexities of needs analysis, and to "Rossett the outsider," who does us all a service by drawing conclusions only after her objectivity is assured.

Some writers thrive on rewording what others have said and laying claim to it as their own. Not Rossett. She is quick to credit those whose work has helped shape *Training Needs Assessment*. Gilbert, Harless, Mager, and many others are cited repeatedly. It is important to her that purpose-based training needs assessment be viewed in context—as a step forward but one that is part of a *performance legacy*.

While Professor Rossett is active as a consultant to agencies and corporations, she maintains that her strength lies in a full-time faculty appointment at San Diego State University. You hear a different level of excitement in her voice when she talks about job placements for her graduates, or recent honors bestowed on a former student. The seasonal preparation of new performance analysts and program designers helps keep her "eye on the ball." Fresh ideas, experimentation, enough distance and time to reflect—these are the ingredients she prizes.

Allison Rossett has poured four years into writing *Training Needs Assessment* and, in four years of editing it, I have been the beneficiary of her efforts. Now, the rest of you can benefit by using it as a guide to understand and respond to performance problems. And even if you simply read it for pleasure and never apply it to your work, I have no doubt that you'll still recognize it as one of the best books ever in the training and performance arena. It's that good.

Joseph W. Arwady

PREFACE

When I started working in this field, both in companies and at universities, the subject of needs assessment lured me most of all. Why that topic? Why not objectives or procedural training or interactive video or transfer of training?

I was attracted to it because it came first. It served as the foundation for the decisions that had to be made by training and development professionals. I also liked it because intriguing questions were asked of varied sources with sometimes enlightening and often ambiguous or controversial results.

The potential range of useful information also suited me. It involved soliciting both the opinions of people and the data that the computer spits out. It presses professionals to dig in files, observe, interview, lead groups, and distribute surveys. Acting like a detective or a dog with the other end of a sock, needs assessment involves professionals in diligent, complex, varied, purposeful activities.

I think I also gravitated to it because I felt needed. From what I could see, practicing and aspiring training professionals launched projects and responded to problems idiosyncratically. While there was lots of verbal support for *analysis, needs assessment and front ending*, there was no agreement on what constituted a good one. The important writings of Robert Mager, Joe Harless, Tom Gilbert, Roger Kaufman and Ron Zemke provided groundwork. Yet, if you presented a group of human resources and training professionals with a typical initiating situation, there was little accord on the particulars of what ought to be done or even on the questions that the effort should answer. The problem was the absence of a sturdy, inclusive way of **thinking about analysis, needs assessment and front ending**.

I've attempted to provide that in this book. I've presented a conceptual model for *front ending*, one which is equally useful for launching a project on office computerization, pizza oven maintenance, the life cycle of lard or manufacturing safety. Those are just the kinds of examples that pepper the book and illustrate what I call *purpose-based training needs assessment*.

In addition to *purpose-based training needs assessment*, the cases, studies, dialogues, exaggerations and models in the book provide exposure to the diverse wonders of professional practice in our field. You'll meet a group of professionals who are struggling to agree upon optimal customer loop design. You will encounter public housing tenants with real live problems with cockroaches. You'll hear people talk to each other, reading the words that a training professional uses in a needs assessment interview for point-of-sales registers. You'll be exposed to the endless challenges that surround performance appraisals. And you'll hear numerous tales about sales—in financial institutions, insurance companies, baseball parks, fast food emporiums and retail computer stores.

This book is for you if . . . .

- you know you want to do a needs assessment but you're not sure how to start, proceed and finish;
- you're not sure if you should be recommending training as often as you are;
- you've been handed a big, murky project and told that the solution needs to be up and running ASAP and you don't know what the solution ought to be;
- the company keeps introducing new technologies and you're supposed to get people *up to speed*;
- you know that front end study is essential but aren't sure what questions to ask and what sources to use;
- you want to do lean analyses but the surveys and interview schedules just keep getting longer and longer;
- you wonder what the difference is between needs assessment, task analysis, critical incident analysis, subject matter analysis . . . and how and when to use them;
- you're eager for another and more robust way of thinking about this topic.

I believe that *Training Needs Assessment* will be immediately useful to **practitioners**. There are descriptions of real problems, tangible suggestions about steps to take to solve the problems and many, many examples of directions, words, phrases, questions, memos and reports. The models will convert into approaches and instruments that you can use today.

I'm also interested in tomorrow. I've tried to write a book that also serves **aspiring** trainers, instructional designers, human resources specialists and instructional technologists. There is selected background literature, detailed examples and juicy descriptions of what goes on in corporate and agency settings.

Needs assessment. Gaps. Surveys. Interviews. Front end analysis. Critical incidents. Supervisors. Ticket sellers. Sales approaches. Harless. Remote sensing. Limp fries. Motivation. Walt the insurance man. Orin the banker. Suzanne. Subject matter analysis. Shortage control. Bob Hobbs. Gilbert. Zemke. Telecommunications. Auto mechanics. Funny money accounts. Optimals. Actuals. Feelings. Causes. Solutions. They're all in the book.

I've tried to write a useful and occasionally entertaining book. You'll let me know if I've succeeded?

Allison Rossett

TABLE OF CONTENTS

Training
Needs
Assessment

Part One: INTRODUCTION

Chapter One: THE TRAINER'S CHALLENGE

Introduction

This is a book for people who are in the business of affecting human performance. These professionals are called trainers, performance technologists, instructional designers, education specialists, training managers, course developers, industrial relations managers, curriculum planners, documentation specialists and instructional technologists.

The book focuses on **one** topic: **training needs assessment, or TNA.** TNA is the umbrella phrase I've coined to encompass activities like analysis, front end analysis, needs assessment, needs analysis, discrepancy analysis, etc. **TNA is the systematic study of a problem or innovation, incorporating data and opinions from varied sources, in order to make effective decisions or recommendations about what should happen next.** Sometimes that recommendation involves training; sometimes not.

While most professionals would agree that they ought to do front end study, there is little agreement on how to do it. Where do you start? What do you say or write or observe? In what order should the study occur? When are you finished? What do you do with what you've learned? The purpose of this book is to describe the way I answer these questions.

The book has three broad goals:

1. to **conceptualize** what we do **before** we train people or recommend non-training solutions;
2. to introduce and use the concepts of **purpose-based TNA** and **stages of assessment** in light of three kinds of challenges;
3. to describe and exemplify specific **steps, tools and techniques** for carrying out TNA.

3

To achieve these goals, the book is divided into four major parts:

Part One: INTRODUCTION

Part Two: TNA TECHNIQUES

Part Three: TNA TOOLS

Part Four: CONCLUSION

In **Part One**, the reader is provided with a very brief review of a systematic approach to training, and to the focal point of the book: TRAINING NEEDS ASSESSMENT (TNA), an umbrella term for what we do to understand performance problems and introduce new systems and technologies. The chapters in Part One introduce TNA as purpose-based assessment.

Three powerful **analysis techniques** are presented in **Part Two**. Extant data analysis, needs assessment and subject matter analysis are described, highlighting their uses in acquiring certain kinds of information about problems and systems.

Part Three presents and clarifies the steps involved in using TNA tools: interviews, observations, group meetings and surveys to gather TNA information. These TNA **tools** are described in detail with examples which illustrate their uses.

The conclusion of this book responds to the person who says, "OK, I now know about the purposes for front end analysis. I am more familiar with a range of analysis techniques and with tools like interviews and surveys. How do I put it all together? What do I do first? next? And when am I finished?" **Part Four** is about planning TNA and then about disseminating the results of your TNA efforts.

The Challenges

What are the kinds of challenges that come across the desk of training professionals? **Just as the nature of the "request for training assistance" or the plea for "HELP!" affects the kind of solution(s) the trainer proposes, it also affects the TNA that should be done.**

Let's look at some typical situations:

• Last year the Speedy corporation spent almost $500,000 on a new shortage control program. However this year's shortage figures are unimproved by this innovation. While theft is a reality of the convenience store business, diligent franchise owners, dutifully implementing the shortage control program, should improve the bottom line. The corporation charges the Training Department: "Teach them this shortage program AGAIN. And get them to use it so we can all benefit from the results."

• Ponce de Leon Inc. manufactures computerized home and hospital life support systems. Acknowledged by the health industry as highly effective but difficult to use and maintain, the continued life of this corporation is threatened. The Technical Support Division is charged with rapidly changing the industry's perception of the Ponce de Leon systems by developing print materials that will make them easier for people to use and maintain.

• Solid Gold, a midwestern bank which was started by former MOTOWN executives, aggressively takes advantage of new regulations in the financial services industry and develops new investment and savings programs for customers. Management wants to be certain that tellers are fully informed about the new financial packages available to customers. The Marketing Vice President leans on the Vice President for Human Resource Development for assistance in developing a solution. The financial products will be available in just over a month. "Everybody has to be up to speed on this."

• Metropolitan Hospital is administered by a group that believes in customer service. Every spring, no matter what, the newest member of the training staff is given the task of setting up and offering telephone training workshops, and every staff member with responsibility for answering phones is expected to attend.

• The telephone company develops a new computer-based technology for diagnosis of residential phone problems from remote locations, without ever leaving the office. This innovation means that thousands of employees will need re-training. What courses? What content? Delivered through what systems? Who gets trained first? Next? Next?

• The company is suffering declining sales. In a competitive business atmosphere, but one full of opportunity for the sale of personal croissant baking machines, Le Perfect Taste is getting beaten for shelf space by a rival machine. Upper management decides to hire an instructional technology consultant to work on this problem. They know they want a sales training package but are willing to consider other options too.

• Palmer Inc., the second largest producer of undergarments in the USA, has nine factories in the north and southeast. The CEO at Palmer likes to bring management from all nine factories to headquarters in Augusta, GA. at least twice a year for management development seminars. This CEO is a believer in training and development, and he makes it clear that he wants his upper level managers to "get a lot" while they are at headquarters.

Are these situations familiar to you? Are they the kind of circumstances that might launch you on a project?

At first glance, they appear to be just like each other. But they're not. When you look at them carefully, they are different from each other. What's important is that they reflect the range of challenges that training professionals confront.

There are **three kinds of initiators** of TNA:

1. Performance Problems: These are the most familiar circumstances which involve training professionals and launch TNA. You can recognize performance problems because managers say things like, "What's going on here? They used to be proficient with the equipment," or "We taught them how to use the shortage program. Now why don't we see results?" or "We believe in Le Perfect Taste as a product. So why aren't our sales people getting us that shelf space?" "Why are we having so many requests for repair of our products?" Performance problems happen in the midst of *ongoing* efforts in situations when employees ought to know how.

2. New Systems and Technologies: While it varies with the setting and industry, the introduction of new systems and technologies is capturing a greater share of the time of the trainer or instructional technologist. Here are the words that professionals will hear under these circumstances: "Teach our people to use the new system!" or "We know our equipment is highly technical. We also know it's good. The problem is helping people to get comfortable with it. We need documentation for the Ponce de Leon models which is as strong as the equipment"; or "The course for service order takers has to show them how remote sensing of telephone problems is going to improve the situation for everybody"; or "Our tellers need to know enough about these financial products to introduce appropriate customers to them. Can you make that happen?"

3. **Automatic or Habitual Training**: In some cases training happens because it has *always* happened, because the *law* mandates for it to happen or because it *looks good* for it to happen. This situation is represented above in the annual telephone workshop at the Metropolitan Hospital and the bi-annual management development experiences for the Palmer Corporation. There is no *particular* problem here and no new system of technology for which employees must be trained.

These broad initiators of action usually appear in mundane and varied formats:

- printouts which present bad news
- complex technology which demands user support
- changing regulations which alter products and services
- hiring, promotion and turnover trends
- not enough sales, or occasionally too many
- regulatory action
- shareholders who demand better return-on-investment
- management hunches, concerns, priorities and intuition . . .

These are the challenges. Now we turn to solutions.

The Solution

One solution most often requested by management is to "train'em" and "teach'em" so that "the problem will go away and fast" or the "costly new system will get the use it deserves." The prudent training professional is going to have to look carefully at the problem or system before he or she commits resources to training as the answer to the problem. That look, that careful examination, is called training needs assessment (TNA); it's what this book is about.

Before we focus on TNA, let's talk about systematic training, in general. We'll review the broad steps a trainer carries out, and the place that TNA has in that process.

Systematic approaches to training or instructional systems development (ISD) was developed during World War II to address the pressing and technical needs of the military for trained personnel. Intuitive, random and varied ways of teaching soldiers to fly, march, maintain equipment, lead others and generate battle strategies were undependable. ISD provided a broad prescription for looking at the men and women and their work and figuring out ways to teach them to do it.

Robert Gagne's name is associated with the early days of ISD, as it is with so many major contributors to this field. He and his colleagues at Florida State University, most notably Leslie Briggs, Robert Morgan and Robert Branson, developed and popularized the big box model which eventually turned into the Interservice Procedures for Instructional Systems Development (IPISD). Mandated by the military and adapted to meet the needs of large corporations like AT&T, this systematic approach in its dozens of iterations is the basis for much of what goes on in training and development today.

Briefly, let's look at the big boxes and what they mean. (See Figure 1.1.) This book concentrates on the first box, on providing a new conceptualization for the techniques and tools inherent in analysis. Yet as we focus on the first box, on analysis, we need to understand how the outputs, the information gathered during this stage of effort, relates to everything else that is accomplished in training and development. That's what makes this a "system." What we do and find out in each phase has a direct and predictable bearing on the next box or phase of the effort.

ANALYSIS OR ASSESSMENT (A)

The challenge is to find the problem, to understand it sufficiently so that it can be solved. Why aren't salespeople getting Le Perfect Taste more shelf space? What could Palmer managers do better? What do tellers know and not know about these accounts? about selling financial packages? What kinds of documentation will enhance Ponce de Leon systems? Is it the store owners and operators or is it the quality of the shortage control program? What is going on and why is or isn't it happening?

DESIGN (D)

If the problem is one which can be solved through training or job aids, then trainers or instructional designers will establish clear and useful training

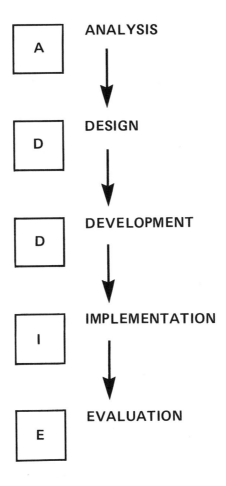

Figure 1.1

intentions in this phase. Just exactly what behavior and knowledge will the trainees possess? What accomplishments will we expect? Once training goals and objectives are established, decisions are made about appropriate strategies and technologies. In this phase, Ponce de Leon Inc. health equipment would have to decide on the specific and different expectations for family members vs. medical personnel and on how to achieve these different objectives. They would also consider the different demands of using the equipment in a hospital vs. at home.

DEVELOPMENT (D)

Working from goals and objectives, training strategies are planned and developed. The work of Dave Merrill, Barbara Martin and Leslie Briggs, Robert Gagne, and Sue Markle enlightens this phase as we use their research and ideas to make decisions about how to achieve given objectives. In development we write courseware, make videotapes and plan and execute the details of courses. There are tangible learning products developed in this stage.

IMPLEMENTATION (I)

This is where we try out the training solutions that have been developed. Palmer Industries holds a motivational seminar led by Norman Vincent Peale. Ponce de Leon tries out a series of workshops and job aids in hospitals. Solid Gold puts on seminars for tellers and pairs these seminars with a major sales incentive program.

EVALUATION (E)

Did the interventions work? Is there anything that needs changing? Should the training product or system be used again? Are hospital employees operating the equipment? Are the managers more motivated, if that was the problem? Is Le Perfect Taste getting more shelf space? Are financial packages getting sold? In evaluation, trainers are concerned whether the problem has been solved, whether the reason for doing all this has gone away. Evaluators seek data to judge the worth of the training effort. In a goal based evaluation, judgments will be only as effective as the quality of the goals. That takes us back to the first box, TRAINING NEEDS ASSESSMENT OR ANALYSIS, since that's where goals were derived. (See Figure 1.2.)

Training Needs Assessment (TNA)

When management presses for a video program to show how to lock up a store or a remote sensing course to detect telephone breaks or a home study course to deter turnover, trainers need to talk about UNDERSTANDING PROBLEMS or CONTEXTS FOR

What happens during ISD???

ANALYSIS:

People who know about the subject and
who care about training and development
ask questions like:
- who will our students be and what
  do they already know? want?
- why do we want them to know this?
- what within this topic is it most
  essential that they know? how will
  we decide?
- what might/will they do with this
  information? are there any problems at
  work that have been caused by not knowing?
- what is the cause(s) of the problem?
  will a course or training help?

DESIGN:

In this phase of ISD, trainers and
educators get very specific about
the goals and objectives of the course,
unit or program. What skills *exactly*
would they have? What kinds of goals
and objectives are we talking about?
What are the options and constraints
under which we will be planning?

DEVELOPMENT:

During this phase decisions are
made about HOW to do this.
Using earlier stage data, educators
select methods, technologies, sequence,
materials, practices, etc.

TRY-OUT:

This is where you do it: offer the
course or send out the program.

EVALUATION:

Did it work? Are the students able
to achieve course objectives? Will
it affect their work?

Figure 1.2

NEW SYSTEMS BEFORE ENACTING SOLUTIONS. What we all must do is make professional, convincing cases for ANALYSIS PRIOR TO PARTICULAR SOLUTIONS. This book will show how to make that case and carry out that analysis.

The effort to understand performance problems goes by many names:

Training Needs Assessment (TNA)

Training Needs Analysis

Pre-Training Analysis

Front End Analysis

Analysis

Trainers need access to more detailed and sturdy prescriptions for understanding performance problems. The worthy trainer or performance technologist or education specialist wants to do a front end analysis. What questions does he or she ask? What data is sought? What critical incidents are gathered? What sources are consulted? How is subject matter selected? ignored? In what order are those noble analyses conducted? May any be omitted? How do you know when you're finished and can report your results or start to develop training? Those are the questions that this book, *Training Needs Assessment*, answers.

Resources

Briggs, L.J. (1970). *Handbook of Procedures for the Design of Instruction*. Pittsburgh: American Institutes for Research.

Briggs, L.J. (Ed.) (1981). *Instructional Design: Principles and Applications*. Englewood Cliffs, NJ: Educational Technology Publication.

Dick, W., & Carey, L. (1985). *The Systematic Design of Instruction* (2nd edition). Glenview, Ill.: Scott Foresman.

Gagne, R.M., & Briggs, L.J. (1979). *Principles of Instructional Design* (2nd edition). NY: Holt, Rinehart & Winston.

Kemp, J.E. (1971). *Instructional Design.* Belmont, CA: Fearon Press.

Logan, R.S. (1982). *Instructional Systems Development: An International View of Theory and Practice.* New York: Academic Press.

Markle, S. (1978). *Designs for Instructional Designers.* Champaign, Ill.: Stipes Publishing.

Martin, B.L., & Briggs, L.J. (1986). *The Affective and Cognitive Domains: Integration for Instruction and Research.* Englewood Cliffs, NJ: Educational Technology Publications.

Merrill, M.D. (1983). Component Display Theory. In C.R. Reigeluth (ed.), *Instructional Design Theories and Models: An Overview of Their Current Status.* Hillsdale, NJ: Lawrence Erlbaum Associates.

Popham, W.J., & Baker, E.L. (1970). *Systematic Instruction.* Englewood Cliffs, NJ: Prentice-Hall.

Romiszowski, A.J. (1981). *Designing Instructional Systems.* London: Kogan Page.

Rowntree, D. (1982). *Educational Technology in Curriculum Development* (2nd edition). London: Harper & Row.

Part One: INTRODUCTION

Chapter Two: TRAINING NEEDS ASSESSMENT

Introduction

Training needs assessment (TNA) is an umbrella term for the analysis activities trainers use to examine and understand performance problems or new technologies. You've heard it called problem analysis, pre-training analysis, figuring things out, needs assessment and front end analysis. What you call it doesn't matter. What matters is whether you get the information you need to effectively solve problems in the corporation or agency. That detailed information, from the perspective of the various sources or stakeholders, is the **purpose for TNA.**

Purpose-based TNA

Purpose-based TNA is the central concept in this book. The things we must know before we train or report are the **purposes of our TNA study.** We are referring to the information we need to make informed decisions and recommendations.

There are a finite number of specific **reasons or purposes** why we do TNA. **Once these purposes are fulfilled,** the training professional moves on beyond TNA into the latter stages of instructional systems development described in Chapter One.

Purpose-based TNA tracks front end activities for you. These questions demonstrate how it works:

1. Why am I conducting analysis on this problem? What are **all** the possible purposes for my inquiry?

2. What do I *now* know about which I am confident? which I can support with data? which represent opinions and hard data from many sources?

3. What remains to be discovered? What *purposes are unfulfilled?*

This brings us to the **purposes of TNA.** What are they? **Our purposes are to seek information we seek about . . .**

- **optimal** *performance or knowledge*

- **actual** *or current performance or knowledge*

- **feelings** *of trainees and significant others*

- **causes** *of the problem from many perspectives*

- **solutions** *to the problem from many perspectives*

My reading of the literature and my experience with analysis suggest that these are the only *substantive kinds of information* we must have. **For each initiating situation that we confront, we must examine where we are in the quest for information about EACH of these purposes.** Let's look at TNA in light of these purposes.

SEEKING OPTIMALS: visions of desired knowledge or performance. It might be proper procedures for installing a phone, explaining a croissant maker or foreclosing on a house. It might be the principles involved in selecting a computer system for a small business or in designing office stations. The emphasis is on the knowledge, skills and attitudes which trainees must have to get the job done well.

SEEKING ACTUALS: the way it is, what people know and do. What are phone installers currently doing? How are foreclosures transpiring? What do salespeople say when they explain the croissant maker or assist clients in selection of computer systems? We can only talk about problems when we know there is a difference between what ought to be occuring (optimals) and what is occuring (actuals). The gap between optimal and actual is called a discrepancy or need. Roger Kaufman (1979, 1982) has emphasized the importance of identifying discrepancies, prior to launching any solutions.

Purpose-based TNA includes a familiar subtraction (next page):

OPTIMAL
- ACTUAL

PERFORMANCE DISCREPANCIES (NEEDS)

The trainer or course developer's job is to erase or diminish performance discrepancies (needs). This can't happen until the **details** of the performance discrepancy are known. That necessitates a search for information about optimals and actuals. Then the information about optimals and actuals is plugged into the subtraction presented above, yielding the **nature of the problem . . . in detail**.

Information about the nature of the problem isn't enough. Other purposes must also be satisfied.

SEEKING FEELINGS: opinions about the problem or task or competence related to it. Trainees, supervisors and significant others will have feelings about a performance problem or a new technology. A stickier challenge within TNA is to find out what those feelings are. Consider sales people who are not placing as many croissant machines as headquarters anticipates. Perhaps the sales staff has doubts about the product or its strength compared to its competitors. Or consider the introduction of a new and expensive computer system. Do employees like the one that has been chosen? Do they feel confident that they will be able to learn to use it? Do they have prerequisite keyboarding skills? You don't really understand the problem until you have unearthed the surrounding feelings.

SEEKING CAUSE(S): why is there a problem? What's causing it? There is usually some reason people do things, and some reason they don't. When you seek cause or causes, you attempt to find out what various sources think is contributing to the problem. Do not expect unanimity on the topic. Trainees may think there are environmental causes of a problem, like computers which *go down* or improper forms. Supervisors may think trainees don't know how. And other employees may wonder if there are any incentives for doing it and doing it right. The four possible causes of performance problems are discussed in detail in Chapter Four. The quest for the causes of the problem is central to TNA.

SEEKING SOLUTIONS: ways of ending or diminishing the problem. It is hard to resist thinking about what to do to end or diminish the problem. Many training professionals found their ways into this field because of an interest in teaching classes or producing video or writing educational software. It is natural and democratic to want to ask sources how **they** think the problem might be solved. If you think their answers will shed light on the cause(s) of the problem (e.g., *"Just re-write that form and those performance appraisals will improve."*) then ask. And if there is some chance that their preferences will be considered in selecting the training mode, include them. In most cases, however, trainees have very little to say about whether and how training transpires. In most situations, decisions about the nature of the solution will be based on management preference. Ideally, that management preference will be enlightened by what training professionals have found out about the *cause*(s) of the problem.

Using Purposes to Think About TNA

Initiating Challenges

Three kinds of initiating situations were described in Chapter One: the need to solve performance problems; the introduction of a new technology, product, policy or system; and habitual or automatic training. Those situations affect TNA because they influence the kind of purposes which must be fulfilled.

Purposes and Challenges

Purposes	Challenges		
	Problems	*New Systems*	*Automatic*
• OPTIMALS	X	X	X
• ACTUALS	X		
• FEELINGS	X	X	X
• CAUSE(S)	X		
• SOLUTIONS	X	X	

This approach is based on some assumptions about the relationship between challenges and purposes. I've assumed, for example, that TNAs undertaken for performance problems will necessitate the search for information relating to all purposes. I am also assuming that a **new** system is very new. In reality, there may well be information about actuals which must be collected. And finally, I am assuming that habitual training situations are based more on upper management whimsy or legislative fiat, rather than any particular, identifiable problem in employee performance. If habitual training matches a nagging problem in the corporation, I'd treat it as a performance problem, emphasizing the search for cause and actuals.

Use purposes to think about TNA:

1. Examine the initiating situation to determine if it is a performance problem, new system or habitual demand for training.

2. Identify purposes associated with that kind of training challenge. For example, if you are charged with teaching bank employees at SOLID GOLD about *new* financial products, then you know you will be seeking detailed information about optimals, feelings and preferred solutions. Another example is the Speedy Corporation and its problems with shortage control. Since they have spent a year in training employees on the new system, and some are *getting* portions of it, and the results are nowhere near what they anticipated, the training group confronts a classic performance problem in an ongoing system. They will need information in regards to all purposes, with an emphasis on **why** there is a problem with the shortage system implementation.

3. Track your progress based on fulfillment of these purposes. Don't seek information that you already possess. Do you now know enough about the financial products to create job aids for employees? Are you certain about employee feelings surrounding these products? surrounding the role of sales person? Chapter Twelve presents forms, models, examples and practices which demonstrate how to use purposes to move through TNA to gather the information you need.

What You Have and What You Need

Optimals

If you have only the optimals, the noble *oughts* in the situation, you are only part of the way there. You lack the touchstone of reality, of what is actually going on. Consider the manager who says, "They just don't understand our shortage control system. Teach them about it so they will know how to open, close, conduct surveillance, apprehend and monitor. We'll look at these documents and even more clearly spell out what they should be doing." That's a pretty good start on optimals, right? This instructional designer, however, lacks information about actuals. That means there is insufficient **detail** regarding the nature of the problem (optimals minus actuals).

Actuals

Instructional designers are more frequently flooded with data on actuals. You might be handed printouts which detail the bad loans being made by the loan documents. You will be subjected to descriptions of how loan documents have been going wrong. But management will resist clarifying or altering lending policies or philosophy. It just wants **better** loans, fewer uncollectibles which lead to costly legal procedures. Data on loan problems abound, but management doesn't much want to get into a precise discussion of optimal lending judgment. In a real situation I once heard it described as "sort of something like undefinable good sense." Once again, the designer can't move forward on a detailed definition of the problem because one portion of the subtraction is missing: clarity about optimals related to loan judgment.

Feelings

A worthy legacy of John Dewey (1933) and the student-oriented 1960s is appropriate concern about the feelings of potential trainees. It is often overdone or underdone. I've seen needs assessments which fulfilled no other purpose than to determine how secretaries felt about the new telephone system or how teachers felt about computers. I've also seen full scale front end analyses which never bothered to find out how much employees value the introduction of a new system or technology and whether or not they feel competent to learn to handle it.

Cause

Some front end studies will dwell on cause and avoid other issues. While the question of what is causing the problem is crucial to figuring out what to do about it, it is by no means a sufficient concern. Employees may feel attacked if queried endlessly about **why** they are messing up. It is inappropriate to ask trainees why they are not proficient on a *new* system or technology. They don't know it because no one has taught them. As Mager would say, even with a gun to their heads, they couldn't use the computer language or maintain the numerical control lathes. Cause usually isn't a relevant concern when you are dealing with innovations.

Solutions

This is a less frequent problem, but one which does appear. It is the behavior of a training professional who isn't sure about what else to ask, so he or she asks how incumbents want to get trained or where or when they want it. Admit it. You too have seen needs studies which are filled with questions about locations, times and modalities for training. This is particularly irresponsible because the opinions of job incumbents on solution preferences is not often considered when final decisions are made about how to solve the problem.

TNA Purposes and Techniques and Tools

We use analysis techniques and tools to fulfill purposes. The kinds of information we seek determines our technique. Some techniques enrich our knowledge about optimals. Other techniques meet the need we have to know what is currently happening. Still others lead us to information about feelings and causes. When we are trying to figure out what to do first and next in TNA, we have to determine how we have done on the achievement of our purposes. What remains to be discovered? Do we need more information from sources in order to be confident about optimals, actuals, cause, feelings or solutions?

Examples

Consider these examples of slivers of data from TNAs. As you look at them, ask:
- Is this information about optimals?
- Is this information about actuals?

- Is it information about feelings? or cause(s)? or solutions?
- Do I need more information to feel confident that I know what is happening here and why?

☐ Of the 89 accident reports involving hands, arms and fingers, 74 percent of the victims had been on the job for fewer than 6 months. The accidents involve several different pieces of equipment.

☐ Sixty-one percent of reporters anonymously agree or strongly agree with the statement that they "are not the kind of person who would use a computer." Fifty-five percent disagreed or strongly disagreed with the statement that "with a good class, I could get comfortable using the portable computer." Only 8 percent of the current reporters have requested use of the portable computers on which they've already received some training.

☐ Call-backs for improperly installed phones are driving management wild. Even though installers have a manual which details every step in the installation process, they are still not getting the phones in and operating.

☐ In his video address to new hires, the CEO describes the kind of safety effort he expects on the job. The Vice-President of Personnel also writes a memo specifying additional efforts that each unit is expected to undertake to diminish accidents and work-related illnesses.

Think now about **purpose-based TNA**. Think about what we know and don't know in our quest to fulfill each of the purposes. In the first accident problem, we know something about actuals, probably not enough, but something. Clearly we lack information on causes and can infer optimals and feelings. The last example, also about accidents, provides information about optimals. Charged with developing safety training for this CEO, the trainer would need to know a great deal about actual performance. The training professional assigned to increase reporter use of portable computers has information about actuals and feelings and nothing about optimals and cause, although the feeling data (*"no way I can learn to use computers"*) has obvious implications as you ponder the cause of this problem.

ANALYSIS TECHNIQUES & PURPOSES

PURPOSE   **TECHNIQUE**

	Extant Data Analysis	Needs Assessment	Subject Matter Analysis	Task Analysis
• Optimals		X	X	X
• Actuals	X	X		
• Feelings		X		
• Causes		X		
• Solutions		X		

Figure 2.1

TNA Techniques Link to Purposes

TNA is the quest for what is and ought to be going on. It is also a systematic effort to find out causes, feelings and solutions. While I think energy and marketing to senior management should focus on purposes, it's useful to link purposes to familiar phrases: extant data analysis, needs assessment; and subject matter analysis. The other dominant technique, task analysis, is effectively treated in Ken Carlisle's *Analyzing Jobs and Tasks*, the first book in the series of which the present volume is a part.

Chapter Three introduces these analysis techniques, pairing them with the purpose(s) for which they are best suited. In an attempt to nail down the mushy language surrounding front end analysis, I've taken familiar front end phrases and linked them to the reasons we do all this interviewing and assessing and surveying. (See Figure 2.1)

Resources

Carlisle, K. (1986). *Analyzing Jobs and Tasks.* Englewood Cliffs, NJ: Educational Technology Publications.

Deden-Parker, A. (Fall 1980). "Needs Assessment in Depth: Professional Training at Wells Fargo Bank." *Journal of Instructional Development, 1*(1), 3-9.

Dewey, J. (1933). *How We Think.* Boston: DC Heath.

Edwards, B., & Fiore, P. (1984). *Conducting the Training Needs Analysis.* New York: Training By Design.

Gilbert, T. (1978). *Human Competence: Engineering Worthy Performance.* New York: McGraw Hill.

Kaufman, R., & English, F.W. (1979). *Needs Assessment.* Englewood Cliffs, NJ: Educational Technology Publications.

Kaufman, R. (1982). *Identifying and Solving Problems: A Systems Approach.* San Diego: University Associates.

Mager, R., & Pipe, P. (1970). *Analyzing Performance Problems.* Belmont, CA: Fearon Press.

Rossett, A. (February 1985) "Nailing Down Needs Assessment." *INFO-LINE,* 11, 14.

Rossett, A. (October 1985) "What to Do Before You Do Anything." *Data Training,* 31-33.

Part One: INTRODUCTION

Chapter Three: INTRODUCING ANALYSIS TECHNIQUES AND TOOLS

TNA Techniques and Tools

The heart of this book is a belief that there are **five central purposes for TNA**. These five purposes are described in Chapter 2. Figure 3.1 presents the relationships between techniques, tools and purposes. Analysis techniques and tools are introduced and briefly described in this chapter.

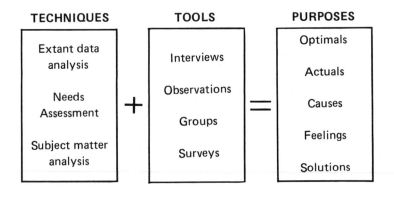

Figure 3.1

ANALYSIS TECHNIQUES

Extant Data Analysis (EDA)

Extant data is the "stuff" that the company collects that represents the **results of employee performance**. It might be sales figures, accident reports, call-backs for non-repair, shrink reports, letters to management, attendance figures or exit interviews. The key is that we seek aggregate results of employee behavior, not just a single letter of complaint or call-back. **In EDA we do not look at what the employee does; we look at effects and then we infer back from results to draw a picture of actual performance.** We seek the outcomes of employee actions in light of the goals of the corporation or agency. We can infer a great deal about current employee performance from results.

Thus, extant data analysis unearths ACTUALS, providing a picture of what is actually happening in the work place. While EDA presents a stark vision of the effectiveness of employees, it does not tell you WHY there is or is not a problem or how employees feel about it.

To understand EDA, we have to think about the distinction between behavior and accomplishment, action and the results of that action. This useful distinction was highlighted by Thomas Gilbert (1978) in *Human Competence*. Consider the salesperson who makes many cold calls, but sells few products. Or consider the instructor who talks and talks, points and gestures, but then her students begin their jobs not really able to carry out the procedures which were taught in the course.

The training professional does not go out and generate extant data anew. Rather, he or she asks for access to that which already exists, to the records and files which reside within the corporation or agency. That might mean asking for computer printouts on sales, completed performance appraisals or requests for transfer. Extant data analysis is treated in more detail in Chapter Five.

Needs Assessment (NA)

In addition to providing the name for this book, NEEDS ASSESSMENT is also a specific front end technique which fulfills the entire range of TNA purposes. **It is the way we go out and seek *opinions* on the optimals, actuals, feelings, causes and solu-**

tions from a variety of sources. Extant data is about inferences based on results. Needs assessment is about opinions. Unlike extant data, which is already in existence, needs assessments involve contact with sources to seek new information and perspectives on why sales are down or requests for transfer are up.

During needs assessment, training professionals seek opinions from relevant sources. What is the nature of optimal performance or expertise? How are things going now? What are employees currently doing that works? that doesn't work? What are the feelings that surround this portion of their job or new technology? What do sources think is causing the problem and, sometimes, how do they think it ought to be solved?

Think about the problem of training telephone operators to relate to customers in the new, computerized context. For extant data analysis, the training professional would look at figures on number, nature and length of contacts. He or she would also ask to see letters of complaint or commendation from customers. Needs assessment, on the other hand, might involve conducting interviews with supervisors, operators and customers. A printed survey might also be distributed to get an anonymous picture of operator feelings about the new system and their ability to handle it. Needs assessment is the subject of Chapter Six.

Subject Matter Analysis (SMA)

During subject matter analysis, trainers or instructional developers seek the nature and shape of bodies of knowledge which employees need to possess to do their jobs effectively. It is a quest for the details of OPTIMALS, the information that an informed employee possesses which enables him or her to get the job done. It might be information about resources appropriate to handling customer questions or rules about accessing the computer system. Or it might be the ways that different diseases manifest themselves, or information about the compatibility of a line of computer peripherals. The search is for mental schema or connections that represent what the effective performer knows.

Subject matter analysis is conducted through interaction with subject matter experts and documents to derive essential information. This information then serves as the basis for training programs and job aids.

The challenge in subject matter analysis is to ferret out the details of invisible bodies of knowledge. Think about the difference between successful sales and successful telephone installing, or between brilliant medical diagnoses and effective drawing of blood. Sales and diagnoses are based on facts, concepts and principles, invisible to the naked, observing eye, and stored as schema in the mind. Watching the salesperson or the physician won't tell you what they know which enables them to make decisions and be effective. Certainly some of it might be inferred. But not the essential details and relationships. Those optimals must come from interviews with the subject matter experts and reference to the literature which surrounds their work. This analysis technique is covered in Chapter Seven.

The details of phone installation, deck swabbing and taking blood are more accessible through observation. That leads us to task analysis.

Task analysis is a TNA technique that derives OPTIMALS attached to visible tasks. Relying primarily on observation, during task analysis model performers do what they do well so that a comprehensive description of that excellence can be recorded by the training professional. These elements of visible, optimal performance then serve as the basis for training. Task analysis is not treated in this book because it has been successfully treated elsewhere (Carlisle, 1986; Zemke and Kramlinger, 1982; Davis *et al.*, 1974).

Analysis Tools

Interviewing

The interview is the most prevalent TNA tool. We interview as part of needs assessment, subject matter and task analyses. During interviews, we pursue information related to all TNA purposes. It is also possible that an interview might provide access to extant data. Chapter Eight describes how to use interviews as a TNA tool.

Observing

While observation is a useful and highly touted front end tool, my research suggests it isn't used in TNA very much at all. I'd like to encourage a rekindling of interest in the tool. We might use observations for perusing extant data and for capturing the details of optimal or actual performance during subject matter and task analysis. Observation as a TNA tool is discussed in Chapter Nine.

Facilitating Groups

One cost-effective way of getting and disseminating information, and of garnering support, is through the use of TNA groups. The use of groups for TNA is based on a belief in synergy, that the product of the interaction of many participants transcends a traditional sum of the parts. Groups are often used as a jury of experts to derive a consensus opinion on optimals. They can, of course, be used for every other TNA purpose. Chapter Ten is about the use of groups to carry out TNA.

Surveying Through Questionnaires

In Chapter Eleven, steps and examples are presented for planning, writing and disseminating TNA surveys. The questionnaire or survey is an excellent device for acquiring information relevant to all possible TNA purposes.

Resources

Carlisle, K. (1986). *Analyzing Jobs and Tasks.* Englewood Cliffs, NJ: Educational Technology Publications.

Gilbert, T. (1978). *Human Competence: Engineering Worthy Performance.* New York: McGraw Hill.

Davis, R.H., Alexander, L.T., & Yelon, S.L. (1974). *Learning System Design.* New York: McGraw Hill.

Martin, B.L., & Briggs, L.J. (1986). *The Affective and Cognitive Domains: Integration for Instruction and Research.* Englewood Cliffs, NJ: Educational Technology Publications.

Zemke, R., & Kramlinger, T. (1982). *Figuring Things Out: A Trainer's Guide to Needs and Task Analysis.* Reading, MA: Addison-Wesley.

Chapter Four: PERFORMANCE PROBLEMS AND THEIR CAUSES

Introduction

One of the purposes of TNA and a concern which runs through the training and development literature (Harless, 1970; Gilbert, 1978; Mager & Pipe, 1984) is the quest for the *cause of the performance problem*. It is a concern that is close to my own home and heart.

Ten years ago, soon after I got my first cat, I worried about why she was always mewing, begging and looking skinny. I fed her and fed her and fed her. Still she mewed, begged and looked gaunt. Not to be beaten by this thing, I changed brands of cat food and gave her more of it. I figured she had a hefty appetite and an enviable metabolism.

So I kept feeding her and she kept doing the things that assured I would keep up the feeding schedule. Months later, as I told the story to a friend, he diagnosed the cat as having worms. Which she did. I was feeding my cat and her insatiable worms. I also was rewarding her begging and mewing with frequent food.

This cat tale from my life focuses on **a problem and its cause**. All the food in the world would not have solved my cat's problem because the problem wasn't too little or the wrong food. Similarly, there are performance problems which training can't alter because they aren't caused by an absence of training.

The cat story has another lesson for us. My cat was *doing a number on me*. I reinforced her mewing and toe nibbling with food. She reinforced my incessant feeding by behaving like an angel for a few hours just after I fed her. She gave me a brief illusion that she was sated so I continued to stuff her.

There were two causes of this problem—the worms AND the incentives we were both using on each other. **Problems often have several causes. We're only able to solve problems if we can ferret out their cause or causes.**

Brief Description

Chapter Four presents performance problems, their possible causes and the options human resources professionals have for solving these problems. While earlier chapters drew our attention to the quest for the nature of problems in the work place, to the use of TNA to clarify optimals and actuals, this chapter highlights **CAUSE.** We are concerned about cause(s) when performance problems have initiated our efforts.

Think about . . .

- middle managers who fail to turn in their performance appraisals;
- breakdowns which indicate difficulties with maintaining certain switching systems;
- office workers who ignore powerful capabilities within their word processing systems;
- teachers who leave the microcomputer in the closet at the back of the room; or
- tellers who sell few financial accounts.

In all of these instances, somebody or several people think there is a problem. When the desired performance is, or should be familiar, we seek the cause of the problem.

That's different from when we're attempting to integrate a new system or technology into the corporation. Determining cause is rarely a front end purpose when introducing innovations. People don't know how because it's new to them.

Therefore, in this chapter we focus on problems in familiar situations. The managers, engineers, office workers, teachers and tellers aren't doing something that somebody thinks they ought to be doing. There is a gap between optimal and actual, albeit a non-specific one, but a gap all the same, in an ongoing situation. In addition to the quest for details about the gap, the performance professional must find out **why** there is a discrepancy.

Even though we often bear the title of **trainer**, responsible practice of our profession involves searching analysis of whether or not **training** will fix this problem. Joe Harless, Thomas Gilbert, Robert Mager and Peter Pipe, with excellent work in this area, **focused the trainer's attention on conducting an analysis of the CAUSE(S) of the problem BEFORE using a training intervention.** We must seek cause(s) of performance problems because problems have four different kinds of causes and **different causes necessitate different solutions.**

Kinds of Causes

Problems have causes and performance problems are no different. There are four types of causes of the problems that trainers encounter.

☐ **1. Absence of skill or knowledge**

This is the employee who, as Mager and Pipe (1984) pointed out, can't do it even if you put a gun to his or her head. They can't because they **lack the skill or knowledge.** They don't know how to climb the telephone pole or swab the deck or lay the cables or clean the turbine or explain the new product or diagnose the illness. No matter how much management wants them to or how much they want to, they are unable to pull it off. They don't know how or they don't know how to do it up to the desired standards. They just can't. Or they can't do it quickly enough or accurately enough. A subset of this kind of cause is the absence of **prerequisite skills or knowledge.** I encountered this example while involved in a project to assist a very large corporation in setting up standards for course development: Course developers were provided with spiffy, new computers. Management thought many of the course developers were ungrateful when they failed to make immediate and significant use of their computers. For many of the developers, the problem with using the computer was that they had never learned keyboard skills. These were highly skilled, technical and operations people, mostly male, and typing skills were not in their repertoire. Naturally they did not pitch themselves into the wondrous functions of the word processor when they were hung up on and embarrassed about hunting and pecking.

☐ **2. Absence of incentive or improper incentive**

The feedback, appraisals, incentives and policies surrounding job performance have everything to do with performance problems or the lack of them. **Consequences of job performance matter.** Is desired, continuous, successful performance treated differently than flawed employee behavior? Can you point to a situation where the employee gets something good as a result of doing a good job? Or is productive performance ignored, possibly even punished, by leading to additional work?

Our own profession presents numerous examples. I was working with a telecommunications company to train course developers in better, sleeker course development procedures. As I conducted my TNA, prior to training anybody in anything, I kept hearing the same complaint, "While I put in 50+ hours on getting this course together, I watch Hiram sit in his cubicle and produce nearly nothing. That's the way it is throughout the company. The Hirams of our great company are ignored for their inactivity, while productive instructional designers are expected to do the work of their slothful colleagues. And do I get a bigger paycheck? Only by a few pennies! No, it's not worth it. I'm disenchanted."

Think about the baseball free agency and the incredibly productive years that players so often have before they go out on the open market. Or consider the dulling affects of tenure on academia.

We are talking about **CONSEQUENCES**, and the way people perform if the results of their action are **known to them and linked to more optimal job performance.** When we are looking at a situation in which people **could do it if they wanted to, flawed incentives are often a contributing cause of the problem.** That's the telephone operator who could provide courteous assistance; she or he knows how. That's the professor who could advise students in career and course options; she or he knows how. That's the instructional designer who could get that CBT course finished on time; she or he knows how. Often they will do it if there are incentives associated with the desired performance.

The emphasis here is on two things:

- **Strong, suitable** incentives, appropriate to the employees
- **Known**, public and consistent incentives

Strong incentives are things, activities or opportunities that employees want. If you want to figure out what works with a group of employees, look at their behavior. If it has increased with a particular incentive program, then you probably have one that works, for now anyway. The traditional programs involve money and promotions, but there is no reason to limit the company to those. Career development opportunities are a definite possibility, as are tickets to sports events or keys to the corporate cabin in the woods. But just because you think you'd like the incentive, don't assume it will serve as an incentive for all employees. Administrators at my University give football tickets to productive faculty and staff. Well, while it is a sweet gesture, few professors leap at the opportunity to watch San Diego State's losing football team.

On the other hand, Mary Kay Cosmetics knows what it's doing with incentives. They offer lots of little incentives keyed to lesser, but desirable, performance. Then they offer big, visible incentives distributed to a few highly productive sales people. The incentive program works because this sales staff likes the money, the group vacations and the image and dream of a pink Cadillac.

I've heard corporate personnel and training directors lament the ungrateful nature of employees who fail to recognize just how wonderful an incentive is. You can't strong-arm people into being entranced with an incentive. Talk to them and watch what they choose for themselves; that will provide clues to strong incentives that can be tied to effective performance.

Nor can you expect employees to be thrilled when their excellent labors increase their workload. There are endless tales of the repair person who gets more work orders because of superior speed and accuracy. Or the training specialist who is assigned more and tougher problems because the trainer (a Hiram clone) in the office next door isn't performing. Or consider the engineer whose excellent research and development earns her the opportunity to give numerous public presentations; in addition to having more work to do, she is kept from the laboratory and rewarded with what she considers to be a less desirable task.

Imagine yourself as the trainer in that last example. You are charged with getting star engineers up to speed on presentation skills in a context where those engineers are not volunteers; in fact, they dislike anything that keeps them away from the work that made them stars in the first place. Will training solve the problem of engineers who make perfunctory public presentations? Not likely.

What about management attention? An employee who is productive, makes numerous contacts, comes up with many ideas, puts ideas on paper, is going to get some attention from management. Is management putting a damper on activity by providing negative feedback? Sometimes the non-performer is ignored while the prolific performance gets tons of attentive **CRITICISM**.

Do employees know what will happen to them as a result of performing the facets of their jobs? **It is incredible to conduct TNA and repeatedly hear employees say that doing or not doing X or Y makes no difference.** Especially when queries to management just about always yield assurances that there are policies surrounding that performance. Do these policies find their way into practice? **Strong, carefully selected incentives must be KNOWN TO EMPLOYEES AND CONSISTENTLY PRACTICED BY MANAGEMENT.**

☐ **3. Absence of environment support**

Incentives and environment are directly related. After all, what is a more telling component of the environment than supervisors, managers and the policies they enact. The overlap between incentives and environment is useful. If you overlooked some problems within the incentive system, you are likely to pick it up here, when you look once again **at all that surrounds the worker as he or she does the job.**

Are there factors outside of the trainee's direct control that prevent him/her from doing the job? Many of the problems traditionally purported to be training/instructional problems actually stem from policy, personnel or other contextual factors. There are three areas to scrutinize when determining if the environment is blocking effective performance: **personnel, policies and tools.**

Personnel. Who touches the lives of the employees who have been identified as having the performance problem? Ask these questions as you seek the causes of this problem:
- On which other employees must the trainees depend?
- Do those employees affect the problem in any way?

- Do *related* employees think this is important?
- Does the supervisor know enough about what his/her employees must do?
- Does he/she provide incentives for proper performance?
- What does he/she do if they don't perform?
- Does the supervisor agree that this is a problem or is it just a concern of higher management?
- Does the manager or supervisor want his or her people doing this?
- Are managers appraised for supervising this? What happens to them if they ignore it?

A large telecommunications company sent its curriculum developers off for intensive training in instructional systems development. After a week of training and preparation to use numerous job aids and forms to manage this course development system, they headed back to their operating companies. Their managers met them with a heap of cynicism. Within three weeks, most developers were back to doing things in the good old intuitive way. After all, nobody looked at what they were doing and turning in. It doesn't matter whether you think these developers have a problem caused by flawed incentives or environment; it could be called either. The important point is that you recognize that more training for these curriculum developers won't make a dent in this problem. In this case, the managers are the ones whose performance is causing the problem.

Policies and Procedures. What does the company or agency tell the employee and his supervisor about this particular facet of the job? Look to related policies and procedures.

- Consider the flight attendant who fails to act with sufficient responsiveness to the passenger. Is there a policy warning against fraternizing with passengers? Might the fine line between fraternization and responsiveness be causing problems?
- Or consider the assembly workers with frequent accidents. Has there been introduction of a new procedure for production without lowering the productivity expectation? Maybe the worker is attempting to maintain productivity

levels before he/she is sufficiently adept with the new procedure.

- Another example is the employees who only rarely use the Centrex telephone system. A related factor is that they are never evaluated for using it or not using it. There are no formal policies which manifest themselves in performance evaluations that give teeth to the platitude . . . *"Employees will attempt to conserve corporate resources . . ."*

Tools. What does the company or agency give the employee to do the job? For some jobs and problems this is not a significant factor. But for others, especially in skills training, tools are crucial to efficient and safe task completion. Look at some examples:

IDENTIFIED PROBLEM	TOOL PROBLEM
1. Increased scrap production	1. Gloves which were recently issued to lathe workers are too thick for rapid, easy, fine-tuned adjustments.
2. Lost paperwork	2. Desk storage systems are unlabeled. No designated trays or colored files.
3. Telephone repair people are taking excessive time diagnosing problems for the past 60 days.	3. Trouble-shooting kits do not include equipment appropriate to the rain and flood problems of recent months.

☐ 4. Absence of motivation

Joe Harless places motivation and incentive together when he talks about the possible causes of performance problems in *An Ounce of Analysis Is Worth a Pound of Objectives.* Mager and Pipe do the same. Their point is that consequences, external results, weigh heavily when we are attempting to improve performance. Often, if you alter and systematize the incentives, you've fixed the problem. With that I agree.

But I'd like to go a bit further. If you look at enough performance problems, you eventually become dissatisfied with a solely behavioral explanation of what's causing performance problems.

Recent, more cognitively oriented literature in training and development (see Bandura, 1977; Harmon, 1979; Keller, 1979; Sprague, 1981; Nuttin, 1985) focuses our attention on **what's going on inside the employee**. When we lump incentives and motivation together, we ignore the difference between internal and external factors and focus only on the more traditional external variables like incentives and environment.

What is motivation and how can the work that has been done in this area contribute to our understanding of performance problems and their causes? In 1979, *The Journal of Instructional Development* published John Keller's discussion of the implications of motivation theory and research for instructional designers. Acknowledging the roots of our field in **both** behavioral and cognitive psychology, he lamented the omission of attention to the internal aspects of trainees, "to the heart or spirit of the learner." Citing the earlier work of Porter and Lawler and Bandura, Keller presents a useful explanation for motivation:

VALUE X EXPECTANCY = MOTIVATION

VALUE is the worth individuals attach to things or outcomes as evidenced by their choice of it given other options. Trainees have to have a sense of what *it* is, what they will be able to do *with it*, and why *it* is worth doing. They must be able to cogitate on what is good, worthy and valuable about that which they are about to learn, either for its **immediate or future implications**. Think about your own professional development. You are likely to be attending a seminar or reading this book because you are conducting or anticipate conducting front end analyses.

EXPECTANCY, confidence or efficacy is the trainee's perception of personal likelihood of success at the task. Will the staff be able to operate and maintain the new intravenous units? Will I be successful at mastering PASCAL? Will my mother acquire hangliding skills? Here is an illustration of expectancy, a concept which Bandura contributed to our repertoire.

The setting is lovely; the workshop leaders are competent. And my mother is there because my brother dragged her. She however is not paying attention, wiggling even, making comments which annoy the other beginning students, most of whom are college students. She is the classic unmotivated student. She wants the class to be over. She tells my brother she wants to go shopping. For hangliding, she manifests low value ("she can't imagine why she is there, of what possible use hangliding is to a 60-year-old woman") and no expectancy ("she is positive that her old bones can't fly.") **Multiply little value times no confidence and you can see exactly what's going on inside the trainees we so often dismiss as *unmotivated*.**

We can even pretend to quantify our examination of motivation as the cause of performance problems. It's a pretense because the numbers we assign are subjective and illustrative; they are our opinions of where trainees stand in relation to the subject matter. Still the numbers are suggestive and useful—as you will see in the following example:

- There are two groups who need to learn how to use the slightly complex Centrex system for corporate telecommunications. One group is composed of college graduates, successful recipients of numerous corporate workshops, all eager for promotion. The other group is hourly employees, mostly high school graduates who do filing, data input and message transfer.

Which would be the more motivated group? Which group would you rather train? If we assign some squishy hypothetical numbers, you can see the way the different factors contribute to trainee motivation. These numbers spring out of my imagination. **In the real world, on the job, you would assess potential trainee's perceptions of value and confidence through stages of needs assessment.** Assume you can assign numbers from 0 through 10 with 0 being no value or expectancy at all and 10 being lots of it. Remember, as you think about the centrex system and the two different groups of trainees . . .

VALUE X EXPECTANCY = MOTIVATION

Trainee Group	Value	Expectancy
College graduates	7	10
Hourly employees	9	3

The first group enjoys approximately a 70; that's substantial motivation, dependable interest in the subject and in their ability to pick it up. The other group values the skills (9) even more than the first group but isn't confident about their ability to pick it up (3). The absence of "can do" feeling kills motivation. They wind up with only a 27 and would be a more challenging training assignment.

Back to my mother: If I interviewed her at the time, she would have had a zero expectancy and only a 1 or 2 value figure. When you multiple that out, it is 0 motivation, representing a near impossible training task. Her college student classmates, on the other hand, are a delight. We can assign these volunteer students a 9 or 10 in value and high expectancy. They would rate somewhere between 80 and 100. Now that's a fun class to train!

Herein lies the theory behind what we've all felt in our bones. We'd much prefer training volunteers (high value). It is far easier to work with trainees who have had positive schooling and training experiences (high expectancy). When we lack a motivated group, we want to have strong incentives to offer for desired performance, the way the military does in its training. The worst possible situation, and a common one in business, is gazing out at a group of trainees who didn't much want to be there (low or no value), doubt their ability to perform on the task (low expectancy) and have a supervisor who didn't much want to release them to come to the training session (impossibly difficult incentive system.)

Let me then introduce what I hope will be a useful distinction between motivation and incentive. What employees believe and value about a product or procedure and themselves in relation to its contributes to their **MOTIVATION.** What management does to them and for them as they work is the **INCENTIVE** system. There is what they know and feel; that's internal. Then there is what happens to them in relation to the way they carry out elements of their job; that's external.

Let's look at an example which illustrates the difference in perspective when seeking motivation vs. incentive causes:

- A chain of hospitals purchases new intravenous feeding equipment because it is purported to be more comfortable, safer, cleaner and precisely controllable. Approximately 1/3 of the total units are in place in the hospitals. And few of them are being used. The new equipment has validated job aids on how to maintain and use it. Still staff avoid the new and rely on the old. Prior to purchasing thousands of additional IV units, management wants to make sure that the new ones are as good as promised. They can't check them out or provide better service to patients if the staff avoids the new equipment.

This situation needs to be examined for its CAUSE(S). Here's a hypothetical examination of the intravenous case. **Note the way familiarity with the different kinds of causes structures the nature of the inquiry.**

CAUSE TYPE	QUESTIONS
SKILL/KNOWLEDGE	• Does the job aid work? • Can they set up and maintain the IV? • Is it a tougher or lengthier process than the former IV?
INCENTIVE	• What happens if they use it? If they don't use it? • Do they know what is supposed to happen? Does it happen? • How do supervisors respond to it?
ENVIRONMENT	• Is the new equipment there? • Does it work reliably? • Is the old equipment equally accessible? • Is the job aid where it is supposed to be?
MOTIVATION	• Does the staff know why this IV has appeared? • Are there good reasons, reasons which can be shared with staff? • Does the staff believe they can master the use of this new technology?

These questions illustrate how motivation and incentive are different causes of performance problems and how that conceptu-

alization influences the way we question sources. There are different domains covered by the questions attached to incentives and motivation. Here is a hypothetical ending to the TNA portion of the intravenous case.

1. Skill/knowledge discrepancies do not appear to be a factor. The job aid works. When training professionals asked randomly selected employees to use the aid to set up and operate the equipment, they handled it just fine.
2. Supervisors understand the reasons for the new equipment but express doubts about whether employees know why a change has occurred.
3. There are no policies relating to rewards or punishments for use of this equipment and supervisors would prefer not to add such a policy. They feel it would be inappropriate because staff attitude might be communicated to patients if staff is coerced into using certain equipment.
4. The new and old equipment and the job aid are there and equally available.
5. While there are good and uncynical reasons (e.g., safety) for introducing the new equipment, staff are pretty much unaware of them. They don't value the new IV units and think they are a hassle. As far as they are concerned, the old way was good enough.

This is primarily a problem caused by an absence of motivation. Hospital employees don't know enough about what's so great about this new system to begin to embrace using it. When pressed, they can't provide reasons, causes and benefits to attach to the hassle of using something new when they were already so comfortable with the old. It's not that they feel they are unable to master the system. With the job aids, they do fine using it. The problem is that they lack an internalized sense of value which would compensate for the hassle of figuring out the new one.

Having the old and new equipment in close and tempting proximity also contributes to the problem. People will stick with the familiar. Removing old IVs until the new units are more familiar might contribute to their integration into the wards.

But remember the concern of the supervisors about forcing staff to use the new system. They thought that patients might be affected by staff hesitations or dislike of the new IVs. This also could be the case if management uses an environmental solution (removing the favored old equipment) without addressing the motivational aspects of the problem.

In 1978 Thomas Gilbert wrote, "There is more nonsense, superstition and plain self-deception about the subject of motivation than about any other topic." (p. 308) He goes on to describe a foreman who used a pep talk to *motivate* his employees to carry out an unpleasant task. An operational definition of **pep talk** which uses the conceptual model I'm proposing would be one which **raises the value, importance and worth attached to the task and their confidence that they can do it—at least for long enough to get it done**. In keeping with the distinction I'm drawing, Gilbert suggests another possible solution: to provide incentives for this onerous job.

Incentives are, no doubt, very powerful. However, rarely do trainers control them. On the other hand, we can exert a powerful influence as we build value and confidence in employees. Thus, the distinction has significance for interpretation of the problem and for steps to resolve it.

Figure 4.1 summarizes and illustrates the most likely causes of performance problems. Remember problems can be caused by any combination of these kinds of causes.

Solutions Linked to Causes

While TNA costs money because it takes time and personnel, it is far more costly not to do it. Why? Because training is an appropriate solution to problems which are caused by an absence of skills, knowledge or motivation. Training will not solve problems which are primarily attributed to flawed environment, policies or incentives. Figure 4.2 highlights cause and appropriate responses.

Performance Problems & Their Causes

There are four possible causes of performance problems. Some problems have one cause; some problems have several causes. Before you start to solve a performance problem, you have to know from whence it comes.

1. They lack skill or knowledge.

Even if they want to, they just don't know how to write purchase orders or operate the word processor.

2. The environment is in the way.

They don't have the tools, forms or work space to enable them to perform. The classic example is the computer that keeps "going down" during registration or the clerk that is supposed to answer questions at the counter and file at the same time.

3. There are no, few or improper incentives.

This is so often the case at universities! What does excellent performance matter? What does sloppy or non-performance matter? Who isn't familiar with case after case of competent staff who get loaded with work and weak employees who are ignored, to their joy and delight.

4. The employees are unmotivated.

There are two factors that contribute to motivation and are multiplicatively related: value and efficacy. What good do the employees see in it (the system, form or technology)? Do they believe they are able to learn what is involved in doing the job the way it is now defined?

Figure 4.1

SOLUTIONS LINKED TO CAUSES

Kinds   Solutions
of causes

Skill/knowledge discrepancies   Training
                                           Job aids

Flawed incentives   New policies, contracts
                                           Training for supervisors

Flawed environment   Work redesign
                                           New and better tools
                                           Better match between person
                                           and job

Lack of motivation   Training so can see benefits
                                           Better processes or tools if
                                           there are no benefits to cite
                                           Training which provides early,
                                           tangible successes to build
                                           confidence

Figure 4.2

The following chart presents cause, examples and associated solutions:

Problem Cause	Example	Solution
Absence of skill or knowledge	Can't troubleshoot the D-4 bay, even with the supervisor standing there (skill)	Training
Absence of knowledge	Can't compare our FUNNY MONEY package to the competition's (knowledge)	Training
Flawed environment	Old directories and reference guides hamper social worker's referrals	New guides
Flawed incentive	After developing effective CBT program, trainer gets new product with hostile expert	New work assignments
Absence of motivation	76% of the reporters at the paper admit to being either uncomfortable or slightly uncomfortable composing news stories on the computer (low expectancy)	Training
	Of these same reporters only 16% could list one reason for converting from paper and pencil to computers (low value)	

There are four basic causes of performance problems (absence of skills/knowledge, incentive, environment and motivation) and two broad kinds of solutions:

1. **Training**: Interventions which through presentation, examples, practices and feedback teach someone to do something they were never taught, or never learned or forgot how to do. Job aids are an intervention which are often linked to training. A product knowledge seminar on a new insurance program might include preparation to use several rate and benefit computational job aids, for example.

2. **Reporting and Restructuring**: Professionals with training-related titles are now more frequently perceiving themselves as *performance specialists*. That kind of vision, one which relies upon skills in job redesign, climate interventions and organizational development leads to solutions which have little to do with training. Non-training solutions, or remedies, as Joe Harless calls them, should be recommended or effected when the cause indicates. Our options are varied. For example, new policies, a new personnel appraisal form, a different work schedule, new tools, rewards for desired performance, or managerial action regarding non-performance might be suggested as remedies. The key here is to look at the problem, figure out what is causing it and act accordingly. It isn't unusual to be told to develop training for a group, then to conduct a TNA, only to discover that your original, presumed trainees are not the cause of the problem. Rather, their managers are the ones who are the major contributors to the discrepancy. Or that all the training in the world isn't going to increase sales. Again, report on it. The purpose of TNA is to gather information so you can bring managerial attention to what is really going on and to WHAT IS CAUSING IT. That will reserve training interventions for appropriate problems and innovations.

Resources

Bandura, A. (1977). Self-Efficacy: Toward a Unifying Theory of Behavioral Change. *Psychological Review, 84*, 191-215.

Gilbert, T. (1978). *Human Competence Engineering Worthy Performance*. New York: McGraw Hill.

Harless, J. (1970). *An Ounce of Analysis Is Worth a Pound of Objectives*. Newnan, Georgia: Harless Performance Guild.

Harmon, P. (February 1979). Beyond Behavioral Performance Analysis: Toward a New Paradigm for Educational Technology. *Educational Technology, 19*(2), 5-26.

Keller, J.M. (1979). Motivation and Instructional Design: A Theoretical Perspective. *Journal of Instructional Development, 2*(4), 26-34.

Nuttin, J. (1985). *Future Time Perspective and Motivation.* Hillsdale, NJ: Lawrence Erlbaum Associates.

Porter, L.W., & Lawler, E.E. (1968). *Managerial Attitudes and Performance.* Homewood, Ill.: Richard D. Irwin.

Mager, R., & Pipe, P. (1984). *Analyzing Performance Problems or You Really Oughta Wanna* (2nd edition). Belmont, CA: Fearon Publications.

Sprague, G.A. (February 1981). Cognitive Psychology and Instructional Development: Adopting a Cognitive Perspective for Instructional Design Programs in Higher Education. *Educational Technology, 21*(2), 24-29.

Part Two: TNA TECHNIQUES

Chapter Five: EXTANT DATA ANALYSIS

Brief Description

Extant data analysis directs the trainer or personnel specialist's attention away from what Thomas Gilbert (1978) calls "the great cult of behavior" towards "accomplishments" (p. 7). While I admit to retaining fascination with behavior, I've too often seen colleagues and students count motions and detail stimulus-response chains, rather than capture the subtleties associated with meaningful performances linked to accomplishments. Effective TNA captures the details of optimal and actual behavior and knowledge, while at the same time examining results or accomplishments attached to that knowledge or skill.

Extant data analysis is the effort training professionals make to ground front end analysis in *performance and accomplishment.* Just how much breakage is occurring? For how long has this been going on? How many repair call-backs are there? How many complaints? What kind of complaints are recorded? What about sales figures? What about requests for assistance? How many questions? What kinds of questions? What do the exit interviews say? The accident reports? The letters of appreciation? Turnover? The bottom line?

- Extant data is sales not salesmanship.
- Extant data is satisfied customers not any particular greeting.
- Extant data is better mileage not any one way of tuning a car.
- Extant data is fewer call-backs not a particular repair technique.

- Extant data is people in the ballpark not hot dog cooking or grounds maintenance.
- Extant data is the team's standing in the league not batting stance or ability to scoop up a ground ball.

In this chapter we focus on where upper level management so often places its focus—**on outcomes**. It is hard to get a Vice-President of Marketing and Sales to talk very long about closing techniques; he or she wants to look at sales figures. It is difficult to fix the attention of a Board of Directors on kinds of communication skills; they want to see those skills manifested in retention rates for the engineering staff. And Hospital Directors do not want to dally over the details of equipment storage on the floors; they want approvals from safety regulatory agencies. Usually, management attention can be represented like this:

Performance – – – – – – – – – > **Accomplishments**

If, however, sales dip, engineers flee or regulators deny approvals, management will temporarily focus employee behavior on selling, communicating and safety. Then, management concern, for the moment, looks like this:

Performance – – – – – > Accomplishments

During TNA, the trainer must examine the problem from **both** perspectives, because both yield essential information. **During extant data analysis, we look at outcomes and accomplishments and use them to make inferences about current employee performance.** In extant data analysis, the natural products of ongoing employee effort are examined to better understand performance and performance problems.

Extant data analysis is appropriate only in those front end situations where you are looking at a **performance problem**. Because extant data analysis looks at what is **actually happening and not happening**, the study must be of an **ongoing** situation as opposed to the TNA work which accompanies the introduction of a new technology.

Purposes of Extant Data Analysis

1. **Scrutinizing Results to Perceive Behavior:** The major purpose of extant data analysis is to determine the OUTCOMES of employee effort and then to use them to understand employee performance. Think about the carnival hawker who sells and sings and implores, but few customers choose to visit her exhibit. Or consider flight attendant behavior. All the drinks and food are distributed and collected on time, change is made and returned to passengers, but still there are complaints that this airline's attendants are *less responsive* than those of competitors. You could have watched the hawker and the attendants and not known that there was a problem with performance. By focusing on accomplishments, you know there is a problem, even if surface indicators suggest that they are *doing* OK.

2. **Seeking Truth Through Trends:** Extant data doesn't lie. While it may not give a complete picture of what is going on, it does offer a snapshot of the results of what is actually and naturally transpiring at the carnival or in the airplane. When the training professional uses extant data analysis to seek truth, he or she is looking for **trends in outcomes** which shed light on **trends in employee performance**. One letter of complaint from a customer or one quarter of weak sales represent a kind of truth to management. The challenge for a personnel or training specialist is to determine if that sliver of extant data (the letter or sales blip) is indicative of larger truths about what employees are doing or not doing.

3. **Using Results to Shape the TNA Effort:** These larger truths then enlighten TNA, becoming the basis for framing questions for latter stages of the study. Instead of queries like, "What's the problem with selling the 'Salt of the earth' account?," you can frame questions which are grounded by reality and detail. For example, "Third quarter sales of money market accounts, prior to the introduction of 'Salt of the earth' were stable, nearly identical to third quarter of last year. Since 'Salt' we're down 11 percent in *teller* generated new accounts. Why are tellers selling so few of these accounts?" is a better question. It shows you know what is going on and it stimulates more specific responses. Here's another example: "Let me quote to you from some letters from

passengers. Do you think they accurately reflect passenger treatment?" In the 'Salt of the earth' question, the trainer uses extant data to get information on CAUSE of the problem. In the airline example, extant data is grounding the search for more information about ACTUAL flight attendant performance.

4. **Matching Corporate or Agency Goals**: Extant data may be used to measure the company or agency against its goals or *reason for being*. Think about it this way. The nuclear power plant is really about producing energy, doing that for less than it costs to run the plant, doing it safely, and being permitted by regulators to keep operating. No particular employee performance, in and of itself, is of interest to management. Employee behavior matters, in the eyes of management, for how it contributes to the achievement of organizational goals. That is why extant data analysis is such a powerful tool for negotiating with management, employees and even unions. The issue is not what employees swear they know or do; it's how it turns out in light of the goals that have been established. The issue is the results of the aggregate of employee effort in comparison with the reasons that the group exists. Do employees respond properly when an alarm activates? Do passengers report having had a certain kind of experience on the airplane? Are the accounts being sold by tellers? The Human Resources group can train *ad nauseum*, and new employee behavior might even result, but applause will come only when all that effort results in ACCOMPLISHMENTS LINKED TO GOALS.

5. **Saving Money While at the Same Time Gaining Understanding of the Problem**: Because extant data analysis relies upon examination of **existing** information within the company or agency, trainers avoid the cost of generating **new** opinions and data. When we use the extant data analysis technique, we gather no new information. No interviews. No questionnaires. We seek nothing which is not already and naturally present in the organization. What we want is ACCESS to records, files, forms and print-outs, usually collected and retained for purposes other than analysis by training professionals.

6. **Verifying What You Hear During TNA**: As you carry out stages of TNA, you will often hear, "They don't know how to . . . ." or "We know all about that. We don't need training.

We need more . . . or better . . ." Use extant data analysis to go back and find out if they do, in fact, know how to explain the account or fill out the form. Several years ago I got involved in a TNA for word processing training. The word processors told us they knew all about the system, that there was no need to bother with training. If there were any problems, it was with the system and with their supervisors. What we did was examine the documents they had already created on the system for errors and frequency of kinds of uses. Inferring back from this extant data, we were able to verify their statements and to derive a clear picture of what they could actually do as well as what they chose to do with the system.

Description of the Extant Data Technique
Extant data analysis . . . .

☐ unearths the results of employee behavior

e.g., sales figures, accident reports, enrollments

☐ makes it possible to determine the relationship between employee effort and organizational goals

e.g., matching sales with expectations

☐ assures that internal, *regular* corporate data is part of the front end inquiry

e.g., accident reports or exit interviews as part of the study

☐ involves cajoling and negotiating for information

☐ is gathered and examined by human resources professionals but not originally generated by them.

When Do You Use This Technique?
Early and repeatedly when confronted with performance problems in **ongoing** situations—usually not new systems, products or technology.

Under ideal circumstances, a supervisor or manager has used extant data to determine the details of the problem before you are assigned to it. He or she then provides you with an initial description of the situation based on review of the records. That doesn't always happen.

What most often happens is that one sliver of extant data (like an accident or a letter to the CEO) gets the momentum going. *"Put together a course on this thing so we don't have any more of these accidents!"* or *"Do something on communications for our flight attendants. It's obvious they don't know how to keep our passengers happy."* Before doing anything, make certain that you have *first* taken a close and careful look at all natural, related records and information.

Once you have examined records and are now involved in all the stages of TNA, you will want to keep referring back to natural records. Extant data is a reality touchstone; it doesn't lie, especially if it is based on results of employee performance gathered over time. For example, you may be told by employees that they know all about the 'Salt of the earth' account. Go back to the extant data to check the records and see if there are any customer complaints about inaccurate information. Are the cards filled out correctly? Have customers been properly qualified? Match what you hear from sources during needs assessment with extant data. Pursue discrepancies.

How Is Extant Data Analysis Done?

Extant data analysis is a sleuthing technique which gets developers and trainers to outcomes of performance. Extant data analysis is unlike other front end techniques because it involves use of INFERENCE, OBSERVATION and PERSUASION only. Trainers will not interview or survey, instead they will pore over and paw through records and files. The keys to the technique are **figuring out what kind of information you need, determining where it is, gaining access to it and incorporating what you find.**

Here is a series of steps which will enable training professionals to carry out this technique:

Step 1: Examine the job and its outcomes.

Step 2: Identify quantitative results of the job.

Step 3: Identify qualitative results of the job.

Step 4: Determine how to get extant data
and eradicate obstacles.

Step 5: Examine the data.

Step 1: Examine the Job and Its Outcomes. Examine the job, focusing attention on the duties or tasks which have been identified as problematic. Think about what employees do, might do, and the opportunities or challenges with which they are confronted. For example, look carefully at the tellers' opportunities to sell 'Salt' accounts. Examine the materials that they have been given to give to customers who inquire about "Salt of the earth" accounts. Look at recent directives related to customer *wait time*. Has there been any recent corporate pressure to diminish the moments that customers stand on line? What else is going on in the branches now? Has there been a major ad campaign that might increase traffic for purposes other than 'Salt?' Are there any other new, competing products? When tellers were informed about 'Salt,' what else did they learn or get?

Step 2: Identify Quantitative Results of the Job. List the **tangible and possible quantitative outcomes** of that portion of the job. There are **enroute** outcomes and there are **terminal** outcomes. For example, an enroute outcome is the forms that the teller must fill out to initiate an account. The terminal outcome is the number of accounts sold and the size of the accounts. Word processing provides another example. Enroute quantitative outcomes would be the telephone and electronic mail questions logged regarding the system and its uses. A terminal outcome is the number and kind of documents generated per employee. Establishing quantitative outcomes is based on corporate or agency goals. It is entirely possible that the number and kind of documents is an enroute outcome. What the company is seeking to achieve is job stability and satisfaction. If that is the case, then a more appropriage terminal outcome would be the number of requests for transfer and information collected during exit interviews. Note that this step focuses on the kind of results which can be counted and measured objectively. When you begin to seek subjective information, for example, the kinds of aggregate feelings which might appear on exit interviews, then you are talking about the qualitative effects of employee performance. That moves us to Step 3.

Step 3: Identify Qualitative Results of the Job. List any likely **reports of qualitative impact of performance on people.** What are others, like customers or users, saying? Are there letters or telephonic comments that have been collected? What about performance appraisals or exit interviews? Most companies or agencies gather information about others' responses to them. What are they? Where are they? The classic example of this kind of subjective and important data is letters of complaint and appreciation. For whom? What are they saying? Remember that you are seeking the recorded and natural collection of opinions and responses. When thinking about qualitative outcomes, it is important to do more than count comments. You will be pressed to do a *content analysis*, a serious examination of the recurring and often subjectively derived themes within the extant data.

While both steps 2 and 3 involve systematic creation of lists, don't forget the richness of what Joe Arwady calls "eureka finds." There are piles of interesting indicators hidden within companies and agencies: old newsletters, exit interviews, requests for transfer, union mailings, etc.

Step 4: Determine How to Get Extant Data and Eradicate Obstacles. Now that you have a list, you need to do something with it. Where is the information? Who has it? Who else has it? Will there be resistance to your efforts to dig into files and peruse computer print-outs? Have there been any reports produced for other purposes which might relate to the problem or situation?

Not all extant data is equally accessible. **Usually, you can gain access to enroute outcomes more readily than the extant data which is very close to the bottom line.** The company might, for example, give you copies of the account slips and cards that have been filled out by tellers. Where they will balk is at the computer print-outs which present sales per teller, per supervisor and per branch.

It is not unusual for managers throughout the company to want to know *"why somebody from training wants to look at accident, breakage or cold call reports?!?"* You might have to construct elaborate justifications to gain access to extant data. I remember a performance appraisal project like that. Upper level management was dissatisfied with the quality of performance appraisals filed by middle managers. They turned it over to training and to an external consultant. They wanted a course to fix the problem. Before progress could be made, a verifiable picture of **actual**, current middle manager performance on these appraisals was necessary. It made sense to examine randomly selected performance appraisals that had been submitted over the past 18 months. Sounds reasonable? Sure. Still, the group had to justify, implore, reason and nearly beg to get their hands on this extant data. Finally, with names appropriately masked, the training group was allowed to scrutinize those appraisals and use them to infer actual middle manager skills and knowledge. If you are clear about what the extant data does for you, how it contributes to your TNA purposes, you will be more likely to be able to make a clear and compelling case to examine that data.

Step 5: Examine the data. What are you going to do with it once you have it? Look back at the list of possible uses for extant data included at the beginning of this chapter. Which are appropriate in your situation?

In the performance appraisal example, hand in hand with a subject matter expert from the Personnel group, you would examine these randomly selected appraisals for frequently recurring problems. Where are they? On which lines? What exactly are they? Is it a lack of specificity? Failure to use behavioral statements? Failure to substantiate? The exact nature of the errors which appear on the forms must be analyzed and then summarized.

Let's turn to the 'Salt' example. It is possible that extant data analysis will prove that tellers are filling the usual number of cards and that they are filling them out correctly. The problem is that they fail to fill them out for people who are *qualified* by income and circumstance to purchase the 'Salt' account. If that is the case, you need to ask questions about **why** they don't qualify purchasers. In that example, extant data directed the instructional designer to seek very specific information on **cause**.

The flight attendant problem might involve very different existing records. For that case, let's say the trainer examines all the unsolicited customer letters that have been received at the home office in the past three months and analyzes them for their content. The following issues, concerns and complaints about flight attendants were raised by letter writers. The percentage figure indicates the percentage of letters in which the comment appears.

- *not friendly enough, curt*   *17%*
- *inadequate food and beverage service*   *07%*
- *improper safety orientation*   *04%*
- *unprofessional appearance*   *10%*
- *uninformed about services, frequent flyer options*   *19%*
- *enforced rules inappropriately*   *04%*
- *unable to help on information about connections*   *11%*
- *miscellaneous problems about failure to meet needs*   *04%*

The content analysis of the letters clarifies the general areas which must be studied during this TNA. What exactly did the letters say the attendants actually did which was incourteous? What did they do which made the flight less pleasant than anticipated? What questions went unanswered or were answered incorrectly? Partial answers to these questions come from the letters; others must come from interviews with customers, supervisors and attendants, providing a reasonably detailed picture of what is actually transpiring on the planes. Additional information comes from observations of the attendants as they communicate with passengers. Can you look at the above list and begin to see the performance problem(s) which might be addressed through training?

Analysis of extant data provides information on what employees are **actually doing**, at least in the opinions of the customers who choose to write to the airlines. What needs additional confirmation? As you look at these figures, you are probably wondering WHY they are or are not doing something? **What are the implications of what you have discovered?**

An Example of the Five Steps of Extant Data Analysis

Not too long ago, a state legislature passed a law mandating "informed patient consent" prior to surgical procedures. This meant that the medical establishment was responsible for providing patients with information that would enable patients to make intelligent, individual decisions about their medical treatment, especially surgical treatment. Universal Hospital is expected to serve as a model enterprise in pre-surgery patient education. Imagine that you are the training director who is responsible for painlessly training 107 physicians to do this competently. Interns and residents will also participate in the program. The law has been in effect for nearly four months when the training director is tasked.

Step 1: Examine the job and its outcomes. We are focusing on the interpersonal interaction that accompanies information about common surgical procedures. Usually it occurs in a hospital room, often with family members present, and rarely is received as a welcome event. Most patients are nervous, uncomfortable with the problem and the impending solution, frequently viewing the surgery as the lesser of evils. Some patients are in awe of the physician, doubting that they have even the vocabulary to pose *good* questions, and stating that they don't want to waste his/her valuable time. Physicians, although most admit to the benefits of an informed patient, were not supportive of the legislation. They raised questions about just how much information would add up to an *informed* patient.

Step 2: Identify quantitative results of the job. The objective, *terminal* outcomes of this portion of the job are: medical record/ recovery of the post-surgery patient, number of malpractice suits, size of settlements, number of complaints to the hospital and legislature; and selection of the same surgeon for other procedures. Enroute quantifiable outcomes are: the number of times the physician must come back to the patient to secure permission for the surgery, length of contacts, time elapsed between explanation and consent, number of times that the individual changes his/her mind about the surgical procedure, reports of additional questions to other staffers about the procedure; and number and length of family contacts with the physician regarding the procedure.

Step 3: Identify qualitative results of the job. The most notable and useful qualitative result of this portion of the surgeon's job is a satisfied, informed patient who feels he/she has been treated well. Extant data indicating that kind of physician and hospital accomplishment are letters and calls of complaint and commendation from patients.

Step 4: Determine how to get data and eradicate obstacles. Terminal, longitudinal data like deaths and repeat choice of the physician is unavailable after only four months. Enroute quantitative indicators have not been collected by the medical or nursing staff, although they admit such information would be useful to have.

The training director turns to the qualitative extant data for a picture of how well doctors are actually handling this new and expanded responsibility. Letters to the legislature are unavailable, but those to hospital administration are readily turned over for perusal. Since patients are well aware of the new legislative thrust in this area, they have chosen to write with more frequency than usual. The Assistant Director of the Hospital is willing to allow the training group to examine the letters with a promise of confidentiality from the training director.

Step 5: Examine the data. Just under half of the 24 letters were complimentary. Patients felt that their physicians eased their minds and informed them prior to the surgery.

The other half were not at all satisfied with their educational experience. The problems, when subjected to content analysis, predominate as indicated below. The percentages reflect their appearance in the 13 letters which are judged as generally negative.

- *vague and confusing information*   *69%*
- *weak or absent post-surgical care explanation*   *54%*
- *failure to solicit or respond to questions*   *38%*
- *lofty and technical vocabulary*   *61%*
- *discomfort with role of educator*   *23%*
- *made patient more anxious*   *15%*
- *incorrect or biased information*   *23%*
- *got no information, took no time*   *08%*

A narrow majority of the patients who chose to communicate with the hospital are not satisfied. They do not feel that the physicians are in compliance with the law, and say so in useful detail.

They also are reasonably clear about the problems they have with the doctors' performance on this aspect of their jobs. Collapsing the areas of *lofty vocabulary* and *vague and confusing information* provides a clear picture of what patients think is the number one problem with their doctor as teacher. The other recurring problem is the doctors' failure to provide systematic and memorable information on post-surgical hospital and home care. A distant third is the physicians' omission of time for the patients to ask questions.

What are the implications of this information? The training director decides to verify these findings through follow-up interviews with patients and physicians. Given the OPTIMALS spelled out in the legislation and further specified by hospital administration, if this information on ACTUAL performance holds up after latter stages of assessment, she has clear directions for a lean training program.

However, before she trains these doctors in use of concrete and familiar words, examples and other educational techniques, the trainer must ascertain WHY they are not doing it satisfactorily. Since almost all of them are trying (only 1 out of 13 letters complains of no effort) and doctors agree that educating patients is important (though it shouldn't be legislated), why are they doing it poorly? Don't know what to say? Don't know how to say it? Can't tell appropriate from inappropriate detail? Same problem with vocabulary? Think there is no time to do it right? Try to say too much? Are they attempting to comply with the letter rather than the spirit of the law? That takes us to other TNA techniques, techniques which are appropriate to the search for the causes of performance problems.

Conclusion

Extant data analysis is the front end technique which directs attention to outcomes. Then, based on those outcomes, inferences are made about employee skills and knowledge. In extant data analysis, we look first at what employees accomplish, then at what they have done to bring about those effects.

Outcomes — — — (inference) — — — > Performance

A certain kind of information comes when you ask an employee about his or her ability to do the job. Another kind of information comes from watching employees do their jobs. This chapter has been about still another kind of front end technique and data. It is the powerful perspective and information which is derived from looking at outcomes and **then inferring back to the nature, quality and quantity of employee performance**. Extant data grounds the training professional in the real world surrounding the performance problem.

Resources

Gilbert, T.F. (1978). *Human Competence: Engineering Worthy Performance.* New York: McGraw-Hill.

Mager, R.F., & Pipe, P. (1970). *Analyzing Performance Problems.* Belmont, CA: Pitman.

Mager, R.F. (1972). *Goal Analysis.* Belmont, CA: Pitman.

Witkin, B.R. (1984). *Assessing Needs in Educational and Social Programs.* San Francisco: Jossey-Bass.

Part Two: TNA TECHNIQUES

Chapter Six: NEEDS ASSESSMENT

Brief Description

In 1933 John Dewey first drew national attention to the importance of including the learner's perspective in curricular decisions. Today, training professionals solicit opinions and feelings through an activity called "needs assessment." While most professionals agree that needs assessment is an activity that is worthy and useful, there is no consensus on procedures for doing an effective one.

Needs assessment is the systematic effort that we make to gather opinions and ideas from a variety of sources on performance problems or new systems and technologies. Let's look at each component of the definition:

"Systematic Effort." Needs assessments are carried out through three TNA tools: interviews, surveys and small group interactions. Whenever one of these tools is employed, it is for the purpose of acquiring certain kinds of information. Needs assessing is not random activity. As information is gathered, the findings shape the questions asked during latter needs assessment stages. While the training professional must remain open to the serendipitous morsel of relevant information, for the most part, he or she is very clear about why the interview, meeting or survey is transpiring.

"Opinions and Ideas." The trainer or personnel specialist is conducting a needs assessment to gather subjective data about a problem or new system. He or she wants to know how people think and feel about the situation, system, subject matter or problem. During needs assessment, training professionals seek opinions and ideas relevant to **all five** TNA purposes. What do sources think **ought** to be happening? What is **actually** happening?

How do they **feel** about it? In the case of a performance problem, what is **causing** the performance discrepancy? What might be done to **solve** the problem or to **introduce** the new system? Those are the broad questions which ground the needs assessment technique.

"Sources." Incorporate the ideas of groups and individuals with opinions on the job or the system. Stakeholders might include job incumbents, supervisors, customers, subject matter experts, upper management, members of the community, etc. An effective case study of a needs assessment by Ann Deden-Parker (1980) described the perspectives of the constituencies at Wells Fargo Bank.

"Performance Problems or New Systems and Technologies." Needs assessments are appropriate for learning about the people and conditions which surround **performance discrepancies**. Needs assessments are also essential to the **introduction of a new system or technology**. Through them the trainer or personnel specialist acquires answers to questions about how the system will optimally be used, how employees will receive it, as well as options for successfully introducing it.

Needs assessment is the most comprehensive and challenging TNA technique. It involves a quest for many kinds of information, from different sources, through interviews, print surveys and group meetings. Because so many people and perspectives are touched, often at disparate levels in the organization, needs assessing is a politically sensitive activity. Still, it is crucial to seek a clear picture of the affected source's opinions and ideas on the problem or system. The needs assessment technique is the primary vehicle for acquiring that information.

Needs Assessment and Extant Data Analysis

When using the needs assessment technique, the training professional is interested in all sources' **opinions** about optimals, actuals, feelings, causes and solutions. During extant data analysis, on the other hand, the trainer focuses on **results** and makes inferences about **actual performance from those results**.

Information from extant data analysis often provides the springboard for effective needs assessing. Let's look in on a needs assessment interview: *"You've said that middle managers don't have problems filling out the performance appraisals, and that the form is straightforward and simple to complete. I need help, then, in figuring out why the 24 appraisals that I randomly selected to examine had so many errors in them. In fact, only two of them are completely and correctly filled out according to Personnel. Take a look at these. I've masked the names and departments. What do you think is causing this problem?"* Here, as it should, extant data is significantly enriching the needs assessment interview process by grounding it in what has occurred at work.

Once opinions are collected during needs assessment, it makes good sense for the trainer to double back to look once again at the extant data. For example, after getting nearly unanimous expressions of confidence from middle managers on their ability to fill out appraisals and shrugs as to why that confidence didn't result in wonderful performance appraisals, this trainer went back and did a serious content analysis of the errors in the forms. It turned out that 70 percent of the problems and omissions appeared in the lines which request specific suggestions for employee improvement. He then took that information out to the field and was able to ask better and more targeted questions about current skills in that area. Confronted with dozens of middle manager entries like, *"better attitude," "more interest in the job," "take more initiative," etc.,* responding middle managers admitted the uselessness of those entries and talked in a more revealing way about not knowing how to accurately and realistically fill out that portion of the appraisal instrument. It eventually came down to lack of knowledge of how to write more specific and useful behavioral descriptions of arenas for employee improvement. Once upper management made it clear that big, globby statements like *"better attitude"* would not be accepted, managers and supervisors made rapid progress in learning how to correctly fill out that portion of the instrument.

Purposes of Needs Assessment

Imagine walking into a room full of trainees who feel they already know what they need to know about performance appraisals, or the D4 Bay, or the Slurpee machine, or the merit salary system. Or imagine sending out a "suitcase" course to train employees on the computerized service order tracking system and discovering that job incumbents are very hostile to the system, based on the rumors they have heard and their fondness for the system it is replacing.

The purpose of training is change. You must know how the change you are trying to effect strikes the people you are attempting to change. You need to know if they want to change; if they think there is a problem; if they want to adopt a new system or technology; if they feel confident about it; or if they think training is going to make a dent in the problem. Training professionals use needs assessment to find out what the crucial cast of characters think about the situation.

When conducting needs assessments, the trainer or instructional designer is:

1. **SEEKING OPTIMALS AND ACTUALS and, therefore, DE-TAILED DISCREPANCIES:** In needs assessment we try to find out what people think is happening vs. what **ought** to be happening. This lead to questions about **actuals.** *"How are they violating security procedures in their handling of confidential documents?"* and questions about **optimals.** *"What should they be doing with these documents? Try to specifically describe how they handle the documents in their offices and in transport from one locale to another."* A comparison between optimals and actuals yields detailed discrepancies.

2. **GROUNDING TNA IN THE *REAL* WORLD AND PER-CEPTIONS OF *REAL* PEOPLE:** In needs assessment, trainers ask people about their jobs and about their feelings about those jobs. One form of needs assessment is critical incident analysis which presses respondents for *war stories* that detail successes and failures on the job.

3. **SEEKING CAUSE(S) OF THE PROBLEM:** Chapter 4 presents the possible causes of performance problems. One of the purposes of needs assessment is to find out what different sources think is causing or contributing to the problem.

The possible causes of the problem are limited:

- *The employees don't have the **prerequisite** skill or knowledge.*
- *They don't know how to do what is expected of them.*
- *The environment gets in the way.*
- *There is no incentive for doing it or doing it right.*
- *Job incumbents don't think it is a valuable thing to do or know.*
- *They don't have confidence that they can do it.*

During needs assessment we find out if supervisors, job incumbents and other stakeholders "see it the same way." For example, supervisors may think that employees have forgotten check-in and check-out procedures for top secret documents and need to be retrained. On the other hand, the employees claim that they know the procedure, but feel it is unwieldy and unnecessary. If you put a gun to their heads, employees claim they could do that security check-out with perfection. During needs assessment, you must find these differences of opinion and resolve them before you can consider that you have successfully completed TNA.

4. SEEKING FEELINGS/PRIORITIES: Needs assessments should be used to assess sources feelings about:
- the topic, subject matter, system or problem;
- whether or not it is a priority;
- whether training is perceived to be an appropriate approach to the situation or whether some other solution is favored;
- their confidence at mastering it.

What you find out as you assess feelings has implications for determining whether or not motivation is a cause of the problem. Remember, motivation is described in Chapter 4 as the multiplicative relationship between the value an individual attaches to content and his/her belief that he/she can master it.

5. INVOLVING SIGNIFICANT PARTIES TO ACHIEVE BUY-IN: While seeking information on optimals, actuals, feelings and causes, the trainer is simultaneously using needs assessment to get people involved in the instructional product or service or alternative solution BEFORE implementation. A classic professional frustration goes like this:

□ *Methodology and marketing departments introduce a new system or program and order up some training to teach staff about it. They want the course to be ready just as soon as the new system is.*

□ *The course developer works with subject matter experts to design and develop a course which assures that the new thing or method meshes with current systems.*

□ *The course is offered and field supervisors across the company resist sending their people because they ABSOLUTELY NEED EVERYONE THEY HAVE. Supervisors feel strongly that they*

*can't afford to release people from their jobs to go and get trained—
at least not right now.*

Solicit information from managers. Get field supervisors to
share their priorities. Ask them what problems they anticipate in
releasing personnel for training on the new system. The TNA
process **gathers** and **disseminates** information. *Needs assessment
can be an effective marketing tool.*

6. **TRAINING MANAGEMENT IN WAYS OF LOOKING AT
PROBLEMS**: I think that performance technologists and trainers
have major contributions to make to the way companies and
agencies are managed. We can insinuate ourselves into the system
through the quality of the questions we ask, the specificity and
clarity we model for our colleagues in other units, and the uses
we make of the information we gather.

During a consultancy with a military contractor, a training
manager told me this story. She had been conducting a rare and
important needs assessment interview with the CEO of her company. After repeated pressure by her to be very clear, tangible and
behavioral about the optimals he had in mind for a *quality assurance training program*, he exclaimed, "I see what you're getting
at. It's like when John Fitzgerald Kennedy vowed that we would
put a man on the moon before the decade was out. He didn't say
we would achieve superiority in space. JFK talked in tangible
terms about the outcome he expected of the country. I need to
do that when I talk to you about our *quality assurance program*."
This was a breakthrough for the training manager. In fact, through
this needs assessment interview, she carried out significant, induc-
tive training with the CEO.

Description of the Needs Assessment Technique

Needs assessment . . . .

☐ relies upon opinions and feelings gathered through interviews, surveys and group meetings;

☐ seeks information on all five purposes; optimals, actuals,
feelings, causes and solutions;

☐ involves as many concerned sources as you can afford;

☐ is conducted in stages with what you learn in the first
stage influencing the questions you ask and data you examine in
latter stages.

WHEN DO YOU USE THIS TECHNIQUE?

Always. The question is not **whether** you will solicit this kind of information through needs assessment. It's **how much** of it you will do and using which tools.

How can you solve a problem you don't understand? How can you develop training or other kinds of interventions for people whose perspectives you haven't examined? Needs assessment is important because it is the training professional's method of exploring the hearts and minds of concerned parties.

It is rare to use needs assessment **first** in TNA. When you do use it first, it takes on the qualities of what Roger Kaufman (1979) calls an *alpha assessment*. This is an assessment which is not initially limited and defined by managerial focus or extant data.

Alpha assessments involve going directly to the job incumbent or learner and saying, "What can we do for you? What do you want from our group? What might help you do your job better?"

An *alpha assessment* is similar to an unstructured market survey. In such a situation, you are able to go out and ask open-ended questions about preferences. Market conditions permit and encourage educational institutions to conduct *alpha assessments*, as they seek to serve and attract diverse populations. They are far less frequent in corporations, where the range of inquiry is limited by corporate priorities.

It is the rare corporate training director who is afforded the opportunity to think and assess, in an *alpha-ish way*, the needs of employees in the corporation or agency. More often, lamentably, the training director must respond to crisis demands to "get the new system on line" or "plug up the holes we think we have in our security procedures" or "increase sales of the frangarama." Within broad problem arenas or in response to corporate goals, it would be useful for training professionals to perform as strategic planners, not just fire fighters.

HOW IS NEEDS ASSESSMENT DONE?

Needs assessment is active, repeated interactions with sources about a new technology or performance problem. While the professional literature abounds with exhortations to DO needs assessments, it is short on prescriptions for HOW TO DO THEM. There are no simple algorithms for planning and conducting needs assessments. Instead, in this chapter, guidelines in the form of broad steps are presented. These steps focus on the issues each trainer should consider when using this technique. Examples are presented within each step with a summarizing example to pull Chapter 6 together. Chapters 8, 10 and 11 describe the use of interviews, surveys and groups to enact this needs assessment technique.

Here are the needs assessment steps:

Step 1: Select sources for needs assessment.

Step 2: Determine stages of assessment.

Step 3: Select and use TNA tools.

Step 4: Create items.

Step 5: Consider critical incident analysis.

Step 1: Select Sources for Needs Assessment. Who are your sources? Who are the people who know and care or who don't care and should? Who will be touched by changes that the Training or Industrial Relations Departments are attempting to make in people or in their environment? Are there customers, supervisors or even volunteers who might shed light on what has and hasn't been happening? Go to potential trainees and their supervisors as sources, but go beyond them too.

It sounds simple. Of course, you would consult with a wide range of sources during TNA and before launching a training effort. Yet, at least a dozen times in the past year, I've heard colleagues say, "I never thought to talk to a customer"; or "It never occurred to me that the immediate supervisors should be brought in on this thing early on"; or "The people who want this course developed want it so fast that they won't even let me meet with the job incumbents."

Use this brief section of the book to remind yourself about *all* the possible sources, all the constituencies who should be queried during needs assessments. And when management stands between you and those sources, point to this chapter.

Here are some examples of needs assessment sources:

☐ Cordless phone sales are down and management wants sales training put in place to take care of the problem. Query:

- sales staff
- sales managers
- subject matter experts
- customers
- corporate marketing experts

☐ United Way volunteers aren't considered sufficiently "helpful" around agency offices because they can't operate word processing or data base programs. Query:

- volunteers
- office supervisors
- United Way managers
- non-volunteer office employees
- telephone callers

☐ Personnel has changed procedures for initiating disciplinary actions and wants management to switch over to the new policy. Query:

- upper management
- personnel management
- legal experts
- middle managers and supervisors who will implement procedures
- employees

After you've determined the different groups that need to be queried, you confront the question of **how many individuals ought to be involved in the TNA**. It depends on two things:

(1) whether you're getting the **information** you seek from in-depth contacts with small numbers; and

(2) how much information and confirmation you need to feel **confident and to convince others.**

A training professional who is asking good questions can learn an enormous amount from interviews with very few individuals, even just one supervisor and two employees, for example. The quality of information is more affected by the questions asked and the time and skill employed in soliciting information than it is by automatically relying upon large sample sizes.

A good way to start needs assessing is by selecting a few wise individuals to interview. Then, in a latter stage of assessment, you may choose to assure the clout of your findings by using statistical analyses to establish levels of confidence.

"Confidence" is a word that statisticians use in a rather technical way. They are talking about how reliable the results of a study are, how likely it is that the findings are due to the treatment or variable in question, rather than an error in the survey or assessment methodology.

You can only use confidence percentages (e.g., *We are 95% certain that these results reflect volunteers' attitudes towards the use of word processors in social service agencies*) if you **randomly** select subjects for interviews or surveys. That's hard to do when you lack control over your sources and settings. My editor's comment about "random" selection was, "I don't want to *randomly* select; I want to *purposefully* select."

The use of inferential statistics also depends upon a **hefty response rate** upon which to make generalizations. Basically, the smaller the total population or source group, the larger the percentage of randomly sampled respondents there must be. For example, to achieve .05 level of confidence, that's a 95 percent confidence level, you need to sample 23 out of a total population of 25 branch managers. For 250 teller supervisors, you'd need to randomly sample 150; and for 1200 tellers, you would sample 300 tellers. Think of the time, paper and prayer to achieve the response rate you need to employ inferential statistics in your reports.

Both **time** and **skill** are essential if you are going to rely upon inferential statistics to establish statistical confidence in your findings. You need **time** to assure the reliability of the items you are using and to gather large numbers of responses for analysis. You also rely upon **skill** to employ and interpret the statistics you choose. Zemke and Kramlinger (1982) admit that though they have logged many hours in statistics classes, they "wouldn't think of doing a major study without a *real* statistician on the team." (p. 319) They suggest that if you choose to use inferential statistics, you should seek help early in the process, so that your data gathering systems will mesh with your statistical intentions.

You must make a decision about statistics early in TNA, when you are selecting sources and determining numbers. You can't decide to use descriptive statistics (e.g., Fifty percent of respondents feel . . .) if you have only interviewed two people. And you can't use inferential statistics (e.g., We are 99 percent certain . . .) without large numbers of randomly selected respondents.

I am not advocating the use of large numbers over small. Often, as my editor reminded me, there just isn't the time and inclination within companies for that kind of study. The reality is that inferential statistics are powerful tools which time, resources and priorities often deny to training and development professionals. We will come back to these issues when we talk about questionnaires, and using computers to analyze and report TNA results.

Step 2: Determine Stages of Assessment. An effective needs assessment is based on repeated inquiries of different sources. That is what I mean by the phrase, "stages of assessment." Too often, training and performance technology professionals rely on a single, mega-instrument to get a picture of the problem or situation. Usually, that's a mistake.

Far more effective is the use of stages, repeated contacts with sources through a variety of TNA tools, with each stage bringing the developer closer and closer to what Robert Mager has called the "heart of the matter." Each successive stage enables the trainer to define the problem or new system in more specific and accurate terms. In Chapter 12, **all** techniques for TNA are described and planned. In this chapter we focus only on repeated stages of **needs assessment**.

Each stage of assessment uses one of the tools detailed in Part Three of this book for a contact with sources. They are interviews (Chapter 8); observations (Chapter 9); interactions with groups (Chapter 10); and print surveys (Chapter 11). For example, one stage of assessment might be interviews with section chiefs; another might be the distribution of a two-page questionnaire to 125 new hires; and another stage might be a focus group with five shoppers. Each stage of information-gathering permits the trainer to ask better, more targeted questions of the source or sources in subsequent stages. The stages in needs assessment are the mechanisms we use to zero in on the performance discrepancy or the context for the innovation.

Let's look at a specific example. This instructional designer is charged with getting office workers up to speed on word processing.

Stage 1: Conduct telephonic interviews with six office workers who are expected to begin utilizing the new system.

Stage 2: Interview management regarding selection of the particular system, its strengths and weaknesses, anticipated response to the system.

Stage 3: Examine documentation for the word processing system. (Extant data analysis)

Stage 4: Meet with four office supervisors, all of whom participated in the selection of the system. They have been trained in its operation.

Stage 5: Gather a group of office workers to discuss response to the new system and to commencing training on it.

Stage 1 ––> Stage 2 ––> Stage 3 ––> Stage 4 ––> Stage 5

**Interview incumbents––> Interview managers ––>
Examine documentation ––> Meet with SME's ––>
Meet with incumbents ––>**

Why five stages? In this case, perhaps because the designer felt that he needed that much contact with sources and that much information in order to prepare for introducing the new system. In addition, his company was willing for him to spend this time on the TNA because the system and its uses were so important to their work.

Why any particular number of stages? Needs assessments may have any number of stages for which the corporation or agency is willing to pay. Determination of the number of stages is based on two considerations:

☐ how much information you need before you feel confident that you know what is going on or what will go on when the innovation is introduced; and

☐ how much time and money has been allocated to this TNA. Amounts vary according to the importance, complexity and context of the situation in the eyes of the company or agency.

The more experience you have with the industry, the subject matter and the job incumbents, the more quickly you will feel confident that the information you have is conclusive. Therefore you will feel that you need fewer stages of assessment. An example is presented by the pilot who finishes a distinguished military career and immediately goes to work for a private contractor who develops training programs for the armed forces. When assigned to a project for F-14s, he feels confident relying upon only two stages of assessment. He knows the subject matter and the people who will be in the training program. One day, however, this same man gets a promotion. The company asks him to manage a major contract with the Saudi Arabian Navy. Far less confident about the people and their situation, this retired pilot spends time and money in numerous stages of assessment.

Step 3: Select and Use TNA Tools. In the preceding pages we've looked at purposes, sources and stages for needs assessment. Now we must figure out **how to go out there and conduct needs assessments.** It's time to answer the question: Why do we use one method over another to gather information? Our options for conducting needs assessments are presented below:

- I.   Individual or small number needs assessments
     - A. Person to person
     - B. Telephone surveys
     - C. Print
     - D. Small group meetings
- II. Large number inquiries
     - A. Print
     - B. Telephone surveys

In Part Three of TNA each of these assessment tools is described and exemplified in its own chapter. Now we will talk about these options in light of the concerns trainers and industrial relations specialists confront as they determine **which** tool to select for needs assessment.

Two factors influence decisions about tools: (1) purposes for the study; and (2) tool use factors. Let's look first at your purposes.

(1) Purposes and Tool Selection

What is it that you want to accomplish through the study? What are the purposes you seek to accomplish? Examine the list of possible benefits of needs assessment detailed at the beginning of this chapter. These purposes influence the way(s) you will approach sources during needs assessment.

There are, however, no hard and fast rules. Like so much else in front end analysis, *it depends on the purpose and on the situation*. Let's focus first on possible purposes for conducting a needs assessment:

• **SEEKING OPTIMALS:** Usually, trainers don't need to worry about anonymity when trying to get a clear picture of what the optimal performer knows and does. It's just not that controversial. Most often it is speculative, and people are willing to dream for attribution. Therefore, interviews and group meetings are appropriate. The major problem with relying upon surveys for information about optimals is that written responses are rarely provided in sufficient detail.

• **SEEKING ACTUALS:** The quest for what is currently going on—in detail—is more risky. Employees and supervisors are often less able or willing to describe actual performance. That means that the instructional designer will, more often, turn to anonymous surveys, observations or to inferences based on extant data for a picture of what is actually going on.

• **SEEKING CAUSE(S) OF THE PROBLEM:** This kind of information can be a hot potato. Is it that people without sufficient prerequisite skills were hired? That supervision is weak or absent? That the equipment isn't repaired? Isn't sufficient for the job? Or that the employees don't know how to do this portion of the job? The answers to these questions reflect on *real* people who hold positions in the company or agency. In order to get dependable information in response to questions about cause, you must either establish a trusting relationship with interviewees or convince respondents that responses to the print survey are truly anonymous.

• **SEEKING FEELINGS/PRIORITIES:** Will sources tell you how they feel about the problem or the introduction of a new system? If there is a trusting relationship, if they believe that what they say will be used without attribution, then interviews and group meetings may be used for needs assessment. If you're not sure, you will probably have to rely upon anonymous surveys to solicit feelings, priorities and confidence surrounding a situation.

• **INVOLVING SIGNIFICANT PARTIES TO ACHIEVE BUY-IN**: This is a situation of "the more, the merrier." Since you want to solicit support from many people at many levels of the organization, group meetings and surveys are cost-effective. If one or a few individuals are resisting, individual meetings would be appropriate.

• **TRAINING MANAGEMENT IN WAYS OF LOOKING AT PROBLEMS**: A print survey won't accomplish this purpose. Individual interviews are probably best, with small group meetings tailing behind.

(2) Tool Use Factors

Each tool has different characteristics which affect its appropriateness for needs assessment. Let's look at each of the factors; consider them in light of your situation. These comments are summarized in Figure 6.1.

Anonymity of sources: Surveys permit it. Interviews and group meetings do not.

Cost/Speed: It depends on number of interviewees, size of small groups, locations of individuals, length of interviews or meetings, number of phone calls, whether or not you must pay for calls or time with individuals, etc. The cost of surveys builds up in the planning stages and continues as instructional designers wait for instruments to be returned.

Opportunity to Follow-up: This is the great strength of interviews and groups. Once you've asked a question and have heard an intriguing or obtuse or unclear response, you can pursue it further. Not so with surveys. If they are truly anonymous, what you've gotten back is what you've got.

Response rate: The rate is usually high in the more personal tools, interviewing and meeting with groups. Response rates with print surveys are often low but can be affected by techniques detailed in Chapter 11.

Ease of analysis: This depends on preparation to capture responses. All tools create problems if preliminary thought isn't given to what you are going to do with the data when you get

NEEDS ASSESSMENT TOOLS

| FACTORS | INTERVIEWS | | | PRINT SURVEYS | |
| | In Person | | Telephonic | Small n | Large n |
	Indiv.	*Sm. grp.*			
Anonymity of sources	None	None	None	Some	High
Cost	Depends on number distance, length	Depends on number distance, length	It depends on length, number and cost of calls	Low	Usually high especially in devpt of instrument
Follow-up Questions	Good opport'y	Fair opport'y	Good opportunity	Some or none	None
Response Rate	High	High	Usually high	Depends on quality of questions & anonymity	Usually low
Ease of Analysis	It depends	It depends	It depends	Easy with preparation	Depends on quality of questions & data analysis prep.
Risk	Some	High, need group skills	Some	Some, print endures	High, many people receive & print endures

Figure 6.1

it. Obviously, computers facilitate analysis of large number print surveys with forced choice questions.

Risk to the professional: What you do during needs assessment may bring applause or ridicule. Most training professionals say that they feel the greatest professional risk comes during the leadership of small groups and the dissemination of print surveys. Picture the situation. You have gathered seven engineers and field supervisors to talk about improved maintenance procedures for a mainframe computer. They all disagree. They even disagree on whether the corporation should attempt to develop a course to standardize procedures from region to region. Or listen in on this quote about a survey, "I was so embarrassed when I got a call from the southern region. Reggie was furious. He thought my survey questions were 'leading' and he found a spelling error."

A discussion of tool selection for needs assessment is often moot. Frequently, management is pressing us, forcing us to look at our watches, to realize we only have time to get in touch with a few people. Then, because of limitations on time, we wind up doing three quick telephone interviews, and a hurried small group meeting, if that.

Thus, *in the real world*, we are pressed to make that brief meeting and those interviews count. Success depends on the quality of the questions that are asked. That leads us to Step 4 in needs assessment.

Step 4: Create Items. The most challenging task facing trainers as they conduct needs assessment is determining the "right" questions to ask. What do you ask in order to obtain the information you need to move on? to convince others that you understand the problem? the context for the innovation? to convince yourself that you comprehend the situation? The success of needs assessment, and often, of TNA, is based on the substance of the questions you ask. That brings us to a way for crafting items based on what you are trying to find out from sources.

In 1982 I published an article in the *Journal of Instructional Development*, titled, "A Typology for Generating Needs Assessments." That article serves as a basis for the approach that follows.

The item typology is based on the **reasons** we conduct needs assessments. Born, thus, of a purpose-based approach to TNA, it also takes into account the most common errors in needs assessment instruments and reports.

Here is a description of each item type. Then I'll present several examples for each. And, finally, I will link the types to the familiar purposes for TNA.

Type 1 questions: **Seek a general picture of the problem.** Is there a discrepancy? Is there a problem? What is going on that is a problem? What do you wish was occurring? Describe the situation which has led you to initiate this request for training.

Type 2 questions: **Seek details of the situation.** Describe *in detail* the problem which is occurring. What is the *next level of specifics* about the situation?

Type 3 questions: **Demand proof of what job incumbent knows.** Can incumbents do what they say they can do? Do they know what they say they know? While all other types of questions are satisfied by respondent **opinions**, Type 3 questions ask the learner to perform as if he/she already knows how to do it. Opinions don't count in Type 3 items.

Type 4 questions: **Seek feelings.** How do people feel about the situation subject or task? Their feelings tend to revolve around four areas:

    4a: Feelings about the *topic*, skills or body of knowledge
    4b: Feelings about *training* related to it
    4c: Perception of it as *priority* in relation to other topics
    4d: *Confidence* related to it

Type 5 questions: **Seek the cause(s) of the problem.** What is creating or contributing to the problem or discrepancy? Possible answers to this question are derived from the concepts in Chapter 4.

Type 6 questions: **Seek basic information about the respondent.** Who is this person? Age? Sex? Experience? Number of people reporting to them? What does the trainer need to know about respondents which will be looked at in light of their opinions (Types 1, 2, 4 & 5) or their performance (Type 3)? **Only ask for demographic information that is relevant to the purposes of the needs assessment.** For example, if you are doing an assessment related to performance appraisals, it makes sense to ask how long someone has been a manager or how many appraisals they are expected to complete each month. Less obviously relevant in this case is inquiry about income or age. Judiciously select information which will help you understand what is going on.

Here are examples of each type question with brief commentary.

Type 1 questions: **Seek a general picture of the problem.**

    1.1   What errors are they making in carrying out the short-age control procedures?

    1.2   What questions do you have about employing the short-age control procedures?

    1.3   Please make a list of the questions you have about nutrition which contributes to a healthy pregnancy and baby.

    1.4   Do you think employees have problems with the short-age control procedures? What are they?

    1.5   What experiences have you had that have led you to enroll in this PUBLIC SPEAKING FOR INSTRUCTORS class?

    1.6   Circuit pack maintenance has been identified by management as a problem in our region. Do you agree? Explain your answer below.

Commentary: Note that these questions are all fairly broad and that they seek information about what is currently going on, and what ought to be going on. They also press the respondent to begin to define a problem or discrepancy, if possible.

Type 2 questions: **Seek details of the situation.**

    2.1   You have already indicated concern about store closing procedures in our shortage program. Please describe three concerns that you have about this segment of the program.

    2.2   Think about the months of pregnancy that stretch before you and the eating that you will do. Here is a list of topics which relate to nutrition during pregnancy. Rate them as follows:

        2 = of *great* interest to me, 1 = of *some* interest, 0 = of *no* interest at all

        a. planning a basic diet during pregnancy

        b. dieting during pregnancy

        c. appropriate exercise

        d. favorite foods and the fetus

        e. budgeting and eating right

    f. alcohol and cigarettes

    g. preparing to nurse through nutrition

    h. the basic food groups

    i. food cravings

2.3 Rank the following based on their criticality for store shortage control in *your* store. Let the number 1 indicate the area in which your people have the most problems with the control routine and the number 4 indicate the least problematic component of shortage control.

    .....a. Surveillance of customers

    .....b. Cash register security

    .....c. Daily opening procedures

    .....d. Daily closing procedures

2.4 How are employees running into problems in the surveillance of customers? What exactly do you see as the most common problems they confront or errors they make?

Commentary: Note that Type 2 items burrow deeper, seeking details of the problem. Most often these are questions about actual performance, about the errors, problems and questions job incumbents have as they do their work. **The key here is to ask respondents for useful specifics.**

Type 3 questions: **Demand proof of what job incumbents know.**

3.1 Mary Jacobs, a 135 lb. woman, is in her second trimester of pregnancy. She consumes two 4 oz. glasses of wine each day. Is she within tolerable limits of alcohol consumption?

3.2 Please watch this videotape of shoppers in our convenience store. There are three shoppers. One of them has just stolen a package of Contac. Another is displaying behaviors which corporate policy identifies as "suspicious." The third has done nothing to warrant shortage control classification. Identify each of these characters and state your reasons for these identifications.

3.3. The circuit pack bippy is indicating need for immediate attention. Which of the following is the first step to take?

.....a. call the supervisor

.....b. implement blue alert

.....c. hose it off

.....d. throw it away and install new one

Commentary: Note that these questions make the respondents do something. They are expected to act like a competent job incumbent (shortage controller) or knowledge-possessor (pregnant woman). Type 3 questions should rarely lead off a print survey, because people will resist their *testlike* feel. Neither should they be asked questions to which they will not know the answers. That's why Type 3 questions are more likely to occur on needs assessments attached to performance problems rather than new systems or technologies. It is also important to make sure that these queries are job-related. Items 3.1 - 3.3 are grounded in real world decisions, as opposed to questions like, "Who did the landmark research on alcoholism and pregnancy?" Type 3 questions are useful when used judiciously, to determine whether or not employees know what they know.

Type 4 questions: **Seek feelings about topic (4a); training (4b); priority (4c); confidence (4d)**

    4.1 How do you feel about surveillance procedures that have been implemented in stores? (Type 4a)

    4.2. Our circuit pack bippy maintenance program is top-notch. Which best describes your feelings about that statement? (Type 4a)

        .....a. Strongly agree

        .....b. Agree

        .....c. Don't know or not sure

        .....d. Disagree

        .....e. Strongly disagree

    4.3 Which best describes your feelings about taking a class on nutrition and life style during pregnancy? (Type 4b)

        .....a. eager

        .....b. indifferent

        .....c. hostile

    4.4 Describe your response to being selected for the course on microcomputer troubleshooting of circuit pack bippies? (Type 4b)

4.5 Management is considering offering a series of seminars on effective performance appraising. Think about the skills you currently have and those you wish you had. Should we launch this seminar series or would another topic help you more? (Type 4c)

4.6 What are your training priorities? Rank the following according to your interest in training on the topic. Let the number 1 represent your top priority, the number 2 reflect the next most important area to you, and so on. (Type 4c)

.....a. Cleaning bippies

.....b. Anticipating bippy problems

.....c. Using computer to maintain bippies

.....d. Replacing bippy parts

4.7 I know that I will be good at using a computer to troubleshoot circuit pack bippies. Which best describes your feelings about that statement? (Type 4d)

.....a. Strongly agree

.....b. Agree

.....c. Don't know or not sure

.....d. Disagree

.....e. Strongly disagree

4.8 Do you think that you can learn to control your dietary habits during this pregnancy? (Type 4d)

Commentary: Note that each questions fits within one of the four feeling categories: topic (4a); training related to it (4b); priority (4c); and confidence (4d). These four kinds of feeling were not casually generated. The four are the areas of feelings that training professionals need to know about, areas with implications for decisions about the cause(s) of the problem and, eventually, for training design. Do employees value the topic? Do they feel confident about it? Those two factors multiplicatively relate to provide a description of motivation, a finding which sheds light on the cause of the problem. Type 4b and 4c items contribute to a deeper picture of how much employees value the topic or problem, and whether or not they think training is an appropriate approach to it.

Type 5 questions: **Seek the cause(s) of the problem.**

5.1 Why do you think our store personnel are having so many problems implementing this shortage control program?

5.2 While pregnant women in this county have successfully cut back on alcohol and tobacco consumption, they are far less successful at weight control during pregnancy. To what do you attribute this?

5.3 When microcomputers were brought in to assist the Southeastern region in troubleshooting the bippy, the field operators avoided the micros. Which of the following, from your experience with the system and the operators, contributed to the lack of use? Rate each as follows:

2 = major factor   1 = a factor   0 = not a factor

.....a. the hardware is unreliable

.....b. the software is weak

.....c. operators don't know how to use it

.....d. operators disagree with the readings

.....e. the micros are slower than the operators at deciding

.....f. lack of availability of the equipment

.....g. it's too complex to learn

.....h. operators fear that the computers will take their jobs

.....i. our operators don't like computers

.....j. supervisors don't support our use of the computers

5.4 Examine 5.3 above and place an asterisk (*) next to the item which is the major cause of the problem with operator computer use. Place only one asterisk.

Commentary: As discussed in Chapter 4, there are a limited number of possible causes of a performance discrepancy. If you examine item 5.3, you can link each choice to a different kind of cause. For example, 5.3a, b, e, & f indicate environmental obstacles; items 5.3c & g indicate a skills/knowledge problem; item 5.3j suggests an incentive problem; and items 5.3d, e, h & i indicate that employee feelings may stand in the way of successful use of the micros in troubleshooting. Items 5.3d & e might indicate *environmental* or *feelings* problems. The training professional will need to look further at the situation, if respondents rate these choices as a major contributor to the problem.

Type 6 questions: **Seek information about the respondent.**

    6.1   Please check those that are available to you at your desk:

        .....a. calculator   .....b. word processor

        .....c. microcomputer   .....d. computer programs

        .....e. documentation   .....f. printer

        .....g. speaker phone   .....h. first aid kit

    6.2   Please check the category that includes the amount of experience you've had with our company:

        .....a. 1 day to 90 days

        .....b. 91 days to 1 year

        .....c. more than 1 year

    6.3   Please check any of the training courses you have attended since assuming a supervisory position with this company. Check all that apply to you.

        .....a. Motivating employees

        .....b. Setting goals

        .....c. Management by objectives

        .....d. Salary administration

        .....e. Writing performance appraisals

        .....f. Conducting appraisal interviews

        .....g. Encouraging safety on the job

        .....h. Encouraging ethical conduct

        .....i. Enhancing productivity

    6.4   Do employees in your store have the following as they attempt to implement the shortage control program? Rate each as follows:

        2=always   1=sometimes   0=never

        .....a. one way mirrors

        .....b. two clerk shifts

        .....c. Shortage Handbooks

        .....d. shrink tags on merchandise

        .....e. surveillance VCR's in store

        .....f. surveillance VCR's at register

        .....g. manager or assistant manager availability on every shift

Commentary: This is a new item type which I added to help the instructional designer or trainer differentiate between opinions and perceptions (as discovered through Types 1, 2, 4 and 5), proof of current skill or knowledge (based on performance by incumbents on Type 3's), and facts about the respondent and the setting (Type 6's). When Jennifer Burkett-Evans and I solicited needs assessment instruments from individuals who had had no formal training in the item typology, we discovered that a surprisingly large number of questions were of the Type 6 variety. I doubt if the best use of a needs assessment survey is to ask questions about age, sex, equipment, training history, etc. Isn't that kind of information available elsewhere? Just yesterday I pointed at a Type 6 question, *"Are you male or female?"* and asked why it was included in the survey. "I don't know," was the response, "Don't you always ask for that kind of information?" **If you include Type 6 items in anonymous surveys, it should be because you intend to cross-tabulate demography with opinions and performance derived from the other item types.**

Figure 6.2 summarizes the item types.

Figure 6.3 links the item typology with purpose-based assessment. The figure shows the most obvious relationships, with Type 1 and 2 questions contributing to information about performance discrepancies; Type 3 questions providing a picture of what employees actually can do. Type 4 questions represent feelings, and Type 5 questions directly seek perspectives on causes. Type 6 questions are not purpose-related; they seek descriptive information about the respondent.

There are less obvious relationships between item types and purpose-based assessment. If, for example, a job incumbent is unable to respond to a Type 3 question, then he or she lacks the skills or knowledge. Such a finding has implications for decisions about the cause of a performance discrepancy. Type 4 questions also contribute to decisions about the cause of the problem. If employees do not value the subject or skills, or think training won't make a dent in the problem, or see the topic as a low priority, or doubt their ability to master "it," impaired motivation must be taken into account as a causative factor.

SELECTING ITEM TYPES

To Acquire Information On: **USE**

- What problems there are
- Who thinks that there are problems
- Who doubts these problems   ➤   **Type 1's**
- What ought to be going on, in general
- What is going on, in general

- What ought to be going on, in detail
- What is going on, in detail
- Who has opinions on the details   ➤   **Type 2's**
- Where attention should be focused
  during the TNA and training program

- Whether or not potential trainees
  know what they know   ➤   **Type 3's**
- Whether or not trainees are truthful

- How people feel about the job, task,
  system, skill. . . .
- How they feel about training on it   **Type 4's**
- How big a priority this is to sources   ➤
- Whether or not trainees feel they are
  able to learn it

- What sources think is causing the
  problem
- What or which, of the possible causes   ➤   **Type 5's**
  of problems, is causing this problem

- Who are the respondents
- Does demography or situation   ➤   **Type 6's**
  influence answers to items

Figure 6.2

ITEMS AND PURPOSES

PURPOSE

TYPE	OPTIMALS	ACTUALS	FEELINGS	CAUSES	SOLUTIONS
1	X	X			
2	X	X			
3		X			
4a			X		
4b			X		X
4c			X		X
4d			X		
5				X	
6					

Figure 6.3

Step 5: Consider Critical Incident Analysis. Critical incident analysis is a kind of questioning which also gets you from general problems to the specific details of performance problems. It is based on interacting with sources to extract the really juicy details of people's experiences. Based on work done by John C. Flanagan (1954), critical incident analysis is a systematic search for the proverbial "war stories." Critical incident analysts work to ferret out the details of successful and unsuccessful performance on-the-job.

I don't think of critical incident analysis as a separate kind of assessment. Rather, I find it most useful to think of it as a line of inquiry, a special way of asking for information about **optimal and actual** performance and knowledge during needs assessment.

Think back on the yellow highlighting pens and charcoal pencils we've used at other times in our lives. They are what I think of when I employ critical incident analysis. The **highlighter pen** relates to critical incident questions like:

"What is it you say that most often closes the sale?"

"Look at this list which describes the details of our selection procedures for assistant store manager. What is it on the list which you think is most important? Why? Is there anything we've missed?"

"Which part of the performance appraisal form causes the most problems to you as you are conducting the interview?"

"Think about the experiences you've had in the field where you were stumped. What did you confront? What did they say? How did you handle it?"

"When you think about the really great instructors that you've known, what is it that you remember them doing that was most effective?"

The **charcoal pencil** seeks shadowing and detail:

"I heard that you and several of the other salesmen use a technique you call Michigan Conformity to counter a certain kind of skepticism about our product. Tell me exactly what you guys say and do when you use it."

"Chandra Harvard was threatening a grievance up until the meeting she had with you. What did you say that forstalled the proceedings? I know that you 'calmed' her. But what is it that 'calmed' her? Try to tell me how it happened."

"How did you decide to ask for additional lab tests? What is it that you felt or saw that led you to order those tests? What were you thinking?"

"I know that you participated in approving these two bad loans. What I want to do is to try and figure out how these two got past our screening procedures. Will you walk me through your reasoning on this?"

By pressing people to close their eyes and think back on real interactions, thoughts, challenges, successes and failures, descriptions of *optimal* and *actual* improve in quality, depth and detail. That is how critical incident analysis contributes to prudent training and development by drawing the trainer's attention to *the right stuff*.

Example

Let's go back through this chapter and see the way these five steps were used to conduct needs assessments for a problem that was confronted by the San Diego Public Housing Commission. The problem was omnipresent, and acutely annoying: the inability of tenants and maintenance employees to diminish the number of cockroaches in public housing units.

Here are the sources, stages, techniques and instruments that were actually used to front end this problem, with some editing to reflect what we've learned about the needs assessment technique since this TNA was conducted.

The work that Carla Mathison (Sickbert) and Ron Crosthwaite did with Judith Fry, a manager at the Housing Commission, was reported in a 1982 article in *Instructional Innovator*. While the training that they eventually developed yielded statistically significant results (yes, fewer cockroaches!), my discussion of their work focuses only on their front end efforts, specifically their needs assessment.

The TNA commenced with examination of extant data (Chapter 5). What do maintenance inspection records show? tenant letters and calls? requests for pest spraying? Extant data analysis occurred simultaneously with subject matter analysis. See Chapter 7 for a description of subject matter analysis as a TNA technique. Subject matter analysis for this project was the developers' effort to find out just what in the world a tenant can do about cockroach infestation in multi-unit dwellings. The developers consulted Housing Commission experts, two local pest control companies, and a nationally known entomologist from Purdue University. These sources were willing and able to define **optimals** for the program.

Step 1: Select Sources for Needs Assessment

The sources for the three needs assessment stages were:

- Housing Commission administrators
- Housing Commission maintenance workers
- Anglo and Hispanic public housing tenants

While there were other ethnic groups represented in public housing in San Diego, the vast majority of tenants were English or Spanish speaking.

Step 2: Determine Stages of Assessment and

Step 3: Select and Use TNA Tools

Stage 1: Extant data analysis through examination as described above.

Stage 2: Subject matter analysis through in person and telephonic interviews as described above.

Stage 3: Needs assessment interviews with Housing Commission officials (administrators and maintenance workers). This stage of assessment pressed for information about ACTUAL tenant knowledge and skill related to cockroach control. The officials were also asked what they perceived as the CAUSE(S) of the problem. Most interview questions were Types 1, 2 and 5.

Stage 4: Needs assessment interviews with a half dozen tenants. What specific questions did they have about combatting cockroaches? Did they know what to do when questions about cockroach control were posed by the interviewer? Did they believe that they could win the war against the roaches if they had information and pest control tools, or did they see roaches as an inevitable part of apartment living? Interview questions were Types 2, 3, 4a and d.

Stage 5:   Needs assessment surveys to ascertain what tenants thought, knew and felt of the problem. There were also questions to find out whether tenants felt that, given information and tools, they could get control of the roach infestation. The survey was comprised of Type 3, 4a, 4d, 5 & 6 questions. Why Type 3's, if the emphasis is on cause? The developers wanted to find out if the tenants knew what they knew. By asking them to perform as if they already possessed optimals about roach control, Ms. Mathison (Sickbert) and Mr. Crosthwaite were able to make inferences about whether an absence of skills or knowledge was contributing to the problem. (It was.)

Step 4: Create Items. Here are the questions, distributed in English and Spanish, which went to public housing tenants. An individual in each of the buildings was responsible for distributing and collecting the print surveys, and for explaining them in the few instances where people were confused by the questions.

1. List three ways that cockroaches get into your home.
2. List what you might do to get rid of cockroaches in your kitchen.
3. What will keep cockroaches out of your home? Check all the items on the list which help keep a home free of roaches.
    .....a. leave lights on as much as possible
    .....b. keep garbage container lids on tight
    .....c. remove flowering houseplants
    .....d. clean up food crumbs and grease
    .....e. get a cat
    .....f. sprinkle salt in areas where roaches like to go
    .....g. play loud music
    .....h. put garlic in cupboards
    .....i. paint interior walls
    .....j. wash dishes immediately after use
    .....k. wash pet's feeding dishes and area
    .....l. use a heavy, shiny wax on floors
    .....m. leave a bottle of ammonia in the refrigerator
    .....n. clean cupboards regularly
    .....o. keep house at cool temperature

4. The roach problem is the manager's problem, not the tenant's.
.... Agree .... Disagree .... Don't know
5. I wouldn't have a roach problem if my neighbors were better housekeepers.
.... Agree .... Disagree .... Don't know
6. I've done as much as I can do about the roach problem.
.... Agree .... Disagree .... Don't know
7. I'd like to learn more about how to control cockroaches.
.... Agree .... Disagree .... Don't know
8. I think I could get rid of the cockroaches.
.... Agree .... Disagree .... Don't know
9. The topic of "cockroach control" is important to me.
.... Agree .... Disagree .... Don't know
10. I would be willing to attend a brief meeting to learn how to control cockroaches.
.... Agree .... Disagree .... Don't know
11. What do you think is causing the current problem with cockroaches?

Can you identify the types of questions that were used? Questions 1-3 are Type 3's; responses to them enabled inferences about actual knowledge of cockroach control.

Questions 4, 5 & 9 are Type 4a's. Questions 7 & 10 are Type 4b's. Questions 6 & 8 are Type 4d's. Question 11 is a Type 5. While the last question (number 11) is the only one which directly asks about the cause(s) of the problem, every other item contributes to figuring out why there is this problem and whether training or some other solution ought to be employed.

Step 5: Consider Critical Incident Analysis. Critical incident analysis was not employed in this situation. Extant data and Type 3 questions within the needs assessment provided a sufficiently detailed picture of current performance and knowledge.

Conclusion

This chapter began with a definition and purposes for needs assessment. I then detailed and exemplified five steps involved in conducting needs assessments. The chapter concluded with an example from a *true to life* battle against cockroaches.

Needs assessment is a systematic effort to gather opinions and information from stakeholders in relation to all TNA purposes. The question is not *whether to do needs assessment, it is how much needs assessment to do.* Often, while we know that we need that information, we must engage in struggles to gain the time and resources to carry it out. I hope this chapter provides ammunition to justify the needs assessment effort and information to assure that it will be much more than an empty process.

Resources

Carlisle, K. (1986). *Analyzing Jobs and Tasks.* Englewood Cliffs, NJ: Educational Technology Publications.

Deden-Parker, A. (Fall, 1980). Needs Assessment in Depth: Professional Training at Wells Fargo Bank. *Journal of Instructional Development, 1*(1), 3-9.

Dewey, J. (1933). *How We Think.* Boston: D.C. Heath.

Dewey, J. (1939). *Theory of Valuation.* Chicago: University of Chicago Press.

Flanagan, J.C. (July, 1954). The Critical Incident Technique. *Psychological Bulletin, 51*(4), 327-358.

Gilbert, T. (1978). *Human Competence: Engineering Worthy Performance.* New York: McGraw-Hill.

Harless, J. (1975). *An Ounce of Analysis Is Worth of a Pound of Objectives.* Newnan, Georgia: Harless Performance Guild.

Kaufman, R., & English, F.W. (1979). *Needs Assessment.* Englewood Cliffs, NJ: Educational Technology Publications.

Mager, R. (1970). *Goal Analysis.* Belmont, CA: Fearon.

Mager, R., & Pipe, P. (1970). *Analyzing Performance Problems.* Belmont, CA: Fearon.

Miles, W.R. (Fall, 1979). A Constructive Criticism of Needs Assessment. *Planning and Change, 10,* 169-180.

Rossett, A. (1982). A Typology for Generating Needs Assessments. *Journal of Instructional Development, 6*(1), 28-33.

Sickbert, C.J., & Fry, J. (1982). You Can Open New Environments to Educational Technology. *Instructional Innovator, 27*(6), 21-33.

Witkin, B.R. (1984). *Assessing Needs in Educational and Social Programs.* San Francisco: Jossey Bass.

Zemke, R., & Kramlinger, T. (1982). *Figuring Things Out: A Trainer's Guide to Needs and Task Analysis.* Reading, MA: Addison-Wesley.

Chapter Seven: SUBJECT MATTER ANALYSIS

Brief Description

This chapter is about subject matter analysis, a technique for finding and representing bodies of knowledge and skill. Think about the salesperson who really knows the product inside and out. Or the radiologist who sees more in a CAT scan than others. Or the teacher who provides just the right number of examples. Or the architect who somehow knows what you need for that room addition. Or the sergeant who . . . Or the manager who . . .

Certainly a trainer or instructional designer can watch what each of these master performers does and list the *observable, behavioral aspects* of their performance, but are they *the optimals that count, the ones that make the architect or salesperson terrific?* Doubtful. Hidden within the teacher or repairperson or architect is a body of knowledge, some subject matter expertise, some handle on content which enables them to be very skillful. Without that knowledge there would be less skillful performances.

Subject matter analysis seeks the elementary cognitive operations which represent knowing something. The search is for the details of these invisible *schema*, brain connections, that enable somebody to do what needs to be done. **There are two components of subject matter analysis: the quest for agreement on the** *details* **of the knowledge of the master performer and the** *representation* **of it so that elements, structures and relationships are clearly depicted.**

Subject Matter Analysis, Extant Data Analysis and Needs Assessment

Extant data analysis uses **accomplishments** to infer performance.

Needs assessments solicit sources' **opinions**. *Subject matter analysis, on the other hand, is concerned with what ought to be happening, with what performers **must know** to do the job **optimally**. Figure 7.1 compares these TNA* techniques in light of their TNA purposes:

When conducting needs assessment, the designer or trainer will go to numerous sources like bosses, potential trainees or even customers to seek their opinions. In extant data analysis, the training professional asks people for access to the *outcomes* of employee performance. That might take you to performance appraisals, exit interviews or computer printouts. Subject matter analysis relies on experts, star performers and documents. You are seeking the repositories of wisdom and skill. They could be brand new technical specifications or elderly zookeepers who are about to retire and might take their knowledge of the animals with them. In subject matter analysis you are attempting to draw out the details, shape and relationships of what is known and done in order to do the job well. This information then turns into representations of the optimals which are central to TNA.

Subject Matter Analysis and Task Analysis

Task and subject matter analysis really aren't very different. **Both activities, after all, focus on the quest for details of optimal knowledge and skills.** Where they are most different is in their emphases, and their treatment in the literature.

Charles Reigeluth (1983) credits Lev Landa with the earliest work focusing attention not just on the *visible* details of successful job performance, but also on the *invisible* elements, the unobservable cognitive operations that enable the performer to perform. Tiemann and Markle's 1978 work makes a similar point: *training direction will be based on analysis of relevant concepts not just on behavioral observations of job performance.* A 1984 article by the same two authors continues the theme: "Content analysis has outgrown the mere listing of statements the learner will be able to recite. It has advanced way beyond the old conventions of S-R tables." (p. 26) See Figure 7.2.

Just as task analysis leads us to optimals in **visible** job activities, subject matter analysis leads us to optimals in the **invisible body of knowledge**. Task analysis most often uses observation to capture

COMPARING SUBJECT MATTER ANALYSIS, EXTANT DATA ANALYSIS AND NEEDS ASSESSMENT

	SUBJECT MATTER ANALYSIS	EXTANT DATA ANALYSIS	NEEDS ASSESSMENT
Seeking:			
Optimals	X		X
Actuals		X	X
Feelings			X
Cause(s)			X

Figure 7.1

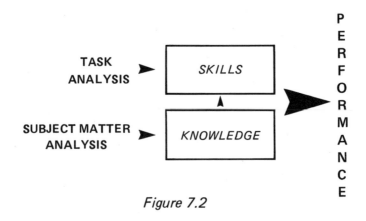

Figure 7.2

the best of what a master performer can be seen doing; subject matter analysis queries to represent what he or she knows. Figure 7.2 presents this relationship. Historically, task analysis has played a significant role in our field, especially in military training and development. Recent work (Tarr, 1986; Carlisle, 1986) begins to expand the definition of task analysis to include the quest for optimals associated with nonprocedural, complex skills like leadership. In this book, I maintain the distinction in order to highlight the emerging importance as well as the difficulty of ferreting out the cognitive components of optimal job performance.

The future will see the blending of task and subject matter analyses, because both seek **optimals**. For most jobs, both task and subject matter analyses will contribute to the picture of optimal performance that the instructional designer constructs, since most jobs include demands on knowledge *and* skill.

Purposes of Subject Matter Analysis

When you look at Figure 7.2, your first impression might be that subject matter analysis is weak because it yields only one kind of information—information about optimals, and invisible ones at that. But it isn't a puny technique. **It, along with task analysis, is the primary source for training directions.** Training professionals use these techniques to unearth the elements and relationships that comprise **expertise**.

Let's look at the purposes of the subject matter analysis technique as **performance technologists** would use it:

☐ *To establish what it is that the knowledgeable performer knows, in useful detail;*

☐ *To provide the details of optimal performance, against which actual performance is* **compared;**

Optimals
_ Actuals
———————
NEEDS
in detail

□ *To flesh out details that represent bodies of knowledge or instructional content; and*

□ *To depict bodies of knowledge based on subject matter research.*

This then will facilitate:

• *Writing objectives.* The standard use of a detailed map of subject matter is to turn it into instructional objectives. The objectives are then used in traditional ways.

• *Deriving prescriptions and selecting strategies for achieving training intentions.* Effectively written subject matter analyses talk directly to training professionals *and trainees* about how jobs are done. We use them to figure out how to teach or train. Trainees can often use the representation of subject matter just as it is, *without adding instructional elements like examples or feedback.* Landa describes them as prescriptive in and of themselves, and they are. Think about the brochures you receive which detail financial options. Or consider the technical specifications which often accompany technical equipment. They are pruned subject matter analyses that *attempt* to teach through the clarity of their representation of the content. Do they? (The problem is that they lack the instructional elements, like examples, nonexamples and practice opportunities which make learning happen.)

• *Examining instructional content in light of the needs and entry skills of varying trainees.* Think about a subject matter analysis of the concept of *hand* for first graders. Then think about that subject matter analysis for physicians who specialize in hands (there really are such people!). Or consider what Sally Ride, the astronaut, needs to know about nutrition in space versus what a junior high school student needs to know. Each necessitates subject matter analyses which match trainee needs with subject optimals.

• *Resolving subject matter disputes.* When subject matter experts(SMEs) disagree, there can be a feeling of overwhelming discord. You can't imagine how a turbine engine ever got fixed with all this disagreement. Detailing content with *each* of the battling SMEs usually yields a picture with more congruence than emotion initially suggested. It also allows you to pinpoint the exact areas which will have to be resolved.

• *Moving towards expert systems.* Subject matter analysis assists the trainer in serving as a knowledge engineer. The quest for elements of knowledge, their structure and rules, is the beginning of what constitutes the basis for the design of computerized programs that can act like *smart* people.

When Do You Do Subject Matter Analysis?

Usually early. And constantly, allowing the subject matter, the "stuff" of the job, the knowledge essential to it, to be part of all of your analyses. It is subject matter analysis, as it unfolds, that enables you to ask meaningful questions during all your stages of assessment.

When you are charged with preparing courses or modules for **new products, technologies and systems, subject matter analysis is the dominant front end technique.** There will be limited extant data because this is something which is *new*. There won't be model performers because this is new to your setting. The needs assessment you do will focus on feelings about value and efficacy surrounding the new thing, certainly not on actual performance *because there isn't any yet.*

Subject matter analysis for an **ongoing task** focuses on a clear expression of optimal knowledge, on finding out what distinguishes the star from the clod. In addition to scrutinizing written documents, you would press stars about what they know which enables them to shine.

Description of Subject Matter Analysis

Your boss might ask you to do a task analysis or to conduct a needs assessment. A mandate to carry out a subject matter analysis is less likely. The phrase *subject matter analysis* is unfamiliar; its purposes are still unclear; it is still confused with task analysis; and the literature presents a murky picture, at best.

In the pages that follow, I attempt to simplify this TNA technique. I apologize for taking enormous liberties in my attempt to firm up a body of literature and opinion which is just beginning to take shape.

Subject matter analysis, like much of the rest of this book, is for the purpose of "nailing jelly to a wall." Subject matter analysis itself is a content, just as product knowledge, or turbine engine troubleshooting is content and SMEs just don't agree. Such controversies sit awkwardly in a **practical** book, where discussions of the disputes are of less interest than their resolutions.

The press to keep this book **practical** leads me to follow Landa's advice about dealing with content which is basically heuristic, or open-ended in nature; he recommends turning it into manageable algorithms. **I've done that in this chapter, forcing out steps or flexible algorithms for a subject matter which is still very mushy.** Use the steps that follow to begin to work with subject matter, but go beyond what I've done to develop strategies specific to your situation.

Steps in Doing Subject Matter Analysis

Step 1: Find Sources of Expertise

Step 2: Elaborate Content

Step 3: Find Structures or Kinds of Subject Matter

Step 4: Represent Subject Matter or Content

ONGOING ACTIVITY: Work with subject matter experts

Step 1: Find Sources of Expertise. There are two kinds of sources of information: animate and inanimate. Your colleagues are the animate sources on which you will rely, and your ability to get them to help you in subject matter analysis depends on your ability to communicate and negotiate.

Documents, engineering reports, equipment specifications, glossaries, job aids, technical manuals and correspondence are inanimate sources of information. An instructional designer once said, "Give me a good technical manual and set of specs. They are easier to relate to than most engineering types I've dealt with." Inanimate sources can't talk back. They also can't interact with you and offer helpful feedback as you try to **elaborate, refine and** represent the subject structure of the system, equipment or product on which you are working.

Who and what are the sources of expertise to which you turn? It varies with every project depending on whether the company or agency has in-house capabilities and familiarity with the area. A training program for corporate auto mechanics to find out why the *repair call back* rate is skyrocketing would rely on existing experts, the people in the field who aren't having the problem at all. There is dependable expertise within the corporation.

A new technology or system would be treated differently. Who knows about it? Was it developed by in-house methodologists? If so, they will be the sources of information on the detailed optimals. If it was developed by someone else, will the vendor provide an expert? Is it possible to send someone from your setting to learn about this new thing? Where can you get your hands on the documentation for the new system? Will the vendor point you to a non-competitor who has introduced it into their corporation or agency?

Don't assume that SMEs will be readily and automatically available for a project. SME reluctance, avoidance, disappearance, evasion and confusion are legion. The concluding section of this chapter is about working effectively with SMEs.

Step 2: Elaborate Content. This is the effort training professionals make to unfold, clarify and analyze content. There are specific ways to get at the details and structure of bodies of knowledge. But first we need common language.

Elaboration theory. This is the recent work that Charles Reigeluth (1983) has done, which is based partially on contributions from M. David Merrill. Let me share the analogy he effectively uses to define **elaboration theory.** He asks readers to envision a lens which is pointed at a subject matter. We can try his lens on my friend's new Isuzu Impulse. Commence by looking at it through a wide angle lens. Note the parts, shape and color, the general spirit of the thing *without details.* Now let's switch to a zoom lens and zoom in on its side; focus on its windows, bumpers, angle, wheels, lights, etc. Now you might zoom in once again, this time focusing on the details of the wheels and wheel coverings. Then you might choose to return to wide angle to look at the larger picture again, especially taking note of the wheel in relation to the side and the side in relation to the whole. This wide-view/zoom-view approach provides detail and relationship information.

Summaries and epitomies. Reigeluth makes a useful distinction between them. Both are a kind of overview, with summaries presenting what happens and epitomes relying upon central themes. Let me try to illustrate summaries and epitomes using familiar content. First, let's look at a familiar concept: the summary. A **summary** is a brief preview or afterview; it is many ideas, once over lightly. A summary of this book, for example, would present its three basic parts and list the major tools and techniques which are presented. A more simple instance brings us back to our childhoods and *The Three Little Pigs*. A summary outlines the plot, briefly describing the three pigs, their differing houses and workstyles and the wolf's effect upon each of them. On the other hand, an **epitome** is one or a small number of selected, key themes or ideas presented through application. An epitome for *The Three Little Pigs* would present its central message: *that doing the best job, even though it takes longer and is harder, works out best in the end.* Then the key events in the story are presented in light of this recurring theme. For this book, the epitome would highlight its key concept: *purpose-based front end analyses, tools and techniques which work together to answer questions about optimals, actuals, causes, feelings and solutions.* Then an example of the use of such a conceptualization would follow. The key ideas that are presented in the epitome then enlighten each section into which you zoom. **It is exactly what I have been doing in this book, tying each tool and technique back to the quest for optimals, actuals, causes, feelings and solutions.**

Concepts. A concept is an object (e.g., Grandma's chicken soup, circulator, scarf), symbol (e.g., stars and stripes, Statue of Liberty, underlining in a sentence) or event (effective therapy, anniversary, successful performance appraisal) with common characteristics and a shared name. Much of the work we do in subject matter analysis is to get at the attributes of concepts, especially those that make a difference. When we talk about concepts, we often want to use bullets to denote attributes. For example, let's say we want to train course developers to interview subject matter experts effectively. What are the elements of the concept *effective* **introduction** *to the subject matter interview?*

- statement of who you are
- statement of why you are there, including what will be done with their contribution
- statement of why they have been selected
- description of the length of this interaction
- inquiry about their questions and concerns
- eye contact, smile, etc.

Atomic components. They are the results, the outcomes, of what Scandura (1976) calls a structural analysis and what I am calling subject matter analysis. **Atomic components** are sought which present the basic elements that represent competence. Scandura focuses our attention on **rules; each rule consists of problem domains, procedures, and range.** The **domain** is the set of problems, issues, conditions or inputs associated with the content. **Procedures** are the cognitive steps that competently address the input or domain. Different kinds of rules represent different kinds of subject matter analysis, a topic treated in Step 3 of this chapter. **Range** is what comes out of the effective performance of procedures on domains. Brock Allen, one of my colleagues at San Diego State, put it this way: *procedures operate on domains to produce range.* He illustrated it this way:

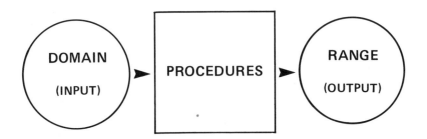

Let's use self-directed, flexible Individual Retirement Accounts (IRAs) as content and tellers as learners. The domains for this example are based on the questions tellers would hear and the empty forms to be filled out. In this case, procedures are the characteristics of this IRA, the flex-IRAs attributes compared to others, and procedures for filling out and routing the forms. The range in this example is IRA sales and properly filled out forms.

The kinds of content elaborations we have been examining lead directly to techniques we can use. Let's generate questions and strategies to carry out Step 2.

Concepts	Elaboration Questions
Elaboration Theory	• Tell me about the *nosilla*? Why is it important? How does it work? What are its key concepts?
Summaries	• Try to provide me with an *overview* of the *nosilla*. What is it like? Is it like this? Give me a general picture of it? There are two kinds of *nosillas* and each has five parts? Am I getting that correct? Is that a *general picture* of what it is like?
Epitomes	• Is there an *organizing principle or rule* to this *nosilla*? What is special or interesting or significant about it? When you think about it, what matters? Is it true that the *nosilla* energizes people and plants, and that there is some ongoing work to use its properties as a substitute for traditional fuels?
Concepts	• What is this nosilla? Is it part of a larger whole? Does it have *parts*? Are there kinds of *nosillas*? What are the *characteristics* of all *nosillas*? How can you tell an outerspace from an underwater *nosilla* if they are not operating? What is unique or important about it?

Concepts	Elaboration Questions

Atomic components:

domains

- What happens that raises our level of con-concern? What do you see on the screen? What appears in the printouts? Are there verbal requests that lead you to implement the *nosilla*? What *issues* do you expect to solve? What are the *conditions* under which you are performing?

procedures

- *Nosillas* work their wonders in a very specific and technical way. Will you *detail* for me? How is it different for the outerspace vs. the underwater *nosilla*? Let's look at its primary part, the one out of five which keeps it going. Can you describe what we need to know to maintain it? I'm not sure I am clear on that third step, am I restating it to you correctly?

range

- How will we know when we've succeeded? What are the *results* of it? Will it be *immediate*? Will there be *anything else* besides light?

Step 3: Find Structures or Kinds of Subject Matter. As the designer or trainer is *eliciting* the stuff of the subject, he or she must also be concerned with the *organization* of this content. In Step 2 we focused on fleshing out the atomic components and attributes of a body of knowledge. **In Step 3, we focus on the way the pieces fit together, and on their classification, organization and structure.** While the concerns of these two steps are distinct, carrying them out often involves moving back and forth between them.

This concern with structure is important. **Once we understand the organization or structure of a subject matter, research provides us with guidance on *how to teach it*.** Also, as course developers and trainers, we seek structure and detail so we can convey it as part of the training that we do. **People learn better when they understand the inherent structure of what they are learning.**

There is, however, little agreement on subject matter classifications and organization. What is agreed upon is that bodies of knowledge all have elements, that these elements are in relationship to each other, and that elements and relationships create structures which matter. Landa (1976, 1983), Reigeluth (1983), Dick and Carey (1985), Scandura (1976), Harmon & King (1985) and Zemke & Kramlinger (1982) all deal with subject matter differently. I've attempted to consolidate their work in Figure 7.3 in a way which makes it useful and accessible to the training and development community.

Let's look at each segment of Figure 7.3. Each of these concepts will then serve aș a basis for questions trainers use to organize the subject matter or task on which they are working.

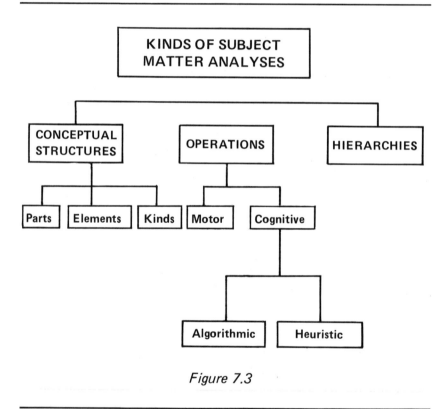

Figure 7.3

CONCEPTUAL STRUCTURES: There are four kinds of concept structures: parts, kinds, elements and combinations.

Parts. A parts structure is just what it sounds like, an organization of a tangible thing and its components. Consider the engine in that Isuzu Impulse or

- your wedding
- a sentence
- a baseball team
- the sails on a boat
- your body
- a disk operating system

Note that parts structures are for **concrete visible things, objects or events**. The large thing which has parts is itself usually a part of something. Often you need to know about the larger whole and the subordinate parts to represent subject matter or jobs.

Elements. An elements structure is used to identify **components of intangible concepts**. Whereas a parts structure is for autos and solar systems, an elements structure seeks the attributes of abstract concepts like fairness and responsiveness to customer needs. Consider a sensitive teacher or

- safety conscious worker
- committed employee
- sexy fellow
- efficient engine

When a course developer or trainer is seeking to identify the attributes of more nebulous concepts like loyalty or sales skill, you will set up an elements structure.

Kinds. The world we live in is full of variety. Kinds breakdowns express that variety. If your mission is to teach extraterrestrials about sports in America, you would need to find the optimals for a **kinds** subject matter analysis. There are many different kinds of sports in this country and you can't just list them. Such a disorganized, unstructured list would be inscrutable to aliens. Will you organize by indoor-outdoor, team-individual, racket or not, etc.? What would mean the most to your learners, while pleasing whoever it is that contracted with you to provide extraterrestrials with sports information? Let's look at some other concepts that come in kinds. Computer systems do. There are also many kinds of phone services and:

- dating services
- diseases
- training methodologies
- bodies of water
- services provided by the union
- VCRs

Combinations. Much of the subject matter with which we deal is conceptual in nature and **combines several kinds of structures**. In fact, I can't think of a job-related body of knowledge which wouldn't be represented by several kinds of structures. Consider product knowledge on pumps and circulators or diagnosis and treatment of types of cancers. You can even expand this to our program on sports for extraterrestrials. First we might seek kinds of sports. Then there are parts, represented by the league structure. There are also parts of a basketball team, parts of a racing program, kinds of bets you can place, elements of an effective fitness regimen or successful betting program, etc. Or think again about the IRA account. There are parts of the application; there are elements of an eligible person; there are kinds of withdrawal plans. As you dig into the content, the training professional unearths numerous elements (Step 2) with significant relationships to each other (Step 3).

OPERATIONS STRUCTURES: There are two kinds of operations structures, an organization influenced by Lev Landa's important work. There are motor and cognitive operations.

Motor. Motor operations describe overt skills. Think about setting up the telecommunications hardware for your computer, or threading a projector, or writing numbers and letters, or break-dancing. **The optimals are obvious and visible**. Ken Carlisle's (1986) book, *Analyzing Jobs and Tasks*, is a useful resource for generating and representing these operations, as is Tarr's chapter in Ellis' book (1986) on military contributions to instructional technology.

Cognitive. Cognitive operations are complex, unobservable mental activities. **The important components of cognitive operations are invisible; they occur in the *minds* of master performers**. While we might hear a physician make a diagnosis, or see an instructional designer recommend a particular training methodology, the important subject matter is in their minds. Landa makes useful distinctions in his discussion of cognitive processes:

   • ***Algorithmic cognitive operations***. Algorithms are processes which consist of a series of steps that solve a certain clearly specified presenting problem. Mathematics is the most frequently used example of cognitive algorithms. M. David Merrill calls these cognitive algorithms "rules." The important point for our purposes is that we are talking about *thinking steps, invisible and significant activities that result in things like computed interest or paint needed to prime a building.* Another example is the thought process that goes into balancing a checkbook or the simple decision-making related to cooking a steak or fish to the desired doneness. We are not talking about the process for painting a building; that's a motor operation. Nor are we talking about how you decide whether you want to repaint, stucco, aluminum side, cedar side or do nothing; that thought process would be represented as a heuristic. We are focusing on **clear, unvarying thought steps in algorithmic cognitive operations.**

• *Heuristic cognitive operations.* Heuristic processes are **considerations, guidelines and rules of thumb which solve a large and varied domain of problems.** Heuristics lack the step by step specificity of the algorithm. In place of steps are numerous ideas, presented *without the comfort of clear, unvarying sequence.* There are heuristics for financial planning, selecting equipment, conducting needs assessments, handling customer complaints and choosing a college. It would be nice if there were **algorithms, guaranteed specific steps,** to handle the problem domain. But life isn't like that. **The knowledge that allows us to handle the hard and challenging parts of life lacks uniform presenting conditions and clear, unvarying step-like solutions.**

Let's look at an example of a heuristic masquerading as an algorithm. *My mother wanted to train teenage me to date what she considered to be the right guys. She said, "It's easy. First you make sure they are Jewish. If they are, then you make sure they are serious students. If they are, then you find out about their families. If there are any genetic problems, terminate. If there are no genetic problems, determine whether the father makes a good living, etc.* My mother had a clear cognitive algorithm going for my youthful partner selection. Her job was to effectively convey her optimals to young Allison. It was a nice, neat flowchart, easy to understand, sufficiently specific to replace the matchmaker she would have preferred. It would be nice if one could choose a partner through an unvarying, step-by-step procedure. But it wouldn't work, I think, even though my mother—and other mothers—want it to be so.

Most tough issues, whether teen dating or conducting TNA or business planning, are **heuristic** processes. While a **mental algorithm** can be followed to determine proper camping spaces for recreation vehicles of different sizes and hook-ups, more complex problems and jobs aren't served by that kind of subject matter breakdown. There are just no simple, invariable steps for choosing an appropriate date or developing a business strategy. A heuristic has to be derived from personal experience or from a SME—or from a combination of both sources.

HIERARCHIES: Hiararchies state prerequisite relationships; in order to do X, you first must know how to do Z. We are talking about **dependent skill** relationships, where you must walk before you can run, for example. Hierarchies also describe **relationships between concepts**. You must, for example, know the difference between the parts of speech before you can tell sentences from fragments and before you can generate good sentences. In hierarchies the focus is on **what must be in your repertoire before you can learn the selected skill**.

Let's look at some more examples of hierarchies. Basic math skills are prerequisite to a balanced check book. You certainly are not going to be able to qualify applicants for loans unless you can define certain concepts like "eligibility." And you are not going to be able to write criterion-referenced test items unless you know how to write objectives.

There are useful resources for the training designer who wants to know more about hierarchies. Dick and Carey (1985) effectively illustrate cognitive hierarchical skill content. Reigeluth (1983) cites Gagne's work on *learning prerequisites*. Gagne and Briggs (1979) urged the search for the facts and ideas which must first be learned before a given concept or principle can be acquired. Recent work by Martin & Briggs (1986) reiterates the importance of identifying hierarchies for their contribution to both cognitive *and* affective training goals. And Rob Foshay (1983) presents a useful comparison of three methods of presenting subject matter and decision-making, one of which is based on hierarchies. While these authors go beyond a singular concern about hierarchies, they treat it as **one fruitful line of inquiry in the establishment and representation of optimals.**

In the past, training professionals most often sought information about hierarchy within visible operations. While those are significant sources of content and organization, they are not the only possibilities. Before you start asking questions, you need to think about job related content in light of the kinds of subject matter organizations discussed in Figure 7.3. How would you classify the content? Find the classification or classifications on the chart below and build your questioning strategy.

Concepts	Structure Questions
Conceptual Structures:	
Parts	• Of what is it **made**? • Of what is it a part? • What are the parts of this piece? • How do the parts **fit together**?
Elements	• Tell me about someone or something that would be most like this: • What are the **characteristics**, in detail, of what you would like to see in place? • If someone or something was absolutely **opposite**, what would they be like? • Think about the **environments** in which this person or thing operates, does that add any attributes to the list?
Kinds	• What is it? • Why is it an example of one? • Are there **others**? What are their names? How is this one different? • Have we forgotten any that also do this? What are their names? How is each one different? • Which is **most like** the one we have been talking about? **most different**?

Concepts	Structure Questions

Operations Structures:
MOTOR

- This is what I **observed**. Is it correct? Should I add anything? Tools?
- This task listing describes exactly what you do. Where are the problems? **likely areas** for mistakes? spots where mistakes will be **most costly?**

COGNITIVE
  Algorithmic
  Cognitive Operations

- What is the **problem** that this solves? What conditions set it off?
- Describe all the **situations** which might present themselves for which you would use this strategy.
- Have we forgotten any ways you might get started on this?
- What **exactly** are the **steps** you use in solving these problems? The **order?**
- Can you describe your **thoughts** as you go through this step?
- What tells you to move from this step to the next? Is that always the way it comes to you? What do you do with maybes?

  Heuristic
  Cognitive Operations

- What are the situations or cases that come to you and cause you to **use your expertise?** Can you describe them exactly?
- List for me the things you consider in making your recommendations.
- Do you always take into account every one of these factors? Can you **skip** one? Which one? How do you decide? Will you still be able to make a decision about which you are confident? In what **order** do you think about this?
- What are the major **decisions** you confront? What information do you need? do you take into account?

Concepts	Structure Questions
	• What do you think it is that makes you particularly skilled in this area? What *do you know which makes the difference*? If somebody else knew this, would they be skillful too? What else is involved? • Let me set up a case for you. What are you thinking, considering as you make a decision?
Hierarchies	• What do you need to *know how to do* in order to do this? anything else? • What *knowledge* are you drawing upon to do this? • Look at these errors. What do you think we might need to teach *to get them ready* to do this right?

Step 4: Represent Subject Matter or Content. Presumably you have been *writing up the subject matter* and sharing it with the relevant SMEs all along. Trainers and designers will also need to present the details of the subject matter and its organization more formally. The important point is to develop a document that communicates. You have laboriously divined the *stuff* of the job, the *key content* constituting expertise. Your vision of optimals and their network of relationships needs to be clearly understood by SMEs and *verified by them.*

Formal and informal representations can take two forms: outlines or graphics. Use the form with which you are most comfortable. Motor operations, cognitive algorithms and hierarchies naturally lend themselves to graphic presentation. Conceptual structures tend to work best in outlines, although a brief, simple part or kind content can be quickly communicated *via* visuals. Heuristics often involve both visual and verbal presentations.

OUTLINES: This takes us back to elementary school days. Words, roman numerals, numbers, letters and capitalization are used to show *detail and relationships*.

Let's pretend that I want to train beginning instructional

designers on *behavioral objectives*. I have looked at the literature
and interrogated a SME; I have pressed hard for information on
the domains (issues, situations) for which this content matters
because needs assessment shows low motivation. While students
have high efficacy in this area, they report low value. Either they
think they know already, or they don't see why they need to
know. This is the outline that came from Step 2 and 3 work.

BEHAVIORAL OBJECTIVES

   I.   What they **look like**
        A. Some examples from real training programs

  II.   What they **do for trainers**
        A. Statement of intentions
        B. Statement of optimals
        C. Planning tool
        D. Source of test items
           1. for practices
           2. for pre-test
           3. for post-test
        E. To communicate with others about the program
           1. supervisors
           2. learners
           3. SMEs

 III.   How you **generate** them
        A. Parts (**ABCD**)
           1. Audience
           2. Behavior
           3. Condition
           4. Degree
        B. What the effective objective writer thinks as he or she writes
           1. What is the behavior of an effective one?
              (e.g., *can tell a passenger is having a medical emergency*)
           2. What exactly is the behavior of somewho who *can tell . .*.
              List in detail all the separate behaviors.
              (e.g., *approach passenger; ask questions in proper order,*
              using job aid; classify answers as "needs emergency care or
              may need emergency care—additional evaluation desirable
              or doesn't need emergency care"; using job aid, determine
              if any in-flight tests should be administered, inform neigh-

boring passengers, request for passenger physician, if indicated by job aid, etc.)

3. What are the stimuli or presenting conditions that set off each of the behaviors?

   (e.g., *certain verbal responses—detail them, test results, if testing is indicated*)

4. What will satisfy us that the flight attendant can do this? How well must he or she perform?

   (e.g., *so responses for given students match expert in 100% of cases; so blood pressure reading is accurate to within . . .*)

C. Common errors in objective writing
   1. Vastness
   2. Methods masquerading as conditions
   3. Unrealistic criteria
   4. Four parts present but content unrelated to real world

Remember that this is a subject matter outline. It will guide you in figuring out how to teach it. But right now it only presents optimals in a clear format. It isn't a lesson plan or specification, not yet. For fun, and as you think about actually doing the training, try to generate a **summary** for this material. How would it differ from an **epitome**?

Look at the way this outline is organized. Can you see how the needs assessment information on motivation influenced the subject matter? A traditional behavioral objectives content outline would have been set up differently, beginning with kinds of objectives, then presenting parts and then focusing on writing them. Note the way the needs assessment technique affected the subject matter analysis. This subject matter outline leads with value-building content because my make-believe needs assessment suggested that they weren't interested in this topic. **TNA works like that, with information from the use of each tool and technique enlightening future inquiry.**

GRAPHIC REPRESENTATIONS: Sometimes it is quicker and more dramatic to present content in a visual format. While outlines show parts and kinds relationships nicely, they lack the dynamic capability of graphic representation. Here is a parts conceptual structure. This structure is easy to understand and appropriate to the static parts relationship.

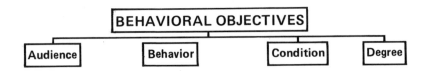

More active content is also effectively treated through visuals. **Arrows show what acts upon what.** Note how the graphics below are more dynamic than the parts breakdown depicted above.

CALORIES CONSUMED – – – – –> BODY WEIGHT

CLASSIFICATION OF OBJECTIVES –––––> TRAINING STRATEGY

These very simple visuals illustrate the way graphics can depict **active** relationships. Diamonds indicate decision points. And rectangles and squares present alternatives. Think about trainers and the process they go through when they conduct needs assessment. Figure 7.4 simplifies that process into a cognitive algorithm; Figure 7.4 is also a review of some of the material we have covered earlier in the book.

Liana Beckett, President of Pantec Training Systems, developed Figure 7.5 to represent optimals for a small component in microchip manufacturing training.

More complex bodies of knowledge and expertise might use computer generated graphics, video and photography to capture additional components, decisions and relationships. While the idea of, for example, videotaping the placement and preparation of complex cable systems is a good one, it is rarely done as part of front end analysis. The expense of these high technology subject matter representations would have to be justified by using the subject matter analysis in two ways: to capture how it ought to be *and* to serve as a model to actually teach trainees.

Example

This is an example of a subject matter analysis for a fast-growing telecommunications company in San Diego. Many new employees are being added to the company and there is a need for a

PURPOSE-BASED TRAINING
NEEDS ASSESSMENT

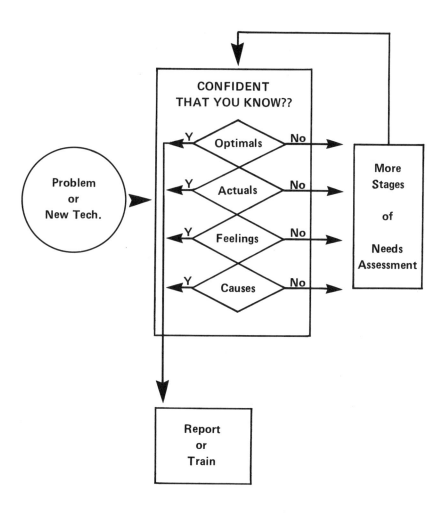

Figure 7.4

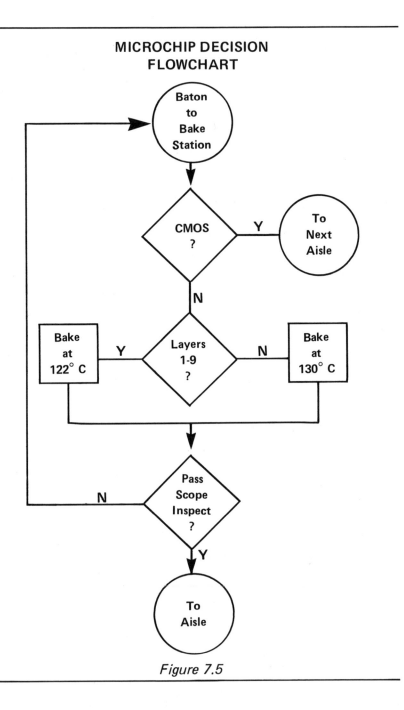

**MICROCHIP DECISION
FLOWCHART**

Figure 7.5

systematic, informative and effective **new hires orientation** which gets people prepared to do their jobs quickly.

The audience for this new hire program is line personnel in jobs from factory workers to top-level telecommunications scientists. The staff in the audience might be secretaries and executives. Approximately 17 percent of the employees are Black, Hispanic, Asian or American Indian. Sixty-four percent are men; thirty-six percent are females. Top level management believes that all new hirees need to know about the benefits, security procedures and intra-company communications systems unique to this young corporation. Most of this discussion will focus on security as subject matter.

Roberta Clarey and Cara Miller successfully carried out this project. It is Roberta Clarey's subject matter analysis of security matters that I present below. I editorialized in Steps 1-3. Step 4 is just as she wrote it and presented it to her client.

Step 1: Find Sources

1. Existing orientation literature.

2. Company literature expressing policies which specify what orientation must include.

3. Brochures and policies from the Personnel department on the topics to be included in the orientation.

4. Employees who know about or need to be consulted about the topics which must be included in the orientation.

5. The published literature on new hire orientations and security procedures training.

Step 2: Elaborate Content

1. Observe current orientation for details of actual subject matter.

2. Interview people who are presenting the current segments of the new hire program for their perceptions of the current content. Seek details of anything they would like to include, not currently in evidence.

3. Press for the optimal information in an overall program and for the **details of the particular sub-specialty**. So questions were framed like, *"In general, what is it that we want new hires to leave the training with?"* and *"You have been doing the presentation*

for new employees on career development and opportunities here at XYZ Inc. What is the theme you want them to pick up as you present the details of job posting, application, tuition reimbursement, etc.?" Or, *"What are the elements of our security program? What makes our program effective? What is it that a new hire needs to know about each of the parts of the program you just described? What are the attributes of a security conscious employee? What would they be doing in their daily work? Is there anything about our security program which we can use as a theme in discussing each aspect of security?"* **Note that the developers** were conscious of issues of summary *and* epitome as they sought details appropriate to the different conceptual aspects of security.

4. As the **elements and nature of the subject matter began to unfold, developers used it to guide their questioning.** In fact, Steps 2 & 3 blended to allow better questionning and elaboration. For example, as the developers noted that security had parts and elements, their inquiry was guided by the quest for the specific parts of the system and the elements of a responsible attitude towards corporate secrets. Another example is the topic of gaining access to secure areas, an algorithm with dependable and simple steps. *What do you do first, next, in order to get to that area of the company* is different than *In what kinds of security are we involved? What's the difference between proprietary commercial product security and sensitive product security?*

Step 3: Find Structures and Kinds of Subject Matter. A brief orientation program is usually conceptual in nature. The goal is to share the parts, kinds, functions, and elements of a *way of doing business*. People can't realistically be expected to walk out knowing **how** to file for a disability benefit or, for that matter, **remembering how** to gain access to secure areas. Rather, they know the pieces of the benefits system about which they may inquire further and where to find their job aid for gaining access to secured areas. **They also know that security matters as a topic has several important parts/aspects about which they need to be concerned: the nature of the physical plant and security gradations; overt security policy related to badges, products and government contracts; personal and corporate property policies; automobile policies; and the Emergency Action Plan.**

The subject matter analysis for **orientation** to these topics is different in its detail than the search for optimals if you were developing a detailed job aid on **how to do something in particular, or a training after which employees are expected to recall what to do, for example, to be in full and daily compliance with government security expectations and regulations.**

Step 4: Represent Subject Matter. Figure 7.6 is a visual presentation of the security conceptual structure for new hires. Any one of the boxes could be further analyzed into its attributes or elements or steps. For example, uses of badges (1.2.1) could be visually presented with arrows as an algorithm, if such detail is deemed a necessary outcome for this orientation. Or proprietary commercial products (1.2.2.1.1) could be presented with a list of attributes defining that concept or specified steps for how to handle it if that is an intention for the orientation program.

Working with Subject Matter Experts:
A Continuous Part of the Process

The success of steps 1 through 4 depends on the ability to work with the people who are the experts. They are the ones who possess the optimals or a portion of them. It is the trainer or instructional designer's job to get them to give you access to the subject matter, and to verify that you have *gotten it*.

Most trainers can tell amusing and occasionally horrifying stories of experiences with SMEs: A heavy machinery company flew SMEs in from all over the world to discuss maintenance of this machinery in desert climates. The SMEs battled for days, with each SME describing the job differently. Peace came, at least for a little while, when they agreed to disagree and returned to their respective parts of the world. The instructional technologist wound up settling issues that she felt ill prepared to handle.

A student at San Diego State told me about her experiences in staff development for a hospital. She went to meet with an Emergency Room nurse who was going to be her SME for an emergency procedures training program. The trainer attempted to launch the interview, but the nurse's questions kept coming back to the trainer and her background. "Where did she go to school?" "Where else?" "Where has she worked? doing what?" "And your **nursing**, where have you done that?" The nurse's response was cold and

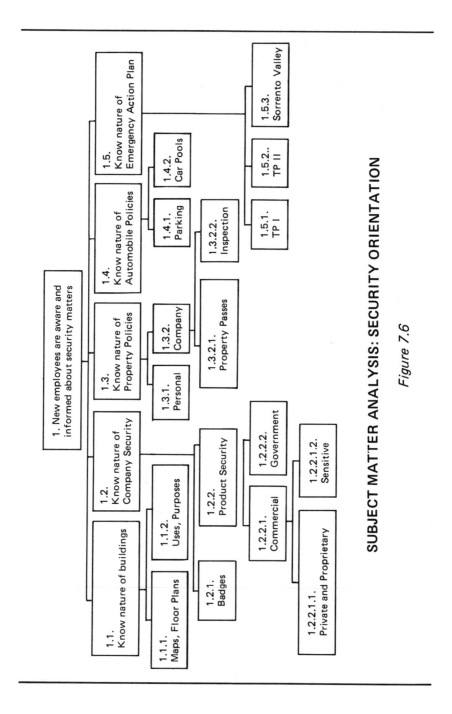

SUBJECT MATTER ANALYSIS: SECURITY ORIENTATION

Figure 7.6

certain, *"Someone who is not a nurse can **not** begin to develop this program! I see no point in talking to you about this."*

Several trainers I know comforted themselves with language. No longer generously and automatically labelling their designated sources as SMEs, they privately called them SKIs (**semi**-knowledge-able individuals) until the SKIs could prove themselves otherwise.

One final true story. Recently, I conducted a three day seminar on needs assessment for 15 corporate course developers in a high technology company. As soon as I presented the concept of purpose-based assessment, all hell broke loose. They liked it. They agreed with it. But they were wildly frustrated by their inability to gain access to SMEs. The SMEs to whom they wished to talk were too busy to talk to them. Other activities (like generating more new systems, methodologies and technologies) took precedence. Often they were given time with people who knew as little as they did about the subject matter. My advice to the course developers was straightforward: **If the company wants an effective course, the developer of the course must have access to subject matter expertise. It's not a negotiable point. Courses without optimals or with the wrong optimals are disasters.**

Once you have a SME, there are some good reasons for the relationship to be at least initially difficult. Why?

• SMEs don't know who you are, and **part of your job is, to admit readily and upfront that you are not a SME.** Most SMEs can't understand how someone who is not an authority dares to develop training.

• They don't know who you are **now.** Many course developers and training professionals were once SMEs. Promoted from excellence in customer loop design or mainframe computer maintenance or bank branch work, trainers assume a new position *and distance from the field and their former subject matter expertise.*

• You are trying to take the knowledge and skills that are within the expert and **package them so that others can become more effective.** What might the successful packaging of a salesman's skill do to his commissions? to the elevated status he enjoys as the *one who knows, while others don't?* How will it make a zookeeper feel to know that the special knowledge she has of the middle sized animals is now accessible to anyone who cares to study

the videotape? Or consider the professor known for his expertise in Ancient Chinese Religions. An eager instructional developer wants to package Chinese Religions to be delivered *via*
interactive video. What might that mean to the professor's likelihood of continuing to teach his favorite course? Will the professor keep his job? the zookeeper? The training that is such
a wonderful idea to trainers can be a threatening one to SMEs.

• **SMEs are people too.** Their personalities are varied, and you
will run into dolls and colossal pains. Sometimes it helps for the
trainer to take some time to think about *who the SME is, the kind
of person he or she is, as it relates to the job that has to be done.*
My graduate students tell me that Coscarelli and Stonewater's
(1981) work presented in Figure 7.7 is a model which they use to
plan approaches to their SMEs. This model is based on how the
SME deals with information and problems: systematically or
spontaneously; internally or externally. Systematic SMEs do
things in predictable, data-driven ways, with purpose always in the
forefront. Spontaneous SMEs respond to the moment or the problem domain; their expertise will not always come to you in easily
structured portions. SMEs that are external share what they think
and feel with little prompting. Internal SMEs will need to be
prodded to provide feedback and details. These variables combine
to yield four kinds of SMEs. My students prefer to work with the
SYEs (Systematic Externals), the folks who organize, structure and
tell you what they are thinking and feeling. The challenge is in
how to deal with the others, given your particular style.

**Coscarelli & Stonewater and Silber & Bratton (1984) concur in
urging trainers to adjust their inquiry style to the SME.** If you can
locate the SME with whom you are working in Figure 7.7, it might
help in planning approaches to this particular person.

David Cram (1981) wrote a useful article in *Performance and
Instruction* which lists six things that a trainer can do to increase
the likelihood of a successful interview with a SME. I've adapted
them slightly:

1. **Create an agenda.** Steps 1-4 should serve as a springboard for
this agenda. Keep asking yourself: *what is my intent in having this
meeting?* You will have very different agendas matched to different purposes.

KNOW YOUR SME

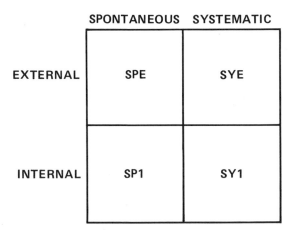

Figure 7.7

2. **Bring something in writing to which the SME can respond.** This might be some extant data on the problem or a task listing which needs elaboration or the subject matter structure you created based on your last meeting.

3. **Question the SME so that he or she is pressed to visualize optimal performance in the real environment.** Look at the list of questions that conclude steps two and three and use them to create your agenda.

4. **If the SME isn't giving you what you think you need, ask again in a different way.**

5. **Pay attention to the SME behavior you want and ignore the unhelpful behavior.** Keep your purpose in mind. Are you there for details of optimals or opinions on why others don't do it well or to find out when and how the two of you can arrange to go on site to talk to star performers?

6. **Avoid discussion of HOW you are going to do the training**. It is too early to commit to any particular kind of training. Some SMEs will want to meander into the details of how to deliver training rather than the innards of the equipment or troubleshooting wisdom you are there to discuss. Decisions about **how to accomplish** training objectives aren't their job; it's yours.

Figure 7.8 is a checklist I've developed that reviews issues in relating to SMEs. It is based on the challenges that trainers confront and some successful tips which I believe will contribute to productive interactions. Joe Arwady, an experienced performance technologist, reminded me of how important it is to "bring something with you to the table." Be certain that you are clear about how this project will benefit the SME, and/or the company, and/or the universe.

The approval process deserves some special attention. An informal nod is rarely good enough. One trainer I know was working on a retail training program for a new fast food product. He presented the Vice President of Marketing with a description of the product that he had gotten from the nutritionists. The VP did what must have been a cursory examination of the task analysis for preparing the new food item. He then urged the trainer to quickly get on with producing the training for the franchises. The worthy developer accepted the informal approval and created the training and job aids. All hell broke loose when the VP eventually saw training for the creation of a **cold** sandwich. The company was introducing a **hot** one.

Get approvals in a serious and formal way. Without them, people can change their minds on you a dozen times, striving to get it just right or to try it out in a different way or to get just a little more for their money. I know of instructional design companies which ask their SMEs to *initial every page as an indication of the accuracy and completeness of the material.* I am not suggesting that you go *that far*, only that you systematically plan and document approvals. Without formal documentation, you are vulnerable to questions about **who it was who got it wrong**. Figure 7.9 is a sample approval form, adapted from one that Pantec Training Systems uses, which you may alter and attach to training development milestones.

GETTING BLOOD FROM A STONE: WORKING WITH SMEs

WHY THEY ARE SOMETIMES DIFFICULT . . . .

- Lack of clarity about your role
- Lack of clarity about their role
- Lack of clarity about the initiating problem
- Concern about job security
- Skepticism about non-styles
- Unwillingness to relinquish control over content
- Not their priority
- No reason to do it

WHAT WE CAN DO ABOUT IT . . . . A CHECKLIST

- explain your role
- explain your expectations for the SME
- describe the problem in terms of what you need
- say that you're not a SME, unless you are
- meet their needs as to time, place, frequency, etc.
- describe the specific outcomes of the project
- describe how management has shown interest in this project
- do what you promise you will do
- share anecdotes about successful experiences working with SMEs
- admit eagerness and selected doubts and fears
- negotiate the approval process

Figure 7.8

REVIEWER APPROVAL FORM

The purpose of this form is to avoid misunderstandings between instructional design students at SDSU and our clients and subject matter experts (SME's).

Designers: Make sure that what you give clients is worthy of their attention.
Clients and SME's: Give careful and prompt approvals. Stand by them.

I have reviewed

. . . .
. . . . for its **accuracy, completeness and appropriateness** for our situation. Where changes are required, I have either marked them directly on the manuscript or have attached clearly marked and keyed insert sheets. I have signed and dated this form to indicate my review.

Check and initial:

...............Approved without changes (initials)...............
...............Approved with corrections (initials)...............
...............Resubmit for review after revisions (initials)...............

Sign:

....
instructional designer   phone   date submitted

....
client or sme   date approved

Figure 7.9

Conclusion

The topic of subject matter analysis deserves a book. It got a long chapter. The effect, I hope, is to encourage professionals to try the steps, use the examples sprinkled throughout the chapter as models, and examine the literature. This is a beginning.

Resources

Carlisle, K. (1986). *Analyzing Jobs and Tasks.* Englewood Cliffs, NJ: Educational Technology Publications.

Coscarelli, W., & Stonewater, J. (1981). Understanding Psychological Styles in Instructional Development Consulting. *Journal of Instructional Development, 3*, 2, 16-22.

Cram, D. (May 1981). Designing Instruction: Meeting with the SME. *Performance and Instruction Journal*, 5-8.

Dick, W., & Carey, L. (1985). *Systematic Design of Instruction.* 2nd edition. Glenview, Ill.: Scott Foresman.

Fleishman, E., & Quaintance, M. (1984). *Taxonomies of Human Performance.* Orlando, Florida: Academic Press.

Foshay, R. (1983). Alternative Methods of Task Analysis: A Comparison of Three Techniques. *Journal of Instructional Development, 6*, 4, 2-9.

Gagne, R., and Briggs, L. (1979). *Principles of Instructional Design*, 2nd edition. New York: Holt, Rinehart, Winston.

Harmon, P., & King, D. (1985). *Expert Systems for Business.* New York: John Wiley.

Landa, L. (1976). *Instructional Regulation and Control.* Englewood Cliffs, NJ: Educational Technology Publications.

Landa, L. (1983). The Algo-Heuristic Theory of Instruction. In C. Reigeluth, ed., *Instructional-Design Theories and Models: An Overview of Their Current Status.* Hillsdale, NJ: Lawrence Erlbaum Associates.

Martin, B.L., & Briggs, L.J. (1986). *The Affective and Cognitive Domains: Integration for Instruction and Research.* Englewood Cliffs, NJ: Educational Technology Publications.

Merrill, M.D. (Fall, 1977). Content Analysis Via Concept Elaboration Theory. *Journal of Instructional Development, 1*, 1, 10-12.

Reigeluth, C. (1983). The Elaboration Theory of Instruction. In C. Reigeluth (Ed.), *Instructional-Design Theories and Models: An Overview of their Current Status.* Hillsdale, NJ: Lawrence Erlbaum Associates.

Scandura, J. (1976). *Problem Solving.* New York: Academic Press.

Silber, K., & Bratton, B. (1984). Interpersonal Consulting Skills: Succeeding with the SME. *A Two Day Workshop Conducted for AT&T Communications*, Morristown, New Jersey.

Tarr, R.W. (1986). Task Analysis for Training Development. In J. Ellis (Ed.), *Military Contributions to Instructional Technology.* New York: Praeger.

Tiemann, P., & Markle, S. (1978). *Analyzing Instructional Content: A Guide to Instruction and Evaluation.* Champaign, Ill.: Stipes Publishing.

Tiemann, P., & Markle, S. (1984). On Getting Expertise into an Expert System. *Performance and Instruction Journal, 23*, 9, 25-29.

Zemke, R., & Kramlinger, T. (1982). *Figuring Things Out: A Trainer's Guide to Needs and Task Analysis.* Reading, MA: Addison-Wesley.

Part Three: TNA TOOLS

Chapter Eight: INTERVIEWING

Brief Description

An interview is an **interactive, verbal, real time communication**. Unlike print surveys or observations, someone with specific intentions is **talking** to someone else to fulfill those intentions. Whether on the phone or in person, the key is reacting to each other **as the interview happens**.

I have no hard data to prove it, but I think that the interview is the most frequently used front end tool. Think about your own efforts to launch your projects. What do you do first and foremost? You talk to people—on the phone and in person. Sometimes you are using it without being aware of it as a formal tool in your TNA arsenal. For example, in an early stage of needs assessment, you are doing it when you saunter into a manager's office to find out the way his people feel about the equipment that is about to be replaced or the way her people are responding to the new service order tracking system. Often, training professionals make formal use of interviews to set the parameters for a project, to find out what got the initiator interested or concerned, and to find out exactly how you do install that automated frang in an underwater location.

Too often we take the ability to interview for granted. Just about everyone can talk. And most think they listen and respond. Then why a chapter on interviewing? My experience is that we don't get sufficient mileage out of our interviews. Take just a moment and think about yourself. *Are you an effective interviewer? Are there any ways in which you are ineffective? Is there anything you do which detracts from your interviewing skills? Have you ever bombed? Why? Do you know?* For example, as

I think about myself as interviewer, I know that I anticipate my interviewee's answers, which blocks me from hearing nuances. What about you? Before you read on, take a moment to think about some experiences you have had doing interviews and consider your skills and liabilities with respect to this front end analysis tool.

Purposes of the Interview

You can employ interviews to gather information in regard to **all** TNA purposes. Interviews are also for making personal contact with people, for sharing ideas, and for engaging in dialogue and problem-solving.

The Interview: A Powerful Tool

The interview is a powerful tool because:

1. It is flexible. The canny instructional designer or industrial relations professional will follow an agenda *and* be very vigilant for opportunities to probe more deeply, inquire about a surprising or conflicting answer, clarify a misconception and add or subtract from the purposes for the meeting or call.

2. It enables you to enlist support and assistance for the project. While print surveys are useful tools for soliciting information, only rarely will they intrigue anyone into helping you solve a problem. Interviews, with two or more people engaged in structured conversation, can occasionally turn a disinterested or opposed colleague into an ally.

3. It provides more information than just words. The astute trainer uses all the clues that are available. Watch eyes, body, position, hands, tone, silences . . . All of them give a picture of the context for the problem or innovation, a multi-dimensional picture that approaches a truth plain words may not.

4. It is a prime agent for carrying out needs assessment and subject matter analysis. Chapter 6 describes the importance of stages of assessment, repeated inquiries of varied sources about a problem or new technology. Interviews are almost always at least one of the stages in needs assessment and often more than one of the stages. Subject matter analysis, also, is effectively carried out through interviews. Sometimes the extant data technique is **launched** through interviews for the purpose of requesting access to information.

The Interview: A Challenging Tool

While the interview is a good way to learn about the problem or situation, it is a tool that challenges the training professional. Why? You can't control your respondent, and you really don't want to for fear of stemming the flow of information, so it is impossible to anticipate all the directions in which the interview might go. It is also difficult to change your interpersonal style to match the inclinations of your respondent. He or she may like a more spontaneous or holistic approach, and there you are with your notes, agenda, and pained expression when the dialogue takes an unforeseen turn. Then there is the challenge of analyzing the data from a real live, free-wheeling interaction. All of us have heard tales of interviews which turned into confrontations with annoyance, skepticism, boredom and outright hostility. It is one thing to send out a survey which goes unanswered or elicits snide comments; it is another to be on the phone or in the same room with it.

Fortunately, we can improve our chances of success by attending carefully to the elements of the interview as identified by Warwick and Lininger (1975): the interviewer, the respondent or interviewee, the topic and the interviewing situation. I'd like to take a look at those four areas as they are experienced by our profession.

The interviewer. That's us. The ones with the need for information. Dressed appropriately, with agenda in hand, the training professional needs to control the interview by knowing what he or she wants and possessing the communications strategies for getting there. Later in the chapter we will focus on creating an agenda. For now it is sufficient to know that we need one and that we will adhere to it, while at the same time retaining flexibility. There's part of the challenge.

The respondent or interviewee. That's them. Zemke and Kramlinger (1982) describe three kinds of questions that interviewees will ask:

1. *Intent Questions*

This is where the interviewee wants to know your reason(s) for this interaction. These are questions like: *why are you talking to me? why me instead of Belinda? what will be involved in this discussion?*

2. *Competency Questions*

The interviewee wants to know what you know and whether or not you are able to engage in meaningful conversation. This might turn into: *are you an expert? will this brief conversation turn you into one? do you disagree with me about any of this?*

3. *Propriety Questions*

These are questions of power and access to information. You might hear: *why should I spend this time? what will happen if I don't? if I do? are you going to be supervising me on this? can I control your activity on this project? do I want to? are there higher-ups in the organization who are interested in encouraging the flow of information or in restricting it?*

Zemke and Kramlinger are right about how interviewee questions cluster. My experience is that most respondents won't ask these questions. They will wait for the information or they will withhold information because of their assumptions, rather than directly inquiring about their concerns. Your introductory dialogue should address these issues, whether the interviewee asks them or not.

To the pivotal questions of **intent, competency and propriety,** I want to add the respondent's appropriate concern with **broader impact.** Interviewees want to know what is going to happen as a result of this interaction, **after the interview.** What are your intentions, not just for the dialogue, but for the project and for them? Sometimes you can only speculate. And other times, the impact is already clear. Share as much as you can. A forthright approach will contribute to building a relationship—for this project and the next.

The topic. Why have you contacted this individual? That sounds silly, but many of the problems instructional designers have during interviews come from not being clear themselves about the specific purpose(s) for this interaction. Get clear about that before you do anything. Your purposes, and therefore the topic(s) of the meeting might be:

☐ Finding OPTIMALS
- what they think ought to be going on
  - how the system should work
    - what they know about it

☐ Finding ACTUALS
- the details of how employees are and are not performing
  - the way the system is operating
    - whether they perceive a problem

☐ Finding FEELINGS
- how this person feels about the situation
  - how they think others feel
    - confidence regarding the topic
      - whether they value/like the topic

☐ Finding CAUSE(S)
- what is causing the problem

☐ Finding SOLUTION(S)
- options for how to solve the problem or implement the innovation

Even before you arrange the interview, it is important to try to anticipate how the interviewee is likely to feel **about talking about this topic**. The engineer who knows he has problems writing technical reports is going to respond differently from the engineer who has been pointed to as a model of excellence in report writing. The supervisor who knows that a new service order tracking system is imminent and that her staff will be pulled away for lengthy training might have a *no problem, they can handle it* attitude leading to brief training. A new customer services manager is likely to have a different perspective on current performance than one who has been in place for three years. A course developer who participated in the selection of a word processing system will feel different from a developer on whom the system has been imposed. And the subject matter expert, the one and only experienced accountant on international mergers and their tax implications, might be ecstatic about sharing expertise or not pleased at all. What will it be? Try to find out from managers, scrutiny of the extant data, and your political experience within the company or agency. You probably won't know for sure before you begin your communication. It is, however, essential to speculate and to be as prepared as possible.

The interviewing situation. There are environmental things that you want to control to increase the likelihood that a personal interview will go splendidly:

- Go where they are, if you can.
- Do it when they suggest it, if you can.
- Schedule ahead of time.

- Make certain that you are hearing the interviewee's opinions in regards to scheduling and convenience. It is possible that holding the meeting where you are fits into his or her plans. The key is to check with the interviewee and *hear* their responses.

- Find privacy and protect it. You are better off in a noisy cafeteria than an open area full of work stations.

- Employ a mental checklist with questions about comfort, noise, privacy, telephones, other distractions, etc. Ask for a different setting if the one you find yourself in is uncomfortable, or presents too many distractions, or isn't sufficiently private. You don't want a good excuse for why it didn't go well; you want the information.

Telephones vs. Meetings for Interviews

It would be nice if I could provide a flowchart of variables which, once considered for your situation, will tell you whether to use the phone or meet in person. I don't have one for you. As I tried to work one out, I kept coming up with **it depends** . . . . For example, while an effective meeting is more likely to contribute to a relationship, it will take more time and a poorly planned one could destroy a budding working comraderie. While a phone call is great for checking something out with lots of people, you certainly won't be able to show exactly what you mean if illustration is called for. There are competing interests as you try to make decisions about how to use the interview tool.

Here is a heuristic of factors to take into account as you decide whether to meet in person or on the phone. Make your decision on the basis of how important the different factors are in each unique situation. Remember it isn't absolute; it is suggestive of the many things you need to consider as you plan.

If You Want   **Then I Suggest**

☐ to inform someone about
the project . . . . telephone

☐ to gather in-depth information . . . . meeting

☐ to discuss difficult, complex
or controversial subject matter. . . . . meeting

☐ to check out a point or two. . . . . telephone

☐ to enlist support from a
disinterested or opposed colleague . . . . meeting

☐ to look at subject matter which
must be illustrated. . . . . meeting

☐ to save money. . . . . telephone

☐ to get to know someone . . . . meeting

☐ to establish a working relationship . . . . meeting

☐ to periodically nurture a working relationship. . . . . telephone

☐ to get an "initial take" on the thing . . . . telephone

☐ to get information from many people . . . . telephone

☐ to get information from a few key individuals. . . . . meeting

☐ to show how important they
are to the project. . . . . meeting

A Step by Step Approach to Successful Interviews

Step 1: Preparing for the Interview

Step 2: Beginning the Interview

Step 3: Conducting the Interview

Step 4: Concluding the Interview

Now let's look at each of them in detail.

Step 1: Preparing for the Interview. Prepare for an interview by 1. knowing why you are interviewing; 2. developing an agenda or interview guide; 3. studying the subject or task; and 4. scheduling with sensitivity.

1. Knowing the Purposes for This Interview. Training professionals need to know exactly why they are talking to this source. That means that *prior to the interaction*, the trainer needs to know which purpose or purposes are involved. **Are you looking for information about optimals, actuals, feelings, causes or solutions?** Several? Then which? Should you try to achieve all your purposes in one meeting?

Let's use the true story of a centralized training organization in a Fortune 100 corporation. They receive a formal request for training assistance to launch a course to train veteran supervisors to train their employees in safe truck driving. It's a truck drivers' "train the trainer." The instructional designers who are responsible for *front ending courses* decide that they had better do some needs assessment interviews to find out more about this request. The trainers are in no way convinced that there is a problem and no extant data is attached to the request. At the same time as they request data on accidents and new hire drivers, they call around the country to ask what is **actually transpiring in the trucks before new hires set out**. They also want to know what the various operating companies **wish was happening**. They are seeking optimals and actuals. In relatively brief conversations with managers, supervisors and safety personnel, they can determine if there is a problem or not, or if this is an aberrant training request motivated by some flukey circumstance.

Now let's pretend that this request for training had appeared with ample documentation of accidents and breakdowns caused by improper driving habits and that this extant data comes from several sites. And let's presume that there are corporate guidelines based on insurance regulations for how drivers should be prepared by their supervisors before being given the keys to the vehicles. So optimals and actuals are in place. No need to pursue those purposes. The question is **why are they concerned about this *now* and what, if anything, ought to be done about it**. You have got to figure out **what you are up to** when preparing for an interview. Nothing else is as important.

2. Developing an Agenda or Interview Guide. Your written agenda has three goals:

1. to help you achieve your purposes;
2. to establish a relationship which will encourage the respondent to give you the information that you need; and
3. to track your progress through the interaction.

Let's talk about purposes and agenda. Some might urge you to write out your questions *word for word*. I don't do it myself because fully scripted questions restrain my flexibility. They also keep me from *being myself* on the phone and in person, and I think that is important. You need to see what works best for you. At the very least you need key phrases (prompts) linked to purposes. Those help you in planning and eventually convert into your interview agenda. A sliver of the plans for the agenda of the truck example might look like this:

Purpose	Prompt
Actual performance problems	Doing now?
	Doing differently?
	Using different trucks?
	Describe how supervisors send them off.
Optimal performance	How train better?
	Exact content drivers must have?
	Insurance regulations sufficient?
Cause(s) of the problem	Why **now**?
	What's different?
	What would solve the problem?

Note how the purposes link with the beginnings of questions. Presented on horizontal sheets of paper, this format would also lend itself to note taking. You can easily fill in the answers as they are offered. Abbreviate your purposes into **Optimals (O)**, **Actuals (A)**, **Feelings (F)**, **Causes (C)**, and **Solutions (S)**, leaving room for prompts and responses.

Purposes	Prompts	Responses

There are reasons we interview which go beyond the traditional TNA purposes described above. You might want to inform someone that your group is looking into this topic. Or you might want to make sure that every region has a chance to hear about the project. Or you might want to display your dazzling interview skills to someone. These additional purposes can be tacked on to the other reasons that you call or meet with people, solidifying your political position as well as your knowledge base about the problem or new technology.

Your agenda should contribute to building a relationship with the interviewee. You do that by attending to the concerns that I described earlier: **intent, competency, propriety and impact.** Make sure that the first moments of your interview do something to address each of those concerns. Here is how it might look on your agenda.

GOALS of the Meeting (*Addressing Concern About Intent*)

*To describe the problem as it appeared on the request for training assistance

*To find out if the experience in your area is the same

*To get details of what goes on and what ought to

*To solicit your help in solving this problem

About ME (Addresses issue of competency)

*With the company thirteen years in operations

* In training and development for three years

*Not an expert on mechanics of trucks

*Served on safety committees at two different plants and instructed one safety course on using diagnostic equipment safely

* Licensed truck driver but far from a subject matter expert

*Intrigued with this thing now that starting to look at figures from across the nation

About this PROJECT (Addresses propriety and impact issues)

*You've been supervisor of guys who drive trucks for seven years so want your opinion

*Rigo suggested you because you commented on the number of times you've heard from management about the various and serious costs of accidents

*Also want you to know talking to me is voluntary

*Total confidentiality

*This conversation won't take more than 20 minutes

*Want to come back to you for another, possibly two more meetings, when I know more, to see if rings true to you

*Might ask you for specific examples later but won't attribute

*Hope this will lead to a clear role for supervisors and tools and time needed to prepare drivers for the field

*Concerns, questions, feedback on how interviewee appears to be responding?

The written agenda for phone interviews or meetings should manage the interviewer during the meeting or call. I use numbers and letters within the agenda because it keeps me on track and helps me match up what I was seeking with what I heard. There is no one ideal format. I suggested a horizontal page above, with three columns: a slim one for purpose; a fatter one for prompts for questions and about half the horizontal page for recording responses. Another possibility would be to retain the familiar vertical format, as shown on page 144.

Name . . . .

Contact information . . . .

Title . . . .

Date of interview . . . .
        Time begun: ....
        Time concluded: ....

Project . . . .

I.   Introduction

   A. About me

      1. remember last time told you just getting to know about details of the problems with performance appraisals
      2. spent past 3 weeks ....
           • read ....
           • observed ....
           • talked to ....

   B. About the project

      1. know most details of the problem
      2. need to know why

   C. About this meeting

      1. your opinion on cause(s)
      2. suggestions on who else might have some ideas on this
      3. call shouldn't take more than 10 mins.

II. Body of Interview (ask if has appraisal form in front of him/her)

   A. Problems I found looking at 35 randomly selected appraisals:

      1. information omitted (espec. items 7-9)
      2. on items which request behavior descriptions (#8 & 9), there are few

        3. only 39 % are filed within 30 days of due date

    B. Problem 1: why?

    C. Problem 2: why?

    D. Problem 3: why?

    E. Vern Madrid suggests that the cause of the problems with appraisals is the way the form is set up. Agree?

    F. What would make the form a more efficient and effective device?

III.   Conclusion

    A. Summarize respondent's thoughts on CAUSE(S)

    B. Ask if anything else wants to add about topic, or ask . . . .

    C. Will probably not have to involve him/her further, but call if anything comes up that would relate

    D. Thanks . . . .

Note that this is *not* the interviewer's first meeting with the respondent and that the respondent is informed that there isn't likely to be any further need for interaction. This is the agenda for a brief telephone contact to find out what this source thinks is causing the problem. Even though it is brief and not the first meeting, the designer or performance analyst is **anticipating** what might happen during this interaction. The purpose is clear; the relationship is already in place; the conversation should be meaningful to both participants. This is obviously a latter stage of needs assessment, and part of a TNA which has involved extant data analysis in earlier stages. **As you look at this sample agenda, you can see that this agenda is not itself the planning device. This agenda is the *result* of planning which is then used to manage the trainer's progress through a successful interview.**

3. Studying the Subject or Task. The trainer has to know enough about the problem, job or subject to ask intelligent questions and respond to inquiries. That doesn't mean turning into an overnight subject matter expert on sonar buoys or switching systems or truck safety. It does mean knowing the basic subject matter or components of the task, learning key phrases, finding out how the subject matter breaks down, in general, and knowing where the major areas of discussion are likely to be. Prepare to hear something like:

"What do you see as the features of our circulators which make them particularly appealing to this vertical market?"

"I don't understand what you mean there. Could you explain it in another way?"

"Would you explain what you heard about how the midwestern group is doing customer loop design?"

"How would you compare the ergonomics of the current system to the one which will be in place in 6 months?"

"What makes you say that?"

"Why are you calling it that?"

"Well, what's the history on this thing?"

"OFTA 11 reverses everything we've been doing on Mark 10s, wouldn't you say?"

These statements are no problem at all for an up-to-date subject matter expert. They pose a considerable challenge to a course developer or instructional designer who has been out of the field for awhile or who never was in the field. What to do?

☐ Admit you are not a subject matter expert, unless you are.

☐ Get someone to provide you with the basic vocabulary and subject or task structure of the thing. Chapter 7 of *TNA* should be a good resource for you.

☐ Study and read so that you can at least distinguish between what you do and do not know and so that you can frame intelligent questions.

☐ Tell the interviewee what you have done to grasp the topic thus far and ask for his/her help and suggestions about how to proceed.

4. Scheduling with Sensitivity. This has been discussed when we focused on the interviewing situation. Remember that you want a time and place which will enhance the likelihood of getting TNA information. That usually means privacy, quiet, comfort, no distractions, and compliance with the source's requests for location and timing.

Step 2: Beginning the Interview. Enhance your chances of a successful interview by being on time with your call or visit. The first moments are crucial. Rather than launching the interview with a good joke or a reference to a recent movie, get down to business. But not heavy business. Don't lead with a controversial or weighty question. For example, "The records that I have seen indicate that your lathe operators produce more scrap than the other shifts. Could you tell me why you think that is happening?" is definitely *not* the way to build rapport, enlist willingness to cooperate, and clarify the purposes of the meeting. Lead instead with who you are and how you came to the project. Don't ask your interviewee to disclose right at the beginning. You do it. Try something like, "I sold for a little under two years and then found myself managing an outlet. Then, after awhile I would up as a regional manager, with a territory similar to yours, only covering rural states. About a year ago, Varda Allen asked if I would consider working in training and development. I jumped at the chance, especially since I had always griped at the training programs and job aids that came to us from headquarters. This project on our shortage control program is my third big project, and it's an important one. You've probably heard that we're working on that."

At the beginning of the interview, the trainer wants to satisfy the interviewee's concerns about intent, competency, propriety and impact. Since you constructed your agenda with those concerns in mind, it should be no problem to follow along with it, allaying your source's concerns as you go.

The example of the performance appraisal agenda in Step 1 illustrates an agenda which will cover the bases. There is explanation of **who** you are, why you are talking to **them** (an opportunity to appropriately compliment them for their expertise and/or experience), **about what** you will be talking, **how long** it will take, and what their **future role** will entail. Respondents' likely questions are addressed with no delays for small talk.

Let them know when you are moving out of the introductory phase of your interview (the phase where you've been informing them) and into the meat of the inquiry (the phase where you will be asking them for information and ideas). Here is a sample transitional phrase: "Now that you've heard about me and the project, let me give you a chance to ask a question . . . ." After they have asked or indicated no need to ask. "Let's talk about thoughts on the shortage control program. I'd like to focus on how you and your people actually carry it out in your stores," will move the interview to its substantive section.

In your introduction you are responsible for building rapport and for meeting the respondent's needs for information about why, what, what for and how long. You are also responsible for getting out of the introduction, where you are the big talker, and into the body of the interview, in which you will encourage the source to do most of the talking.

Step 3: Conducting the Interview. The success of the interview will depend on **asking** the right questions, **hearing** the answers and **recording** what sources say. Your agenda should provide the prompts you need to compose questions. What do I mean by the right questions? First and foremost those are questions which get information appropriate to the purpose(s) for the interview. If you need information about how the shortage control program ought to work, one of your sources will be a manager who is getting good results with this shortage program. Your purpose in talking to him or her is to get details about it, about exactly what they do which makes it work for them. Once you know the purpose of the inquiry, the prompt or the question is included in the agenda. At the moment of the interview (or before if you script questions ahead of time), you must find the exact words:

There are two options for kinds of questions:

    1. **Open**
    2. **Structured or Forced Choice**

Open ended questions are useful early in the interview just as they are during early stages of needs assessment and subject matter analysis. "Please tell me about how a shortage control program ought to treat store closing." or "Describe the way your people actually shut down at the end of the day." or "What do you see as the causes for the problems we are having with shortage control?" While these open ended queries allow broad responses, they are still linked clearly to purpose, with the first seeking optimals, the second seeking actuals and the third keyed to causes. Open ended questions will encourage conversation, show that you lack a preconceived picture of the problem and that you are open to numerous ideas. They also allow the respondent to say a lot or a little, to stay on target or to meander aimlessly.

Structured queries can only be constructed after you know something about the problem and subject matter. In these forced choice questions, you pose a question and ask the respondents to pick an answer. The trainer or industrial relations professional provides the choices from which the respondent selects. Unless you are in a meeting with the source, with a list which is shown at the time of questioning, limit the choices to three. It's hard to keep many bits of information or choices in mind. For example, "When one of your people gets a reading of between 34-40 on the wishbone, which should they do *first*?

    a. issue a telephone alert dialing 1222

    b. recheck the cosmoid

    c. notify the supervisor"

That was a forced choice example of a quest for optimals. Here is one based on extant data and seeking information on cause: "Seventy-one percent of the performance appraisals lack what the Personnel group consider *acceptable behavior statements of areas for improvement*. Which of these two is the **major** cause of this problem?

    a. Supervisors don't know how to write behavioral statements

    b. Supervisors don't know they are supposed to write behavioral statements"

A third kind of statement that trainers need to have in their repertoire is a **mirror statement. You restate what you heard, and sometimes go just a little further.** For example, "You think that

most of the problem with sales is caused by the staff's inability
to manage their accounts and time, and not with a lack of familiarity with new products. Would you say that is true across the
company, in every setting or just in those areas which have a
largely new staff?" or "I hear unwillingness to point to any cause
at all . . . ." or "You've just described a complex procedure for
sanitizing this equipment. Will you watch me as I run it through
for you and check that I've got it all?"

Mirrors work for all TNA purposes. In addition, they are
especially effective at validating a source's ideas, showing your
attentiveness, making sure you got it right and establishing rapport. However, the phrase, **"I hear you saying . . ."** can be overdone. Use it when you need it, when you actually want to make
sure that you did hear the respondents saying . . .

Hearing . . .

An effectively framed question should elicit a response, ideally
a useful one. But sometimes even an excellent question will get
little or no response. That is the time for a mirror, "I've asked
you . . . and you either shrugged or said a terse yes or no. Would
it be better for me to re-schedule this meeting with you? What
can I do to encourage you to tell me more about . . . We really
need to know what you think." I can remember trying to interview a woman who was in the painful beginnings of a divorce.
With typical existential feelings of *"What's it all for," "why go
on," "what does anything matter,"* it was hard to convince her
that she wanted to talk about a mundane corporate performance
problem. I had to *really hear* what she was saying and infer that
this was not a good time to talk. Our communication problems
were out of my control. This woman needed time to heal before
she could help me. I could demonstrate patience or find another
source for the information I sought.

Recording . . .

There must always be a way of recording what you hear from
respondents. It's a mistake to rely on memory. Some people use
a tape recorder. I never do and discourage my students at San

Diego State from doing it because sources often dislike being taped and trainers rarely want to take the time to go back and listen, except perhaps if you have compressed speech capabilities. If you plan to tape the conversation, ask the respondent's permission **before** you pop the tape into the machine. That's true for telephone interviews also.

Preferring to take notes right on the scene, I rely on my old speed writing skills from college. I write phrases, rarely complete sentences and acknowledge that my handwriting will be decipherable only to me. Sometimes I make outlines on blank sheets of paper with numbers matched to the ones on the agenda. Other times I fit my scribbles right within my agenda. If I intend to record responses within the agenda, I prepare one ahead of time which leaves roomy spaces between items.

There are three symbols that are useful as I take notes during the interview:

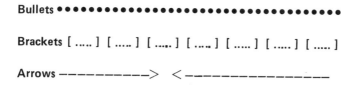

The **bullets** tell me that meaty information follows. That's for responses to my questions which will directly move me along in my TNA. It might be better opinions or details of how the job is done or statements about the cause of the problem, or . . . .

The **brackets** usually follow right after the bulleted information. They signify material which supports or enhances the initial statement. This might be a statistic or a reference to extant data or a page number.

The **arrows** tell me that I have to do something with that particular piece of information. It might mean I need to ask another question about it, or check a reference, or ask for supportive data, or put it in the file on cause, or . . . .

One final trick for assuring useful information from an interview is to look at your notes **immediately after** concluding the meeting or call. Fill in blanks and rough spots. Think about what it means in light of the TNA you are conducting. Prepare to follow up on your arrows. It is difficult to pick up the notes from a meeting even 24 hours after the meeting and make sense of what you find.

Step 4: Concluding the Interview. While you can make good stabs at scripting the introduction and body of an interview, it is much harder to plan the details of the conclusion. Why? Because the conclusion must be based on what transpired during the interview and you won't know your findings ahead of time.

There are, however, five things which should be included in the conclusion of any meeting or telephone interview:

1. Opportunity for the interviewee to ask a question and make a comment.

2. A summary of what the respondent said related to purposes for the TNA and a compliment regarding its usefulness.

3. Discussion of how the interview contributes to the project.

4. An opening to come back to the respondent for additional information.

5. Expression of appreciation.

There is debate about etiquette related to following up interviews. Should interviewees be told what you plan to do next on the project? Should interviewees receive a report which details findings? Should interviewees receive a written summary of the interview which has just concluded? Should their supervisor or manager? The answer, once again, is *it depends on the situation*. In most circumstances, I would say no to all the questions. There are, however, exceptions. Certainly you would report back to a subject matter expert to check for accuracy. If the person is an upper level manager or will be deeply involved in the project in the future, then it is appropriate to tell them what will happen next and to report to them about what you are finding, preserving the confidentiality of your sources. The key is to consider each situation and interview separately and ponder just how much is appropriate to share.

A Brief Example of Steps 1-4

As I have been writing this chapter, the worst fire in San Diego history consumed 70 houses, acres of canyon, and countless memorablila. This fire stopped about 7 blocks from my home. Homes were evacuated throughout my neighboorhood, a process which involved trained volunteer citizens who ran from house to house to prepare us to leave our homes behind. This is a process which involves shutting off gas and electricity and securing the place against looters. Gas and electricity valves and security features vary widely from house to house in this old neighborhood. How could the Captain in charge of training these citizen runners have prepared for and executed an interview which was part of his TNA. Let's speculate on the interviews that he did to determine what the runners had to know to do their job. He turned to subject matter experts.

Step 1: Preparing for the Interview. The Captain knew exactly who his volunteers would be and what their current, actual skills were. They were already signed up from each neighborhood and had filled out extensive questionnaires detailing their knowledge of gas, electricity and security. A few were trained plumbers or electrician, but most were not. The Captain also had the records of other Southern California fires that had threatened homes and the problems which had resulted.

The Captain knew why his volunteers were not able to do these things. They were citizens just like the neighbors they would help out in an emergency. This was a straightforward problem caused by an absence of skill and knowledge.

What the Fire Captain did not know was **exactly what they needed to know in these circumstances.** For this information about optimals he turned to the fire fighting literature and subject matter experts. He planned to interview experts from the gas and electric company and police department to find out:

Optimals   Need to know about
- gas shut off
- electrical shut off
- security procedures

Tools need to carry
Tools need to help others with/lend
Criteria for pre-shutting if resident can't
Anything else they need to know?

His purposes converted into the following agenda for meetings:

I. Introduction
    A. About me: Fire captain in charge of training, concerned with
       emergency preparedness
    B. About Project
       1. get citizens ready to help us out in event of disaster like fire
          which is threatening homes and lives
       2. need trained citizens to go door to door at time of crisis to
          get people ready to leave their homes
    C. About this Meeting
       1. need to know what you think these volunteer citizens need
          to know to help their neighbors and city services (fire, util-
          ities, police)
       2. this meeting will take no more than 30 minutes

II. Body of Interview
    A. Need to know about   1. gas shut off
                               2. electrical shut off
                               3. security procedures
    B. Tools need to carry to help out (bring list for them to look at)
    C. Criteria for pre-shutting if resident can't
       1. age
       2. lack of tools
       3. unwillingness
    D. Anything else they need to know?

III. Conclusion
    A. Ask for questions/comments
    B. Summarize ideas and compliment contribution of respondent
    C. Your ideas will contribute to content of the training program
    D. Thanks

Step 2: Beginning the Interview. The agenda enables you to
imagine just what the Fire Captain said. Presume it went smoothly and that the utility and police persons were willing and eager to
cooperate.

Step 3: Conducting the Interview. Once again, the agenda provides a pretty clear picture of what transpired. The Captain uses
primarily open ended questions because he is just getting into the
subject matter. He does include a forced choice item on tools that
volunteers might take with them. Obviously runners can't carry

everything and the Captain asks his source to rate a list of nine possible tools as to their criticality in this situation.

For entertainment's sake, and to make a point, let's imagine that the representative of the utility company advises you to include content with which you very much disagree. Should you disagree right then and there? I wouldn't. Inquire as to why he or she thinks this is the way to do it. Press for another source or two. Nothing will be gained by getting into a grand debate during the interview. Put a big arrow there and check it later. Be thankful that you have lots of bullets followed by specific ideas, some bracketed references and only three arrows which need immediate attention.

Step 4: Concluding the Interview. The agenda sets the Captain up so that he forgets nothing. The only hard part is summarizing what he found out. He does it within the areas of his agenda, saying what he learned about utilities, security, tools and criteria for stepping in. He also adds the subject of interpersonal and communication skills for informing residents of the disastrous news. His interviewee believes that those are the most crucial skills of all, if volunteers are going to get residents to move beyond panic into effective actions.

The Captain says that he is going to contact the psychologist that the source has suggested, and read the article that was recommended. He doesn't expect to have to get back to the respondent, but urges the interviewee to call if anything else comes to mind. The Captain expresses sincere appreciation for the help.

Resources

Dillman, D.A. (1978). *Mail and Telephone Survey: The Total Design Method.* New York: John Wiley and Sons.

Nickens, J., Purga, A.J., & Noriega, P. (1980). *Research Methods for Needs Assessment.* Washington, D.C.: University Press of America.

Warwick, D.P., & Lininger, C.A. (1975). *The Sample Survey: Theory and Practice.* New York: McGraw Hill.

Zemke, R., & Kramlinger, T. (1982). *Figuring Things Out: A Trainer's Guide to Needs and Task Analysis.* Boston, MA: Addison-Wesley.

Chapter Nine: OBSERVING

Brief Description

During observation, training professionals use their senses to perceive what is going on in the work setting at the time of employee performance.

Purposes of the Observation Tool

Trainers or instructional designers observe to gather the details of **optimal** and **actual** performance and to **infer** the **cause(s)** of performance problems. Observers, through direct means, want to know:

- What does the **exemplary** performer do which makes him a star? How much of this or that is he doing?
- What is the **average** employee doing? not doing?
- What about the performance of the **problem** employee? How does her performance differ from the others?
- What might be **causing** problems? What might be causing the qualitative and quantitative differences between star, average and weak performances?

Observation: An Important Tool

Observation is an important tool because:

1. **It is flexible.** You may have thought you were going into the field to watch star sales employees sell a particular piece of equipment at Phone Stores. Instead you discover how differently store managers deploy their staffs and that these differences correlate with sales figures. While you had clear goals for the observations, you didn't allow those plans to limit what you learned from being where the work gets done.

2. **It grounds your efforts at the work site.** It is easy to be snowed by the wonders of a procedure or a piece of equipment *before it is installed and confronts daily challenges*. Even a single hour in the field shows the context for performance and begins to shed light on **why** things happen (and don't happen) the way they do.

3. **It provides information that goes beyond words.** An employee or a supervisor will say one thing about skills or knowledge; performance may tell a different tale. An employee or supervisor may express one feeling, while what you hear them say or not say, do or not do on the job, indicates a different attitude.

4. **There are two kinds of observations that we can use: observation at the work site and examination of extant data.** They link this tool directly to two techniques: extant data analysis and task analysis. In extant data analysis, professionals seek access to the effects that performance is having, effects which are stored in files and computer tapes. This data is then carefully examined. Task analysis is carried out through observation of employee behavior. You watch the deck swabbing, cable laying, office mail delivery and telephone installing and use those observations to provide significant answers to questions about what is happening, what ought to be happening and why. If the performance about which you are concerned is visible, **can be observed**, then task analysis will be a key technique and observation your main tool. I suspect that tasks whose details can be derived **solely through observation** are probably those most amenable to replacement by robots.

5. **Observation often leads to additional observations or the use of other techniques and tools for TNA.** An observation in a convenience store, for example, might lead to going back and looking at performance appraisals, accident reports or sales figures. An observation of auto repairs might launch the training specialist on a series of interviews with supervisors and purchasing agents. Think about the job of selling personal computers in a retail store. You can observe the details of the overt behavior and the number of contacts which are fruitful, as well as problems which are encountered. But the significant differences between star sellers and the non-stars will be invisible knowledge, things they know to ask customers and anecdotes which they employ to add credibility to

their statements. Thus initial observations are probably going to be followed, in this case, with interviews with star performers, store managers and even customers.

The Observation: A Challenging Tool

It isn't easy to conduct useful observations. Here are some of the concerns which must be addressed as you plan and use this TNA tool.

- **Will an observer affect the setting and the way people do their jobs?**

Usually yes. Imagine your performance if an observer were to sit at your shoulder throughout a morning. Would you behave just exactly as you always do? How could that observer improve the likelihood that you would be natural? Since most of the in-depth observations that trainers do will be with the knowledge of the employees who are being observed, you need to have some techniques to improve your chances of seeing things the way they usually are.

Therefore, the training or personnel specialist who wants to use what he or she experiences to make **generalizations** about how work **usually** gets done must do the following:
- sample performance again and again;
- sample varied locations and performers;
- stick around long enough to blend into the environment;
- assure people that what you see and hear is not going to affect their personnel evaluations.

The training professional who uses covert (hidden and unknown to the person being observed) observation will experience the environment **au naturel**. The drawback is that it is difficult to spend enough time and take sufficient notes to study it **in detail**. It would be hard to stand around an assembly line, repair shop or a retail store for lengthy periods of time taking notes, and not be noticed. Observations which have a very narrow focus (e.g., Do our employees say thank you at the conclusion of each interaction?) or are for the purpose of getting a quick, broad picture of the situation (e.g., How are our cashiers handling Indochinese customers?) can be done using secret shoppers or unobtrusive observers.

- **What do I do about my biases about this task?**

Become as aware as you can of the exact nature of your preconceptions. You can't walk into a store or a maintenance facility and start watching without some notions about why you are there, without prior information about the problem or the new technology. What you want to do is *have a handle on what you think you know and feel already*. Then you can determine if what you perceive in the field supports earlier findings or begins to suggest a different picture of optimals, actuals and causes.

The moments before and after observations are good times to think about issues that Descartes raised hundreds of years ago. He called into question the certainty of our observations, going so far as to pose the existence of a larger power who plants false pictures of reality in our consciousness. Descartes' ideas focus our attention on how reality is shaped by what a manager has told us, the details of a job description or the accident figures we examined prior to entering the facility. What are we willing to take as empirical fact? only that which we have observed ourselves? only that which is corroborated by future stages of TNA?

- **Doesn't an observer have to make assumptions in addition to listing details and counting frequencies?**

Yes. While we can watch for days, even months, and then list **actual** and **optimal** elements of jobs, the conclusions we draw about the **cause(s)** of a problem come through **inferences**. The link between what we see on the job and what it means usually occurs because someone has stuck a neck out and said something like, "Eighty-five percent of all teller sales interactions discuss Account XYZ; only 4 percent mention Account GHJ, the newest option for savers. They obviously don't know enough about GHJ to talk it up." Could be. Additional TNA tools must be employed to check that inference out, since it is possible that opening the account involves filling out an extra form or that a criteria for establishing the GHJ is at least a 12 months residency and that this is a military community with few residents in place for that long. Observations provide a quantitative and qualitative reality which must then be enriched by inferences. Inferences, then, must be substantiated by additional observations, interviews or examination of extant data.

- **Won't an observation guide, something I have to fill out as I observe, limit my perceptions?**

This is certainly something about which to be concerned. A structured instrument which asks about certain things is going to rivet your attention to those things. The alternative, however, is to lose valuable information while you cast around for where to fit it or whether to include it.

- **Won't I be distracted by the newness of the situation or bored by its tedium?**

If you are clear about your reasons for being there, have structured your observation guide to facilitate those purposes, and depart as soon as you have the answers to your questions, then boredom won't be a problem. Distraction might come from the challenge of perceiving the shape of the job and its detailed particulars when the context is new and/or noisy and/or intriguing. Permit yourself time to get over this by doing a two stage observation. In your first stage, seek the gestalt of the task and its broad context. Then come back, less dazzled by the totality, and focus in on the aspects which are meaningful to this TNA.

- **Might this kind of unrelenting observation become a habit?**

I think systematic observation is a habit, usually a good one, for people whose job is improving human performance. You never know when the information observations you have been making of managers and supervisors will become useful, for example, if you got moved from technical training to management development. I know it can also become a preoccupation, slightly annoying to friends not fortunate enough to be in our line of work. For example:

It was a lovely Thursday evening and a friend and I decided to watch the Padres and the Mets at San Diego Jack Murphy stadium. At least that's what I thought we were going to see. Instead I saw performance discrepancies and their causes. There were ticket sellers in desparate need of job aids for handling big bills and Mexican currency. There were beer sellers who took forever to serve up the beer. There were program salespeople who hadn't the foggiest notion how to counter my objections, and there were more than a few problems with the base running of my Padres. My friend griped once about the beer, hissed at the Padres' errors and went no further. I launched into front end analysis, using my observational skills to gather data on actuals and causes(s) of problems. I was babbling away about the TNA I would conduct when I noticed my pal wasn't the least bit interested in my speculations. Oh, the loneliness of the performance analyst!!!

Observation: An Underutilized Tool

This chapter is hard for me to write because I haven't done many observations as part of front end analyses. I found I wasn't alone.

Military training professionals still use observation as one of several tools that contribute to task listings. Here is an account provided by Helen Sparks. Figure 9.1 presents a typical portion of a task listing. Helen Sparks writes of the process, "This Figure is a small section of a total task listing for a Navy aircraft. This sample represents a product which has been validated and is ready to be used as a framework for curriculum development . . . Training analysts used the following sources: existing missions/function data; **observations**; interviews with subject matter experts; design engineering data; and previous task listings for the system under study." Note that observation is only one component in the work.

Observations used to be more popular when there was more emphasis on skills training. Now that so much of training is focused on problem solving, sales, management proficiency and other intellectual subject matter, observation isn't deemed as potent a tool as it was for cable laying, equipment installation and routine maintenance.

I think we might be missing something by failing to go out in the field to look around. A former student, who prefers to re-

PILOT TASK LISTING

TASK	CONDITIONS	*TYP TRN
1.3 PERFORM PRELAUNCH ACTIVITIES		FST
1.3.1 PERFORM INSPECTIONS	Given mission configured aircraft and required equipment; support personnel; appropriate inspection checklists.	FST
1.3.1.1 INSPECT PERSONAL FLYING EQUIPMENT	Given mission required flight equipment.	FST
1.3.1.1.1 PUT ON PERSONAL FLYING EQUIPMENT	Given mission required flight equipment.	NT
1.3.1.2 ASSESS A/C STATUS	Given applicable aircraft maintenance records.	FST
1.3.1.3 PERFORM A/C INSPECTIONS	Given qualified plane captain with applicable ground support equipment appropriate inspection checklists.	FST
1.3.1.3.1 PERFORM EXTERIOR INSPECTION	Given qualified plane captain with applicable ground support equipment; NATOPS manual.	FST
1.3.1.3.2 PERFORM INTERIOR INSPECTION	Given exterior inspection complete; aircraft determined ready for flight/mission; NATOPS manual.	FST
1.3.1.4 PERFORM PRESTART CHECKLIST	Given interior inspection complete; NATOPS manual.	FST
1.3.2 PERFORM ENGINE START PROCEDURES	Given NATOPS Pocket Check List (PCL): appropriate starting power sources; pre-start checks complete.	FST
1.3.2.1 PERFORM NORMAL ENGINE START	Given NATOPS PCL; functional APP or external power.	FST
1.3.4 PERFORM PRE-TAXI/TAXI PROCEDURES	Given post engagement condition with engine and transmission instruments normal; all equipment checks complete; appropriate NATOPS checklist.	FST

*Column refers to training legend: D = Deferred
NT = No Training
RF = Review/Familiarization Only
FST = Full Scale Training

Figure 9.1

main anonymous, shared the way she uses observations and wishes she didn't:

She develops interactive videodisc training programs for manufacturing settings. She relies on documentation, technical reports and subject matter experts—not observations—for details of optimals and actuals. Her maiden exposure to the plant is when she takes a crew there to shoot the video. Then she and her staff wind up furiously altering the scripts to reflect the reality she finds. She wishes that time was allocated for observation during TNA because the quality of the product suffers from haste.

Her story and the encouragement of others leads me to urge personnel and training specialists to attempt to transcend second hand information. Go out and take a look at the situation. When management says there is not time, tell the story of the videodisc producer. An accurate and textured picture of the employee, the duties and the context comes only from first hand observations.

Characteristics of the Successful Observer

Here is an annotated checklist to help you look at yourself as an observer. You need:

□ **Curiosity** about the job and its details.

You are not likely to find out anything particularly useful if you set out to do your observation thinking you already know all there is to know about the situation.

□ **Patience** to stick around, silently, and wait to gather details of performance and insight into the situation.

Usually we are talking about patience applied to sitting and watching. Sometimes you'll need patience to wear down the resistance to gaining access to files.

□ **Tact** which will enable you to crystalize and explain why you are there in such a way as to allay the concerns of the employees who will be observed, and to respond to their questions about your role.

□ **Willingness to blend** into the environment as a thoroughly uninteresting part of it.

□ **Comprehension** of the job or system that is the focus of the observation.

☐ Ability to **do several things at one time**.

An observer must be observing and recording simultaneously. This entails familiarity with the observation guide, ideally gained through having a part in the construction of it.

☐ Proper **reverence and irreverence for the observation guide**.

Most often the observer will follow the guide, presuming it is effectively constructed. There are times, however, when he or she will set it aside because of the surprising and fertile direction which job activity takes.

☐ Ability to perceive **both the forest and the trees**.

Often you will have to pick up on the general structure of the task and its context, as well as note and record the details and frequency of performance.

☐ Ability to record the order in which things occur and then to **transcend that order to infer meaning(s)**.

An observer who is involved in TNA is usually seeking more than a chronology or counting of behavior. We seek the meaning of the presence or absence of performance; we want clues as to how to enhance productivity and the work climate by looking at what is going on.

Characteristics of Effective Observation Guides

The observation guide is a job aid that training and personnel specialists use to get the most out of their time on the job site, when burrowing in the files during extant data analysis, and afterwards, when trying to make sense out of it all. The key is that it is a job aid, something that is part and parcel of the moment of performance, in this case, the moment in which you are using your senses to understand and detail employee behavior. Ken Carlisle's (1986) *Analyzing Jobs and Tasks* includes many useful examples of observation instruments.

An effective guide, in addition to facilitating record keeping, is:

☐ **Simple** to understand and use.

Ideally, someone who hasn't been involved in its development would be able to pick it up and observe, although that it not preferable.

☐ **Linked to the purposes** of this stage of TNA.

While some observations are fishing expeditions, most aren't. The initial open-minded *take on the situation* can be accomplished using a blank piece of paper. The latter observations, those seeking defining details of the situation, must be structured by an observation guide. You are out there for premeditated, specific reasons. These purposes should be listed right at the top of the instrument. Are you seeking optimals from observations of stars, and/or actuals from extant data examination or watching random employees do their work, and/or cause(s) of problem?

An effective guide, in addition to facilitating record keeping, is:
□ **Limited in scope.**

A single observation can't tell you everything you need to know. Decide the part of the work on which you will focus, and structure the guide to help you illuminate and record it.

□ **Accommodating qualitative and quantitative** aspects of the situation.

Your guide must include descriptive elements of behavior, as well as space to record the frequencies attached to those behaviors.

□ **Structured so details of behavior, comments about causes, and miscellaneous information or impressions can be added.**

A student once told me that he had failed to capture some information during an observation in a fast food kitchen because there was no room on the form to get it down. Since systematic thinkers just hate to be scrawling their observations in vertical margins, you need to plan space for additions and surprises. A solution which is gaining popularity is the use of very portable lap computers to record qualitative/descriptive data. The space between items readily expands to accommodate whatever you perceive and files appropriate to different categories of information can be prepared ahead of time.

□ A blueprint for whatever **follow up** needs to occur.

Will you do additional observations? examine extant data? interview exemplary performers? supervisors? customers? What exactly will you ask them? Questions will occur to you as you watch and listen. Why didn't he suggest that other account? Why didn't she mention the new equipment's capabilities? Why did he throw out that part without using the two stage check off? How did he know that he would need that tool rather than the one he had used in every other installation? You need space to note what you want to do later so that it is not forgotten.

Let's take a look at an observation instrument which includes all these elements. Two other stages of TNA preceded construction of this guide: (1) an interview with a sales expert; (2) an observation of a star seller. This observation seeks information on what is **currently and actually going on**. See Figure 9.2.

A Step by Step Approach to Successful Observations
It helps to think about observations as having four broad steps:

Step 1: Preparing for the Observation

Step 2: Introducing Yourself into the Environment

Step 3: Conducting Two Stages of Observation

Step 4: Following-up

Step 1: Preparing for the Observation. The preparation for an observation isn't different from the preparation to conduct an interview or facilitate a group meeting. It involves:

• **Being clear about why you are going into the field.** About what are you already certain? Which questions are you attempting to answer through observation? You will need to figure out if you seek information on optimals, actuals, or causes **through this observation**. In the baseball program example, the field observations were to see what the sellers were actually doing and not doing. Earlier tools and techniques were employed to get the details of optimal sales performance. In fact, a detailed statement of optimals served as the basis for the list of behaviors included on Figure 9.2.

• **Selecting a way of observing which will provide valid results.** You have to decide whether the person or persons who will be observed are going to know you are there; that's an overt observation. The opposite, an observation without informing the person being observed, is called a covert observation. You will also need to decide whether to take suggestions about whom to watch or to use random sampling. There are no strict rules governing observation for front end analysis. Once again we are talking about a heuristic process. Here are some guidelines to help you decide (p. 168):

PROGRAM SELLERS AT BASEBALL PARK

Observation site . . . .
Person(s) observed . . . .
Position(s) observed . . . .
Selection factors . . . .
Date of observation . . . . **Time begun** . . . . **Ended** . . . .

I. **Reasons for this observation** (Check all that apply)
   —Seeking details of optimal job performance
   —Seeking details of actual job performance
   —Inferring the reason(s) for problems or successes

II. **Description of the problem**
   Sales of programs at baseball games at the stadium represent a smaller percentage of admissions than program sales at soccer or football games. The incentive program is based simply on a percentage of sales and is the same for all sports. Sales booths are positioned and decorated identically. The product, of course, is different, as are the sellers.

III. **Actual Sales Performance for One Individual per 3 minutes**
   Sales behavior   *Comments/Details*

Generic mentions of the product

Personalized mentions of the product

Use of adjectives and program details

Mentions of price

Physical movement behind booth

Reasons for success/failure:

Follow-up:

Figure 9.2

If. . . . . , **then I suggest**
  □ you want to assure that employees will be
unaffected by observer's presence . . . . .covert
  □ you seek **details** of **optimal**
performance which will necessitate long observations . . . . . . .overt
  □ you seek **details** of **actual**
performance and **causes** of problems. . . . . .covert
  □ you will need to **query** employee on
why he or she did what they did . . . . .overt
  □ you need to record the **frequency** of
one or two behaviors from many employees . . . . .covert
  □ you intend to observe **many employees**
very briefly . . . . .covert
  □ you intend to observe **a few people**
for a long time. . . . . .overt
  □ you want to **return** again and again . . . . .overt
  □ you want information on **optimals** . . . management selection
  □ you want information on **actuals & causes**....random selection

The ballpark example leads us directly to random, covert observation. Because the instructional designer wants to know what is actually happening, what the salespeople really do when they try to sell the programs, she randomly pulls six sellers' numbers and goes to the gates where they have hawking their wares. Because the sales contacts are brief and many people are milling about, she is able to gather lots of information without being noticed. It would be a different situation if she were trying to observe exemplary computer salespeople as they sell word processing systems. Covert, random observations wouldn't get what she needs.
• **Designing an observation guide which gets you what you need**. This usually entails the creation of something simple which fulfills the purposes for your observation. Jeanne Strayer, currently of Cubic Corporation, provided this example which goes back to her experience in the financial industry. You'll see how simple her instrument was and how readily the information it gathered could be used in her decision-making.
  Jeanne wrote:
  Due to the deregulation of the Savings and Loan industry, Central Savings expanded its portfolio to include some new

"money market accounts." These new accounts were the brain-children of the Marketing Department.

The Training Department, charged with the job of revising the New Accounts class, wanted to be sure that the course focused on what people in the branch actually did with these new accounts. Therefore we decided we needed case studies grounded in the actual work flow surrounding money market accounts.

We decided the best way to obtain information was to go out and observe in the branches, rather than rely solely on Marketing's promotional materials. Our experience told us that the predictions of the Marketing group and the field could be two different things.

Observations entailed a three hour stint in the morning or after-noon on a day that was selected through collaboration with branch management. A call one week ahead of time usually sufficed to set up the observation.

They liked to put us in an out-of-the-way place with close proximity to the action. Branch personnel wanted to be able to get on with their work and ignore us, which is just what we wanted. We learned to accept an absence of overt hospitality because it allowed us to avoid attracting employee and customer attention.

The form I used to record what was actually going on looked like Figure 9.3.

Jeanne Strayer concluded: *What was surprising was not the number of new accounts opened, but the number of **conversions** counselors were making from existing accounts to money markets. The marketing promotional materials were geared towards attracting new money but the reality of the work that counselors did was switching old money about. Conversions were the trickier reality of the branches. The detailed observations enabled us to focus our training on the details of conversions and the problems we saw people have with them—not on generic product knowledge.*

Step 2: Introducing Yourself into the Environment. This step applies to those situations where the people are informed ahead of time that they will be observed. That is what happens in the majority of TNA situations, because most of the information we seek requires lengthy observations and follow-up questioning.

First, the individual who supervises the setting needs to be informed that an observation will occur. If they are to be the focus

NEW ACCOUNT COUNSELORS

Observation site . . . .
Person(s) observed . . . .
Position(s) observed . . . .
Selection factors . . . .
Date of observation . . . . **Time begun** . . . . **Ended** . . . .

I.   **Reasons for this observation** (Check all that apply)
      —Seeking details of optimal job performance
      —Seeking details of actual job performance
      —Seeking the reason for problems or successes

II.   **Description of the problem**
      Marketing conceived new accounts to increase profits and take advantage
of the new financial regulatory picture. Training was charged with updating
the New Accounts class to reflect the new products.

III. **Observation Guide**

Case	Account	Owner	Situation	Couns. Acts	Comment
1	3 month money mkt	indiv	convert savings to new acc't	keystrokes paperwork	sought help coding conversion
2	Money market chk	joint	deposit to bring up balance, convert reg chkg to new acc't	keystrokes paperwork	none
etc.					

Figure 9.3

of your attention, you immediately confront a problem with honesty. If you tell them you are there to observe the ways they motivate their staff, or handle customer complaints about staff performance, you will have to stick around for very long periods of time in hopes of capturing an accurate picture of what **actually and usually goes on.** My suggestion, when management is the subject for observation, is to provide a non-specific purpose for your observation. I would refrain from lying. I prefer saying something like, "My reasons for being here are to see how work flows in this office." That's true; it just isn't all of it.

When the personnel who will be observed report to others, then management can smooth the observer's entry into the workplace. Some observers rely on site management to explain their presence and immediately begin to blend into the setting with nary a nod to the subject who will be observed. I think you are better off saying a few words of introduction rather than depending on management to present your purposes in a non-threatening fashion. That introduction—for employees and managers—should include:

- a general, non-specific description of why you're there;
- a statement that **this is not a personnel evaluation and that nothing seen or heard will be associated with your personnel file;**
- an explanation that this is one of several observations in several sites to familiarize the observer with what is going on in the field;
- some sense of how long you will be there; and
- a reminder to carry on about business as usual

Step 3: Conducting Two Stages of Observation. After this introduction, the observer is responsible for being an insignificant fly on the wall. Here are some things you DON'T want to do:

- help the employee solve a problem or figure out how to do something
- ask a question about why he or she did something (do that later)
- groan, gasp, chuckle, applaud or in any way respond to what is transpiring
- rummage about in your papers or briefcase in a way that will be noticed by employees or customers

- take longer or extra breaks (the Training department usually has enough problems without creating more)

Zemke and Kramlinger suggest two stages of observation and I agree. The first stage is a more holistic *take* on the situation, an effort to look at the broad strokes of the task and the large components of it. A blank piece of paper will suffice as a tool for the observer.

The second stage of the observation, sometimes carried out on a return visit, sometimes done after an hour or so of holistic observation, uses **a structured observation guide to capture details**.

The great challenge is to perceive and record at the same time. I think three things contribute to the ability to do this:

1. familiarity with the work that you will be observing;
2. a guide which helps you record what's going on; and
3. practice.

Maybe a fourth characteristic is the recognition that you won't capture it all, that even videotape would miss some of what transpires. The trainer is charged with perceiving those aspects which will help move the TNA along; that perspective narrows the observer's focus and increases the likelihood of success.

Step 4: Following-up the Observation. During observations, questions will present themselves. You'll want to know why somebody did what they did, or why they deviated from what you expected to see and hear. Occasionally what you see will conflict with the information you already have from other sources. And sometimes an entire new path of inquiry will be initiated during an afternoon watching people do their jobs. Will you observe other employees? Will you interview the people you observed? Will you attempt to gain access to extant data? Will you talk to supervisors? customers?

There is always some kind of follow-up to an observation, if only to rush back to your office and write up the results of what you saw and heard. Be certain to set aside time immediately after the observation to look at your notes and observation guide. I think important details escape us if we let time and other perceptions intervene.

Example

Cora Pendergast provides this first person description of her use of observation to define optimal job performance:

"I used observation as a front end analysis technique as a new instructional design supervisor at a microelectronics firm. I had no previous knowledge of this industry. I had been given a summary of the purpose of the job for which training was to be developed, and I was aware that certain parts of the job were performed once per day at specific times (start of shift, equipment cleaning, chemical checks, etc.). That was about it.

I started out by arming myself with pen and paper, explaining to the operator why I was there, and watching her without questioning for a few repetitive cycles until I had a sense of the flow of the task. I then made a list of the major steps in the cycle and had her complete each step slowly, allowing me to ask questions and write down her answers. From this process emerged a basically sound summary of the major steps in the cycle as performed by this operator. These steps were then verified during interviews with other operators and engineering staff.

I found that this approach worked very well for completing a general job analysis and for detailed analysis of procedural tasks that didn't have very many critical decision points. On tasks that involved quite a bit of judgment, the process deteriorated rapidly if I tried to observe and query at the job site, as the job was being performed. I found it was helpful to do some observation to get a general idea of task sequence. The detailed decision-making criteria were best determined through discussion away from the job.

I have found that the more I work in this industry, the more of a frame of reference I am able to use in discussing jobs with engineers and operators. I now use observation more to verify and enhance information gathered through discussion than for first-time analysis."

Conclusion

Cora uses observation very effectively because she:

- examines the job description first, getting at least a general picture of the position before she begins her observations;

- informs the person who will be observed;
- uses observation to get a broad, general picture of what ought to happen;
- watches, records information, and then questions to acquire necessary details; and
- confirms and verifies what she learned about optimals with other sources, through additional observations and interviews.

This brief example illustrates the potential of observation as professional tool. Through observation, Cora, a new manager at the plant, slowly integrated herself into the work environment, gaining information and trust at the same time.

Resources

Carlisle, K. (1986). *Analyzing Jobs and Tasks.* Englewood Cliffs, NJ: Educational Technology Publications.

Davis, R.H. *et al.* (1974). *Learning System Design: An Approach to the Improvement of Instruction.* New York: McGraw Hill.

Descartes, R. (Meditations). In N.K. Smith (Ed. and Trans.) (1958). *Descartes' Philosophical Writings.* New York: Random House.

Fleishman, E.A., & M.K. Quaintance. (1984). *Taxonomies of Human Performance: The Description of Human Tasks.* San Diego, CA: Academic Press.

Norris, S.P. (1984). Defining Observational Competence, *Science Education, 68*(2), 129-142.

Washington, W. *et al.* (1983). Practical Hints for Observational Research. Paper presented at Southwest Educational Research Association, Houston, TX.

Webb, E.J. *et al.* (1966). *Unobtrusive Measures.* Chicago: Rand McNally.

Zemke, R., & Kramlinger, T. (1982). *Figuring Things Out: A Trainer's Guide to Needs and Task Analysis.* Reading, MA: Addison-Wesley.

Part Three: TNA TOOLS

Chapter Ten: WORKING WITH GROUPS

Brief Description

A meeting is a **purposeful** gathering of **three or more people**, a leader and at least two participants, which affords opportunity for interaction. In most cases the gathering is face-to-face, although teleconferencing and telecommunications offer some interesting possibilities for electronic TNA meetings.

Most of my academic and corporate colleagues dislike meetings almost as much as they dislike taxes and trips to the dentist. While meetings are not as momentarily excrutiating, they are most certainly more pervasive. In Doyle and Straus' classic little book, *How to Make Meetings Work*, the authors claim we average four hours of meetings per week, adding up to 90,000 hours in our lives—more than 365 days—leading or participating in meetings.

Do you eagerly anticipate attending meetings? Do you look forward to leading them? When you are waist deep in TNA, do you consider working with a group to seek optimals? causes? feelings? solutions? Do you have trouble getting people to attend meetings? Have you ever engaged in this dialogue?

> You: *Honey, I'm all tuckered out this evening.*
> Him/her: *Why? What happened at work today?*
> You: *Nothing much. I attended two meetings and ran one.*

Common sense suggests that *two heads are better than one, therefore* ... Working in groups promises synergy, a greater output of ideas and energy than is possible from any one individual participant, the whole turning out to be greater than the sum of the parts. Reality only occasionally fulfills the promise. This chapter attempts to improve the training professional's ability to work with groups of people to achieve TNA purposes.

Purposes of Groups

Meetings are a powerful front end tool because through them you can quickly gather information, dispense information and build affiliation. TNA groups may be used to:

• **Solicit opinions on optimals, actuals, causes, feelings and solutions. Every** TNA purpose can be addressed in group meetings, but not equally well. The most traditional TNA use of groups is to seek a broad picture of **optimals** from a jury of experts. The other purposes are more political and, therefore, more difficult to unearth in public gatherings. While most people are willing to talk publicly about how it **ought** to be, **they are less likely to disclose details of actuals, feelings and causes in front of colleagues.** Still, it does happen. It is certainly possible to imagine a useful group meeting to talk about the plight of performance appraisals in the corporation, focusing on what is actually happening in the appraisal meetings and why so many of these meetings are unsuccessful.

• **Open up options, determine a range of alternatives.** This is what Zemke and Kramlinger call focus groups. Others might call them brainstorming or problem solving meetings. **Evaluation of options is deferred; the goal is to flesh out *all* the possibilities.** These meetings are significant because, for example, they ask store managers to describe all of the problems they have had with the new pizza making equipment or supervisors to tell all the possible ways the new service order tracking system will be used. The key is to generate a wide array of optimals, solutions or causes.

• **Prioritize and make decisions.** This is when options are narrowed and judgments are made. After a range of possibilities has been determined, a decision has to be made. While I know many of my colleagues use groups for this purpose, I prefer to use groups to unearth **many** possibilities and then to work with individuals to **narrow** them. Too often, groups become unproductive debates, as individuals stake out territories and struggle to defend them. Some will win and some will lose, resulting in a trying, **public** group interaction.

• **Inform people about what's going on.** Training and development usually involves many people. There are some who recognize a problem and some who must implement a new system. There are colleagues and managers in the training group, industrial relations or personnel division who are interested in what you are doing and who are handling related projects. Remember the litany, "Why does it take so long to get the course off the gound? What's all the ballyhoo about a needs assessment?" Tell people what you are doing and **what you are learning as you do it.** Then they will be less likely to question the time it takes to complete the TNA process. A group is a good way to keep people informed, to track costs and to receive progress.

• **Solicit support for the effort.** Successful groups can build support for the policies, programs or courses which result from your TNA. While it would be hard to talk individually with large numbers of concerned people, you can involve more of them earlier if you use meetings as a TNA tool.

• **Get more for your time and their time.** Individuals stimulate each other. Ideas can build, one on the other, resulting in a whole which is greater than the sum of individual parts.

Working with Groups: A Challenge

Groups often fail to achieve their potential. Why?

1. **The cast of characters is complex.** There are four roles which must cooperate to yield a successful TNA group. A training professional is likely to find him or herself in any one of the roles or to have to select, train, encourage and beseech people to assume these roles:

• **The planner/designer:** This is the person who knows why he or she is having this meeting. It is almost always the training professional. Are you seeking the **cause** of performance problems? Are you attempting to clarify the **optimals** associated with tasks in a particular job? Do you want to know how people **feel** about a system which will be going on line soon? Do you want to **inform** people about the results of a series of interviews or the direction that you see the course taking, now that you have almost completed the TNA? The planner/designer is responsible for the agenda, the selection and gathering of participants, and the allocation of the other roles.

• **The facilitator:** Should the facilitator of the group be the trainer-designer-planner? **Preferably not.** The trainer-planner-designer often has strong opinions that are best not offered when the individual is functioning as the facilitator. A facilitator should be a neutral, patient, goal-oriented leader. The facilitator carries out the planner/designer's agenda by working with the group in a protective, supportive and responsive fashion. Samovar and King describe three kinds of leaders for groups: authoritarian, democratic and laissez faire. For groups that are a part of a TNA effort, it is folly to use anything but a **democratic and facilitating style.** Doyle and Straus use the word "cop" to describe an effective facilitator, which works well if you concentrate on the benevolent and protective aspects of that job.

• **The recorder:** This is the person who keeps track of what is happening on large, visible displays in full view of every participant. The visible displays serve as what Doyle and Straus call the "group memory." The recorder remains uninvolved in the substance or content of the group. His or her function is to "get down" the utterances of participants without editorializing.

• **The participants:** These are the people who were brought together to make a contribution. They are the ones who are encouraged to express opinions, share ideas, ask questions and achieve the goals of the group. Participants need to know WHY they have been asked to contribute to this effort and HOW the group will be operating.

2. **Training professionals lack authority.** The people assembled for the TNA group rarely have a direct reporting relationship to the trainer. Participants will be there because they choose to or because someone other than the training professional has supported the activity. That is also true of facilitators and recorders. Whether you are attempting to gather participants, a recorder or a facilitator, the training professional will often be pressed to make a strong case within the corporation and agency.

3. **Participants in many TNA groups feel they are there to represent a perspective or constituency, rather than to fulfill TNA purposes.** There is management's position, operations', employees', the Southeast region's, the union's, women's . . . . You may think you have gathered a group to talk about optimal point of sales procedures. Each individual in this situation, however, thinks he or she is there to represent unique interests. Things can bog down quickly.

4. **People like to talk about solutions not problems.** TNA groups are supposed to focus on **analysis** of problems, or to inform people about progress, so that prudent recommendations about solutions can be made. You might find yourself a part of the following discussion:

Mary, the leader/facilitator: We have an escalating number of grievances and requests for transfer as a result of performance appraisal interviews. The reason I've asked you here is to talk about how management can communicate performance appraisals to employees more effectively. I want to know what you think the truly effective performance appraisal interview is like. Wilt is going to record all your ideas on this butcher paper. (Note: this is a group to work on optimals.)

Wilt, the recorder: Please bear with me. I want to write this so everyone can read it, so I'll have to write more slowly than you all speak. I'll do my best.

Mary: Think about the meeting between the manager and employer. What is it that makes an interview like that work? Think about the first few moments? What does the manager do and say which gets it off to a good start?

Rigo: Are you going to use video for this training program? I heard that's what they do for performance appraisals at Transamerica and I like the idea.

Phyllis: If they can do it, we can. Video would be good, expecially if people could look at the tapes on their own. We could introduce the plan at Lake Arrowhead, at the first manager's meeting of the new year.

Bart: That's already scheduled for EEO and EAP. I prefer role plays anyway, in small, feedback groups. How would you know that everyone would watch the tapes on their own? Probably they wouldn't.

The meeting quickly turned into a debate about **how to solve the problem, not the search for optimals that the trainer-designer-planner had in mind.**

5. **Groups sometimes think as one, with individuals failing to contribute their unique ideas and positions.** If individuals do not feel protected and respected in the group, there is danger of what Doyle and Straus (1976) call "groupthink." I've participated in groups where one person volunteers the ideas and almost everyone else nods in unison. When pressed in private settings, the nodders had more to say than a nomcommital nod.

6. **Individuals do have their idiosyncrasies.** One person will fail to contribute; another might talk incessantly; a third might indicate displeasure through body language; and a fourth might waltz into every meeting late and/or exit early. There are many ways that participants can subvert the work of the group. It's important to be ready to deal with unproductive behavior.

7. **It's hard to keep track of the results of group efforts.** Even the most effective recorder can't keep track of every word. Nuances are often lost in the excitement of interaction. And body language can't be recorded on flip chart/butcher block paper or be followed up in the way that it might in a personal interview. As long as you are conscious of these shortcomings and attempt to work around them, you will capture significant qualitative information from group meetings.

A Step by Step Approach to Working with TNA Groups

There are five steps involved in using groups as a TNA tool:

Step 1: Preparing for the Group

Step 2: Launching the Group

Step 3: Facilitating the Meeting

Step 4: Closing the Session

Step 5: Following-up

Step 1: Preparing for the Group. The preparation for a group meeting is similar to the preparation to conduct an interview or an observation. It involves:

• **Being clear about why you are gathering people.**

What do you already know? Which questions are you attempting to answer through this tool? You will need to figure out if this is a session to establish job optimals, or to seek causes, feelings, solutions or descriptions of what is actually happening. While this tool can be effective for gathering all TNA information, it is best to limit a meeting to one or two purposes.

• **Establishing an agenda which will achieve your purposes.**

The training professional (designer-planner of this event) is responsible for translating the purposes for meeting into an agenda which is likely to achieve these purposes. The agenda should clearly detail:

  • participants and roles:
  • **purposes** of the meeting, including content and outcomes
  • **process** rules which have been or need to be established
  • time, place, and length of the proceedings

This agenda, including relevant attachments, should be in the hands of participants **before** the meeting. The agenda orients people to the **nature** of the business which will transpire and to **the way work will be conducted** at the meeting. The agenda itself should be the first order of business at the meeting. It is crucial that participants understand and support the plans you have for their time at this meeting.

• **Selecting participants and allocating roles.**

The four roles in a TNA group were described earlier in the chapter. It falls to the training professional (designer-planner of the meeting) to gather the necessary people and to decide who will do what. There are four major choices you have to make:

  1. **Who** will participate and **how many** participants do we need?
  2. Who will be the **leader-facilitator?**
  3. Who will **record** the meeting?
  4. What will **you, the designer-facilitator** do?

There is no one right number of participants for a TNA meeting. Between 3 and 12 participants seems to work best, although my preferences lean towards the smaller numbers if the training professional is looking for information and priorities. If you have gathered the group to tell them about progress on the project, to "get them on board with the effort," then larger numbers will work just fine.

A person might be included as a **participant** for many different reasons, the best of which is that you want this particular person's opinions and ideas because of what they know and have experienced. If you are clear about the purposes for your gathering, it will be much easier to determine who ought to contribute. There are, however, other reasons people are included in TNA groups:

- their boss wants them there
- your boss wants them there
- they are the boss
- you want to show that you have consulted many sources, regions and constituencies as you planned this program
- you hope that this meeting will "bring them into line on supporting this project"
- you want to "showcase" your skills for a particular individual

If systematically and sensitively probed, even participants included for these more cynical reasons can offer something significant to the project.

The **leader-facilitator** is the person who makes the meeting fruitful. It is the individual who will assure that the meeting stays "on task" while at the same time "feeling good" to the participants. The facilitator is responsible for encouraging everyone to contribute to the efforts of the group. Think about the unsuccessful groups in which you have participated and you will appreciate the magnitude of the challenge. If resources and priorities allow, the training professional should select someone other than him or herself to lead the group. It is a supreme challenge for the designer-planner to act as a *neutral* leader for his or her own TNA group. **After you have been steeped in a project or problem for days, weeks or months, it is difficult to remain equally accepting of all perspectives.**

The **recorder** is responsible for keeping track of the meeting in clear view of all participants. The recorder writes what is said without comment or expansion. Often, after a break, the recorder will be called upon to refresh the group's memory. Once again, if resources allow, it is ideal to bring someone else in to play this role. If the training professional or a participant serves as the recorder, he or she is removed from contributing to the content oriented work of the group.

During the planning of a TNA group, the designer or trainer must determine if the people he or she prefers as recorder and facilitator are willing to serve in those capacities. You do *not* want this to happen:

Mick, the trainer: Now that we're all here; I'd like to get into the meat of our agenda. Before we can do that we need to find a facilitator and a recorder. From our last meeting, you will remember how important those two jobs are and how important it is that the leader and recorder are both neutral and supportive of the group's work. Who would like to volunteer?

Melba, a participant from the Northeast region: If I do that, then I won't get to talk about the job from *our* perspective in the Northeast.

Jan, a participant from the West: I did it last time.

Phil, a participant from the South: I'm not good at that, and besides I like to talk too much.

Fritz, a participant from the Midwest: I promised my boss I'd get our position reflected in this training program, so I can't be an unbiased leader. Sorry. I guess we're stuck.

Mick: OK. OK. I'll do them both. I'll try, anyway. Just keep it slow so I can facilitate and record at the same time.

• **Arranging for the setting and the tools.**

The **setting** for the meeting ought to be as convenient and accessible to everyone as possible. That might mean holding the meeting in a regional headquarters or rotating from location to location.

You will also have to consider the cost of transportation and lodging. While at first glance, it might be compelling to put all meetings at an airline hub city because of air fares, generally lower hotel and food costs at non-hub locations might balance the transportation savings.

Even if all participants work in the same general area, be certain to carefully select a quiet, neutral arena. Don't borrow the conference room which is attached to the Marketing group or any other distinguishable entity. It is far better to arrange to occupy an unoccupied training room or one of the small break-out rooms, so often included in training areas. If there will be several meetings, attempt to use the same location over and over again. You can establish positive meeting habits which will transfer from one session to the next.

There are several ways to physically arrange the environment for a TNA meeting. Doyle and Straus strongly recommend directing the group towards the task as depicted in Figures 10.1A and B. Note that this set-up runs counter to the prevailing habit of gathering the participants around a table for small meetings.

Figure 10.2 presents a more traditional arrangement, one which Doyle and Straus found to be less effective because it directed group energy at people, not the accomplishment of tasks.

Recently, I've avoided round and horizontal tables in favor of U or V-shaped meetings. I think there is small, but noticeable, improvement in the quality of the work that gets done at these meetings.

It takes very little money to gather the **tools** for a TNA meeting. You need comfortable chairs, blank butcher paper on flip charts, brightly colored water-based markers (for writing in at least 1 inch letters), masking tape or thumb tacks and some walls for displaying the recorder's efforts. Some recorders like to write on the flipcharts, tear off the pages and then tape them in front of the group—as the group is conducting its business. Others prefer to place the paper around the room before the meeting and to write on these pages as the meeting transpires. I prefer the latter because I have gotten hung up trying to get the paper off the chart and onto the wall, while simultaneously looking cool and keeping track of what is going on at the meeting. Examine Figures 10.1A and B; imagine that the wall is covered with butcher paper which will soon be filled with legible, bright and comprehensive details of the meeting.

The setting and tools for a meeting must be arranged ahead of time. I know of instructional designers who spend several hours in the room prior to the meeting fussing with its details and ambiance. If you are gathering people from around the region, nation or world, it is certainly worth the time it takes to assure a setting and tools which are conducive to the agenda.

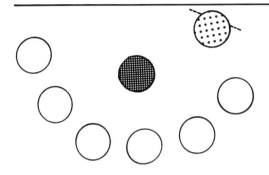

Figure 10.1A

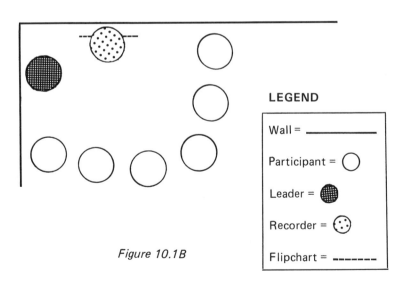

Figure 10.1B

LEGEND

Wall = ⎯⎯⎯⎯⎯

Participant = ◯

Leader = ⬤

Recorder = ◉

Flipchart = ⎯ ⎯ ⎯ ⎯

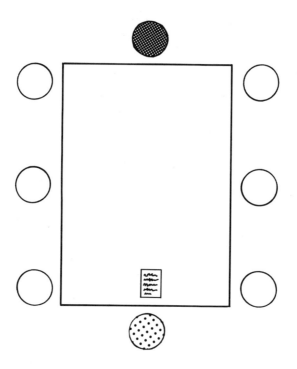

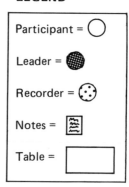

Figure 10.2

Step 2: Launching the Group. The first few moments of the meeting are crucial to its success. Begin with **introductions.** Introduce yourself first. That will enable you to provide a model for the others. Be sure to figure out what it is you want everyone to say about themselves and then to do it yourself. Here is Mark, the instructional designer who is heading up this project.

"I'm Mark Winston and I've been with the company for eleven years. I started off in the stores, in the Midwest—just outside Dayton. I was an Assistant Manager and then a store Manager. Then I became regional supervisor with fourteen stores reporting to me. I eventually wound up doing training out of the Midwest offices and got transferred here two years ago. Two months ago I got the project for computerized point-of-sale registers. And it's a very important one, as you well know. We decided to bring you all here before we set up any corporate-wide training. A few of you have these registers; all of you will have them. This new technology is going to change every job we have in those stores, and I want to make sure we know what you think your people need. I've been the planner for this meeting and will be one of the participants throughout. Let me introduce Joyce Marie, who will facilitate our group."

Note that Mark included:

- his full name
- his corporate experience, especially related to retail stores
- his experience in training and development
- a restatement of the topic
- a personal opinion on the importance of the topic
- his need for their ideas
- the role he will play
- introduction of his group leader, Joyce Marie

After Mark's introduction, he wrote the following on the butcher paper/flip chart and reminded Joyce Marie and the other members of the group to include this information in their introductions:

- YOUR NAME
- WHERE YOU HAVE WORKED AND FOR HOW LONG
- WHERE YOU NOW WORK AND WHAT YOU DO
- YOUR RELATIONSHIP TO POINT-OF-SALES REGISTERS

Joyce Marie has absolutely no experience with the computerized registers. She is a new person in Industrial Relations who has been assigned the function of leader/facilitator for this group. She admits her lack of **content expertise** to the group and emphasizes that her role is to help them get the most and best ideas out of this gathering. She has facilitated four other groups that are similar to this one.

Joyce Marie then introduces Velma, who has agreed to serve as the recorder for this session. Velma, a participant in the group, will do the recording this morning. Jeb, another participant, will take over tomorrow, thus enabling Velma to get involved in the content of the next session. Joyce Marie moves the introductions along, starting with Velma, and prompting the participants to touch on the four categories of information listed on the butcher paper.

After the introductions, the facilitator must turn the group's attention to the **agenda**. While the trainer/planner has created this agenda, it is now up to the facilitator to make sure that everyone in the group understands and supports it. The agenda includes:

- participants and roles
- purposes of the meeting, including content and outcomes
- process rules which have been or need to be established
- time, place, and length of the proceedings

The introductions clarified participants and roles. Discussion of the agenda now must focus on the **crucial difference between the content or purposes of the meeting and the processes which will be used to achieve those purposes. Everyone at the meeting must be able to distinguish between *why they are there and how they are going to operate*.**

The **purposes** of the meeting constitute **why** they have been gathered for a meeting. It might be to find out what supervisors think is causing the increase in scrap production by lathe operators. Or it might be to discuss the nature of optimal performance using numerical control operated lathes. Or it might be to inform managers and foremen about the results of an anonymous survey of first line supervisors. Or it might be to talk, now that significant TNA information is available, about the details of a combined training and incentive program to encourage lead operators to provide on-the-job-training to new lathe operators.

The **process or rules** for the meeting must be clear to participants. This would include discussion of the following:

- the neutral and nurturing role of the leader
- the recorder's efforts to serve as the group memory
- the nature of the meeting. Are we brainstorming, where everything is accepted without evaluation, thereby generating numerous options for later judgment? Or are we gathered together to weigh choices and make decisions?
- the uses of the work of the group. Is the group making recommendations to management or is it in a position of making the decisions itself?
- the nature of productive group participation, including use of "I" statements, substantiating sentences, and avoidance of phrases like "always" and "never"
- how disagreements will be handled
- breaks, lunches, dinners, messages, promptness, future plans for meetings, etc.

Before you launch into the body of the meeting, it is essential that members of the group agree to **both the content (purposes) of the meeting and the way it will be operated (processes).**

Step 3: Running the Meeting. Once beyond introductions and verification of the agenda, you are into the heart of the meeting. It is important to periodically review the body of the meeting from two perspectives: **progress towards achievement of the purposes of the meeting and participation of individuals in the group process.**

Purposes

Continuously track the efforts of the group in light of the **purposes** established before the meeting. Are you acquiring information which helps understand the problem? Is this meeting contributing to what you know about the best ways of doing something? Are you learning about the problems people are having with it? the causes of these problems? the feelings surrounding the situation? any ideas that people have for solving this problem or implementing this new system? Have you disseminated the information that needs to be shared?

Individual Participation

The second consideration is the **participation of each person** in the group. Not only do you want the ideas of individuals, it is important for group members to leave the group *feeling good* about this TNA group process. Remember that TNA groups can build political support for front end and training efforts.

Samovar and King (1981) list the kinds of positive participant contributions which may be anticipated and charted. I've simplified their list for our purposes. The last item was added by a business colleague who complained that the list wasn't sufficiently *real* for his environment. Change it to suit your needs. My point is that it is important to look at member contributions in some systematic way that transcends, "Oh, that Sally. She never does much when we get together." At least, after systematic analysis, you'll know what Sally does and does not do—in detail.

- ☐ Initiates ideas
- ☐ Clarifies ideas
- ☐ Requests
- ☐ Responds to request
- ☐ Accepts or rejects ideas
- ☐ Evaluates ideas
- ☐ Epitomizes ideas
- ☐ Summarizes
- ☐ Reports progress

Consider the nature of the group as you chart the behavior of each individual. For example, a group which has been gathered to *brainstorm* better daily maintenance procedures for a piece of machinery should have few "accepts, rejects or evaluates ideas." On the other hand, a group which is gathered to settle upon the exact procedure for this daily maintenance, based on input from many sources, would have many evaluating, accepting and rejecting contributions.

My modification of the Samovar and King list points towards **effective** group performance from the participants, where everyone is contributing, commenting and epitomizing in tune with the purposes of the session. It just doesn't work out that way all the time.

There are members who remain silent. There are others who talk incessantly. There are habitual arguers and others who nod at everything. Each problem must be handled differently.

Experienced group leaders are encouraged to skip the section that follows. Those of us who have had bad moments in groups, or who anticipate them, may want to review these management techniques.

Problem	Strategy During Group
To much talk, dominating the group, saying **useful** things	Thank the participant and say, "Let's hear from someone else now."
Too much talk, dominating the group, offering **irrelevancies**	Extinguish irrelevant comments, turn away and move on to someone else.
Too little talk, failing to contribute . .	Ask the individual for comments. When he/she does offer something useful, refer to it and praise its usefulness.
Agreeing with everything	Say, "You are nodding and indicating agreement with what Hermie said. What is it that you particularly like about that comment? Is there anything you would like to add or change?"
Disagreeing with everything	Say, "Let's try to put Hermie's suggestions in a form which would be useful for your people. Can you help us synthesize the ideas of the two division managers?"

The best situation is one in which a comment, like those listed above, solves the problem. That won't always happen. Sometimes the facilitator must talk with a participant about dominating the group, failure to contribute, tardiness, early departure, chronic disagreement . . . . Ask the person for a few moments *alone* and say something like, "I've noticed that you make an evaluative comment after every suggestion offered by other members of the group. It happened constantly throughout the day and I am worried about the effect it has on people's willingness to continue to offer ideas. Would you please try to hold back on the judgments when we gather tomorrow morning? We need your ideas, suggestions and clarifications. It's the statements that begin with 'I don't think' and 'I don't like' which concern me."

Note that the facilitator was specific about the problem, said how he/she felt about it yet still attempted to keep the individual involved in the group efforts.

The problem of disagreements in groups deserves special attention. Debates can be epidemic when groups are assembled from varying constituencies. The facilitator wants varying ideas, honest opinions and feelings, and movement towards **consensus**. Majority rule established through a vote is less desirable than consensual ideas, definitions, solutions and opinions which are arrived at after discussion and debate. The problem with a vote to end disagreement is that some participants wind up getting their way and others don't. That is likely to result in TNA results and eventual programs which are mistrusted or avoided by those who lost the vote.

If lengthy discussion and clarification of ambiguous terms doesn't diminish the disagreement, the facilitator may have to **"shift to process."** This means that he or she will move the group away from their discussion of content and into a discussion of **how to resolve this dispute**. The group should have already established some procedures and these can be implemented. Here is a sample dialogue:

June: NO WAY WILL OUR PEOPLE DO IT THAT WAY. Our company has made significant strides in affirmative action by dispersing the responsibility to all managers. Centralizing the functions won't work.

Randy: I'm with Jorge on this. The company needs an officer at each site and we need to agree on his or her functions.

June: I can tell you my people won't be comfortable
            with this.
Bernie: Northern has a model where they control the ef-
            fort through performance appraisals. Functions
            are dispersed, with minimal centralization, and
            their figures look real good.
Jorge: Recruitment and retention activities are specialized.
            Not every manager can be expected to know how
            to do this. Look at our figures on this. We've been
            exhorting and training for six years and we're not
            there yet.
June: A change like this just won't fly. I can tell you
            that.

Thelma, the facilitator: We're at a deadlock here and have been
going around and around for nearly 30 minutes. I am going to
**"shift to process" and ask you all to get off this topic and on to
the subject of *how* we can resolve it.** Let's look at this sheet of
paper, the one with the procedures we developed for handling
disagreements. The first step is to assign a subgroup which will
look at this problem and come back with some written alternatives . . . . Now I want to bring the group back to content, back
to another one of our original purposes. What are optimal procedures for advertising engineering positions in such a way as to
assure affirmative action compliance and sincere effort?

Note that Thelma described the problem, shifted to process,
carried out a mutually agreed upon procedure and then got the
group back on task. The topic to which she turned their attention was one she anticipated would interest them all without
leading to widespread rancor.

Beyond Glittering Generalities

Another major challenge in TNA groups is to move from the
general to the specific. This means taking phrases like, "better
motivator," or "more careful assembler," or "insufficient attention to detail," or "insensitive to the culture of the Hmong immi-
grants," and translating them into clear, operationalized statements. Doyle and Straus suggest a "lasso technique." When a
facilitator uses a "lasso," he or she leads the group to:

1. find unclear or insufficiently specific words and phrases on the butcher paper;
2. circle (lasso) those words or phrases; and
3. work as a group to figure out what the circled words mean by detailing the behaviors, conditions and criteria specific to the murky concepts and procedures.

Bob Hobbs, a talented course developer for a large telecommunications company, offered this example of optimal switch trunk testing:

Job/Function/Subject: GTD-5 Trunk Tester

Description/Background: A GTD-5 is a central office switch. Customer lines terminate here and outgoing calls are switched to other offices. The GTD-5 uses a new call processing technology. The trunk test panel, while similar to existing equipment, has significant differences. Large volumes of inter-office trunks must be tested by employees who possess some background in trunk testing, but have never seen a GTD-5.

The Cast of Characters for this TNA group: Four master performers (subject matter experts (SMEs) on testing trunks from a GTD-5 switch) are convened with a facilitator and a trainer for three days.

Purpose of the Group: The purpose of the group is to define optimals, the skills and knowledge, needed to test trunks from a GTD-5 switch.

The TNA Group: Introductions are made smoothly and quickly. The objective: "define skills and knowledge for testing GTD-5 trunks" is briefly discussed, as are the process and time frames. The SMEs are asked to start by taking fifteen minutes to write down the major functions of the job of testing trunks. The functions are then gathered from each SME and a list is generated and displayed. The facilitator does not see an immediate pattern. There is too much ambiguity and variation in the words that are used.

He tries another tack. Using the standard, reliable *Input-Process-Output* model, the facilitator first finds out what gets a trunk tester started and how he/she knows when the trunks have been successfully tested. Then the facilitator turns to the details of the *Process*. Everyone was able to agree on the *Input-Output* portion. Now they get down to talking about the procedures involved in accomplishing the test, in figuring out what people do first, second, next and so forth. The emphasis is on PERFORMANCE. Murky words are clarified through the "lasso" technique. "Knowledges" are listed on a separate butcher paper, as in "You gotta know how to read the User's guide." The facilitator presses, "Good, if you know how to read the User's Guide, what will you do with what you've read? Format input messages? OK. Let me write that down here. Once the input message is formatted, what do you DO next?"

The complete list of steps takes up several pages. It appears to break into five major chunks. First, identify the trunks to be tested. Second, place trunks in service for testing. Third, call through the trunk. Fourth, record measurements, and five, remove bad trunks from service. While the performance steps are tangible and useful as written by the group, the "knowledge" list will need to be further analyzed.

Step 4: Closing the Session. Before the meeting ends, it is important for the planner/designer to think about where the TNA will go from here. A checklist will help:

□ Have the purposes of this meeting been fulfilled?

□ If not, will additional time as a TNA group provide the information you need?

□ If the purposes for this TNA group were achieved, are there any other reasons to bring them together?

□ Is it feasible to reassemble this group? Do you want to?

□ Are you satisfied with the way the group worked together?

□ Will the "fall-out" from this group help or hinder your efforts on this project?

□ What will you do differently next time? regarding content? regarding process?

□ Is purpose-based front end analysis completed now?

□ If not, what other TNA tools will you employ to get what you need?

Either the facilitator or the recorder should review what happened during the group meeting. Display the butcher paper as the review is conducted as well as any other documents which were generated by group efforts.

The training professional (designer/planner of this meeting) may speak with the group now. It would be appropriate to describe how this information will be used. Will you need more information from these people? Will you be reconvening this TNA group? Will you send them a report on your findings? What is likely to happen next? What is likely to happen to solve the problem or implement the new system or technology? Be certain to tell them what else you need from them, if anything, and what you plan to do with their contributions.

In the last moments of the session, the person who convened the meeting should express appreciation to the participants, recorder and facilitator. Obviously, a three-day jury of experts meeting warrants a greater display of appreciation than a 60-minute gathering to fill managers in on what you've been finding out about point-of-sales registers. Remember, the participants in TNA meetings have learned a great deal about the work you are doing. They might provide you with additional information and turn into good will ambassadors . . . or they might not.

Step 5: Following-up the Meeting. There is only one thing you must do to follow-up a TNA meeting: **Do whatever it is you committed to doing.** That might mean sending the results of a needs assessment to participants, calling them to share what others are saying about the causes of this problem, talking to suggested staff, or sending them an article on a topic which was discussed during the meeting or . . . .

While you never promised a thank you note, it is definitely a good idea to send one. Everyone should receive something which acknowledges their efforts. A few special words to particularly helpful participants, recorders or facilitators will give them the recognition they deserve. Send a copy of the special notes to the supervisors of the people who made your TNA group a success.

Example

Bob Hobbs provided an elaborate and interesting example of the use of a TNA group to detail the skills and knowledge associated with customer loop design.

Background: Customer Loop Design is a function of the Transmission and Protection Engineer and concerns itself with the telephone facilities which connect the customer to a serving central office. A central office is the dial tone source and switches the calls from one customer to another or onto the national toll network. Industry standards exist regarding voice and signal level quality of the facility which connects customers to the central office. The most common facility is a pair of copper wires bundled into a cable and hung from telephone poles. Recent advances in electronics have allowed several customers to share the same physical pair of wires and to be located at greater distances from the central office.

Cast of Characters: We assigned three people to this project: an experienced Jury of Experts facilitator, an evaluator to identify what worked and didn't work, and a trainee charged with learning how to facilitate this kind of meeting. We gathered six subject matter experts from around the nation to inform us about Customer Loop Design (CLD).

Purpose: The group was convened to capture a clear and universal picture of optimal Customer Loop Design.

Preparation for the Group Meeting: We had about 45 days before we were scheduled to start. The project team (three people from the training group) began by talking to a few people in the immediate area about Customer Loop Design. We were trying to build a complete picture of optimal Customer Loop Design before we even met with the SMEs. Our in-house trainer who had subject matter familiarity was grilled for four hours. He also identified some written corporate practices for CLD. Based on our interviews and the written practices, we created a tentative model for CLD. This document turned out to have no basis in reality but it did comfort us and give us an illusion of security, a sense that we knew enough about CLD to talk about it with our Jury of Experts.

The TNA Group: Day 1: We began with an introduction. Everyone said who they were and how they came to be here. We talked about the purposes for this gathering and some of the ground rules for the group. We explained a little about training and defined some terminology: JOB, DUTY, TASK, ELEMENT, SKILL, KNOWLEDGE, and showed a videotape on task analysis in our corporation.

We had prepared a list of questions that were designed to elicit Task statements. These questions had worked superbly when we tried them on each other. Unfortunately we had never tested them on anyone else. What finally got things going was, "Let's take fifteen minutes and write a list of the ten most important things you do when designing a Customer Loop." Our SMEs looked blank and finally said, 'We don't design Customer Loops." The project team called a recess to discuss this surprise.

We pursued this line of discussion with the SMEs. Eventually we determined that Customer Loop Design is a composite activity and that we, fortunately, had a composite group. Each member could contribute a piece of the action and a few could contribute several pieces.

We shifted to the reliable *Input-Process-Output* model. We asked, What gets you started on CLD? What is the outcome of CLD? What exactly do you do in between starting and finishing? The answers to these questions gave us a common basis for discussion and began to iron out differences between operating companies. For example, the size of the California company and the volume of activity it had led to job specialization while the Pennsylvania company's smaller size and volume had dictated a jack-of-all-trades approach.

I casually said that we "began to iron out differences," as if it were easily done. It was not. The facilitator worked hard to allow everyone to express views, protect the interests of the less aggressive SMEs, tone down the comments of the judgmental, and maintain a focus on definition of common steps in CLD. A useful technique for resolving disputes was to post the details of disagreements on a separate piece of butcher paper and to come back to it later. Somehow or other, time and reason contributed to coming to consensus eventually.

The first day ended on an upbeat note. While the SMEs went out to enjoy themselves, the three members of the Project Team huddled to discuss how it had gone. We threw out the initial Task Analysis we had done prior to our arrival at the meeting and decided on the game plan for day two.

The TNA Group: Day 2: While we had finished the first day on a positive note, it seemed to have worn off by the following morning. We looked at what we had accomplished so far and what we still had to do. The facilitator was pressing hard for tangible details, forcing SMEs to move from general to specific statements. It looked like forever until lunch.

We just kept slogging on. What do you do next? Then what heppens? What do you do if this happens? I don't quite understand, could you say it in a different way? **There was constant focus on performance.** The facilitator had to keep bringing people back to the task, "Let's get another description of 'Obtaining the Right of Way.' " Mercifully things began to fall into place. The facilitator's patience and attention to the details of optimal performance for CLD began to pay off.

The facilitator guided the discussion and simultaneously recorded skill and knowledge statements. Input from SMEs was listed on Flip Chart pages and posted on the walls. The facilitator used the pen like a magic wand. He focused attention by tapping on the flip chart at the point under discussion.

When the cap was on the pen, discussion was encouraged. When the facilitator pulled off the cap, and moved into writing posture, the group knew they were being asked to arrive at consensus.

The facilitator capped the pen and said, "John, you appear to be giving this some deep thought. I'd like to hear what you have to say." "How does that relate to what I just wrote for that step?" "Will you explain that to me so I can envision how that would work in the field?" "Good! That helps me understand that. I can see how that would work."

By the end of the second day, we had identified the major steps in CLD and begun to detail the first major step. Once again we ended on an upbeat note.

The team huddled again. The facilitator trainee volunteered to lead the group for the third day.

The TNA Group: Day 3: The SMEs were pleased with themselves and eager to wrap it up and go home. We had allocated three weeks for this process (yes, three WEEKS). If the detailing of optimals was completed early, we planned to involve them in writing the objectives for the training program. After all, there is no law that training professionals always write the objectives. We intended to have the SMEs write *real world* objectives for each task and element with *real world* criteria for satisfactory performance.

The facilitator went back to slogging. Inch by inch—did it have to be this way? For now—yes. The SMEs were used to generalizing from a few pieces of data to make a big picture. Here the process was reversed. We didn't want to group things into comprehensive statements. We sought the nitty-gritty details. Managers often say, "Just give me the baby. I don't want to hear about the labor pains, the pregnancy and the conception." We work in the opposite way. To the statement, "Make a field visit," our facilitator responded, "Why do you make a field visit? What do you look for on a field visit? How do you know to look for that? What do you do when you are done with the field visit? And after that? With which forms?" Could anyone really be interested in all that detail? The facilitator of this TNA group was.

After lunch the trainee started in on the second task. Things went faster. This facilitator knew what is meant by "AC-DC theory" and immediately wrote it on the paper. One of the SMEs got a little hot about this direction from the facilitator. All in all, however, it was a good and productive day.

The remaining days of the TNA group: By the end of day eight, the search for optimals was complete. The trainee-facilitator took over again to coach the SMEs through the writing of objectives. What follows is not for those with weak stomachs. There were no accepted standards for performance. None. If someone were ever fired for incompetent Customer Loop Design, it would not hold up in court.

The SMEs couldn't agree on what is acceptable performance and they couldn't agree on what's not acceptable. At first. Some task statements got restated. Others were reorganized. Imagination and memory were employed. Eventually the statements got reworked into clear pictures of the necessary skills, knowledge and criteria. All the elements were there and approved by participants. They were measurable by real world standards. The knowledge part was crisp and defined. The logic chain from knowledge to task was rational. Our TNA group had accomplished even more than it intended.

Afterwards: We wrote personal letters to the SMEs and included autographed copies of the Task Analysis. We also communicated our appreciation to their bosses. While the project team failed to get the ticker tape parade it deserved, management was impressed with what we did. We have been asked to share our results and process with our colleagues on several different occasions.

Bob Hobbs' anecdotal account of an unusually lengthy TNA group reiterates many of the points in this chapter:

• The project team invested a great deal of effort in preparation. They actually studied the topic of CLD prior to the meeting and produced a document which approximated the charge of their TNA committee.

• They were wise enough to abandon their definition of Customer Loop Design when the SMEs from across the nation contradicted their more static, earlier research.

• The facilitator attempted to remain neutral. Unfortunately the facilitator also served as the recorder.

• The project team evaluated both the progress of the group towards its TNA purposes and the quality of the group process.

• The facilitator moved the group from general to specific through piercing and relentless questioning.

• They focused on performance.

• The group process yielded optimals which went beyond what any one SME knew he knew. Useful standards for performance were developed, where there had been none before. This TNA group was a good example of synergy. Participants and managers deserved their letters of appreciation.

The trick for the rest of us, of course, is to enjoy such positive results with far less time in which to accomplish them.

Resources

Doyle, M., & Straus, D. (1976). *How to Make Meetings Work.* New York: Berkley Publishing Group.

Johnson, D.W., & Johnson, F.P. (1975). *Joining Together: Group Theory and Group Skills.* Englewood Cliffs, NJ: Prentice Hall.

Kemp, C.G. (1964). *Perspectives on the Group Process: A Foundation for Counseling with Groups.* Boston, MA: Houghton-Mifflin.

Mink, O.G., Mink, B.P., Owen, K.Q. *et al.* (1987). *Groups at Work.* Englewood Cliffs, NJ: Educational Technology Publications.

Mink, O.G., Schultz, J.M., & Mink, B.P. (1979). *Developing and Managing Open Organizations: A Model and Methods for*

Maximizing Organizational Potential. Austin, TX: Learning Concepts.

Samovar, L.A., & King, S.W. (1981). *Communication and Discussion in Small Groups.* Dubuque, IA: Gorsuch Scarisbrick Publishers.

Zemke, R., & Kramlinger, T. (1982). *Figuring Things Out: A Trainer's Guide to Needs and Task Analysis.* Reading, MA: Addison-Wesley.

Chapter Eleven: WRITING QUESTIONNAIRES AND SURVEYS

Brief Description

A questionnaire or survey is a **written** and **disseminated** effort to acquire information from **sources**. The questionnaire or survey is prepared for specific reasons, distributed to sources, usually anonymously, returned to the sender, and then analyzed.

Purposes of Questionnaires and Surveys

Written surveys are a popular TNA tool, a method frequently used to find out what large numbers of people think and feel about the problem or new technology. Questionnaires may be used to gather anonymous information in regard to all TNA purposes. They are, however, most frequently used to solicit opinions on **actuals, feelings and causes.**

The Benefits of Surveys and Questionnaires

1. **You can reach many people at less cost than it would take to call or meet with them.** This is the first reason people usually give for relying on print needs assessment instruments. While I agree that this is usually true, there are instances where the time it takes to plan, print, pilot, distribute, harass to get returns, and analyze large numbers of surveys, winds up costing just as much as conducting fewer interviews.

2. **You can promise and deliver anonymity.** This is a strong plus of print. Interviews, observation and group TNA tools are often threatening to participants. Surveys which enable people to express themselves without any fear of recrimination have a better chance of revealing what sources think about the nature and cause(s) of problems.

3. **Respondents get time to ponder**. The problems with which we deal are often sticky and complex. While a source might see it one way on the phone, when the trainer is waiting eagerly for an answer, they may choose to respond differently with time to consider their answers.

4. **Surveys are public, tangible efforts by the training, industrial relations, or personnel group to involve others and incorporate their opinions**. Do not underestimate the public relations value of *effective*, widely disseminated instruments.

5. **They are easier to score and analyze, if properly constructed**. Widespread availability of computers makes this an even more dominant benefit. In Chapter 13, there is some discussion of the uses of computers for the analysis and presentation of results.

The Challenges in Surveying Through Print

Just as an effective questionnaire can be a boon to your career, an ineffective one can be a disaster. Imagine this situation:

In your eagerness to find out what kinds of training middle managers want, you whipped out an extensive needs study. This document queried them on their problems and interests. But it had two typographical errors. And because you knew that long instruments diminish response rates, you squished it into five pages and wound up with insufficient white space. It had good ideas, but didn't look so great, you now must admit. And then there was a little problem with what you meant in item 29.

What happened? Did this instructional designer enjoy the benefits of an effective survey? Hardly. In fact, the good ideas, the comprehensive options and clear directions were lost in the cluttered lay-out. And some sticklers for details were unable to appreciate the quality of the content so fixated were they with the spelling glitches and the ambiguity in item 29.

The foremost challenge of surveying through print is **getting it just right for public consumption**. If you don't, your mistakes or insensitivities are out there for all the world to see. While you can alter a miscue or clarify a murky question during an interview, the print instrument lingers and doesn't improve with time. Sources might continuously note that the training specialist confused *their* and *there*.

You are challenged to find the right words and items. Payne, in a classic 1951 work on questionnaire design, describes research that found question writing to be the biggest problem in survey research. Payne cites Howard T. Hovde, who asked a sample of researchers what they saw as the principal defects in commercial research. Improperly worded questionnaires ranked as the number one defect, with faulty interpretation and inadequate samples lagging just behind. Three experts out of every four mentioned poorly worded items as a problem! That holds true today, I suspect.

Once conceived, printed and duplicated, your questionnaire stands as it is. You may come back with another questionnaire at a latter stage of TNA, or you may use an interview or a group meeting to follow-up. But the following-up, the digging deeper or interacting with sources' responses must come later. **Print is not an immediately interactive tool, the way an interview or group meeting is.** There is no opportunity to clarify, pursue an intriguing idea or seek substantiation. **You need to know what you need to know before you send the TNA tool out.** After that, the survey is what it is, not what you wish it was.

Once you have conceived and disseminated an effective questionnaire, you want to enjoy a hearty response rate, and often won't. In addition to the democratic desire to involve large numbers of people in your efforts, you need high response rates to employ tests of statistical significance. Even if you intend to use nothing more elaborate than percentages, it is absurd to state that "60 percent report some or strong concern with their ability to learn to hanglide" when only 10 out of a total population of 165 senior citizens sent back the survey. Zemke and Kramlinger (1982) claim that a usual response rate for front end analysis surveys is 15-35 percent. We'll talk about strategies for assuring responses later in this chapter.

A Step by Step Approach to Effective Questionnaires

Here are the stages for getting a good survey out and back:

Step 1: Figuring Out What You Need and From Whom

Step 2: Writing Effective Items

Step 3: Writing Good Directions

Step 4: Writing Good Cover Letters

Step 5: Applying a Writer's Checklist

Step 6: Piloting the Instruments

Step 1: Figuring Out What You Need and From Whom
1. KNOWING THE PURPOSES FOR THIS QUESTIONNAIRE
It is essential to know why you are sending out this survey. Statements like, "to get a feel for the situation," or "to see where people are on the new system," or "just to let people know I care" are the harbingers of ineffective print instruments. The statements are far too broad and reflect the good intentions of trainers who aren't sufficiently clear about the problem or innovation to be writing questionnaires. **A print survey is not the place to begin a foray into a new problem or topic**; widely disseminated print must be reserved, in almost all cases, for **later stages of front end analysis**, when you have a pretty good fix on the situation, and can confidently write questions and options for answers.

The training professional who confronts a blank screen and a blinking cursor, or a virgin legal pad, shouldn't be thinking about **what** to write. Rather, think about **why** you are doing this. The **what** will follow naturally.

Concern about the purposes of the particular stage of TNA takes us back to the concepts that are the basis for this book: **purpose-based front end analysis**. What information are you seeking? How does what you want to know **now** flow from what you have found out **before**? Here are the familiar **purposes** which you might have for this stage of your inquiry. The purpose(s) then lead directly into the questionnaire items.

☐ Finding OPTIMALS
• what respondents think ought to be going on
• how the system should work
• what they know about it

☐ Finding ACTUALS
• the details of how employees are and are not performing
• the way the system is operating
• whether respondents perceive a problem

☐ Finding FEELINGS
• how this person feels about the situation
• how they think others feel
• confidence regarding the topic
• whether they value/like the topic

☐ Finding CAUSE(S)
• what is causing the problem
• which of causes detailed in Chapter 4 are in effect here

☐ Finding SOLUTION(S)
• options for how to solve the problem or implement the innovation

2. ESTABLISHING A SAMPLE

Who is going to get the questionnaires? Everyone? People you can depend upon to send it back? The exemplary performers? Lackluster performers? People who pick up their mail? The ones who are planning to attend a certain meeting? Or a random sample of the population? The first and last options are the most desirable; they are the ones which will allow you to make the strongest statements about *all the people in the target learner group.*

There are some terms we need to get straight if we are going to seek the most desirable of sources. The first is **population**. It is the universe about which you are concerned. It might be major league baseball players with a documented history of drug abuse, field engineers who maintain mainframes, or bank tellers from the Bank of America. If you can, it is desirable to send print instruments to to entire population. That will cost in time and energy. It might be reasonable for the ball players and field engineers, presuming limited numbers; it is probably not feasible for the large population of tellers.

The other desirable practice is to send the instruments to a **sample** of the population. A sample is a small portion of the population which possesses the same characteristics as the larger group from which it is drawn. The way you assure this congruence between total population and sample is through **randomization**. Randomization is the process by which you make sure that **all** members of the total population have an **equal** and fair chance of being selected to receive the survey. That must be accomplished by the blind assignment of numbers to **everyone** in the total population and then the use of some computerized or *blindly drawn from a hat* system to select from that population in an unbiased fashion. A random sample is *not* being drawn when you send the survey out to all the middle managers and then wait to see what you get back. What you get back may well be the middle managers who perceive themselves as most expert or the ones who are most dismayed with upper management.

How many do you select for your **randomly drawn sample**? That takes us to the issue of **sample size**. Every statistics textbook presents a table of the minimum number of individuals who must be sampled to make generalizations about the larger population. The larger the total population, the smaller the **percentage** of individuals which must be queried.

A small portion of a National Education Association table illustrates the point:

Population Size	Sample Size
100	79
200	132
500	217
1,000	278
3,000	341
8,000	367
15,000	375

If we want to survey bank tellers prior to launching a major product knowledge program and there are 8,000 tellers in the population, we will need a sample size of 367 randomly drawn respondents. And we will need an excellent response rate from them if we seek to use inferential statistics to add weight to our findings, to assure management that what we found out could not be attributed to chance.

3. ASSURING NUMEROUS RESPONSES TO QUESTIONNAIRES

You can increase the likelihood that you will receive a high or perfect percentage of returns by:

• Writing an instrument which deals with **issues of concern** to the sample. Instruments which treat topics of interest only to you or upper level management are most likely to get tossed. The annual survey on telephone customer relations will get fewer responses than a questionnaire linked to extant data like recent breakdowns or sales figures.

• Clearly stating the **purpose(s)** for this instrument. Once again, avoid, "To get a feel for the thing," or "To see where you all are." Say that you want to know the strategies people are most likely to use to sell the product or the causes for dips in sales. Tell them if there is concern about a problem and identify the survey as part of the effort to figure out the best solution.

• **Following through** on the purposes and enjoying a reputation for doing so. There are few virgin sources out there; many of the people who will get your questionnaires have received them before. If you get a reputation for feigning interest in gathering data, or for not using what you find out from your surveys, then you are less likely to enjoy healthy response rates. Cultivate a credible history of using what you learn and, insofar as possible, of reporting back to people about what you are learning from TNA.

• Making it **easy to respond**. Provide self-addressed envelopes, where possible, for attractively constructed, laser printed, forced-choice instruments. Attach a stamp, if internal mail isn't an option. Remember that most sources will toss this survey at the first hint of inconvenience or confusion.

• Providing a **reason** to send it back. This isn't always possible, and it does conflict with confidence in anonymity, but it helps to give respondents something for their efforts. The results of the survey is the standard return for their effort. I try to go beyond that. My colleague, Farhad Saba, and I conducted research on the ways that TNA is carried out in international settings. In order to encourage responses, we offered those who chose to respond a TNA job aid as a gift. The price we pay will be suspicion that our responses were from the neediest professionals or the most serious professionals or . . . . But since it is a small population from which we draw to begin with and since we did not randomly select a sample from it, we are acknowledging the weaknesses of our sample in favor of getting descriptive information from a unique and elite cadre of training and development professionals who work abroad.

• **Harrassing** non-respondents until they finally turn the instrument in. Sometimes it helps a little, if you use an impersonal system of writing to all members of your sample to remind them to *please* send the survey back. Personalized nagging, however, makes sources wonder just how anonymous they really are, no matter how much you assure them that a secretary is handling this part of it in a blind fashion, or that the questionnaires are numbered with a computer generating letters to non-respondents. They know and you know that the computer or secretary that begs for returns can also generate a list linking returns with respondents.

Step 2: Writing Effective Items

THE CONTENT FOR QUESTIONS

Chapter 6 includes the section, Step 3: Creating Items. That section details the purposes which initiate surveys. Based on these broad purposes, an item typology is proposed which facilitates the generation of individual items for questionnaires or interview guides. The typology that I developed solves the problem of **what to ask.** When training professionals pound a stack of returns and say, "I still don't know . . ." or "I didn't get what I needed," or "Now what do I do with all this?"; they probably are suffering from having asked the wrong questions. **Problems of content can be addressed through the item typology presented in Figure 6.2.** A brief summary of the typology follows:

Type 1 items ask WHAT NEED.
Type 2 items ask for DETAILS.
Type 3 items provide PROOF.

Type 4 items ask for FEELINGS and MOTIVATION.
Type 5 items ask for CAUSE(S) OF THE PROBLEM.
Type 6 items ask about the RESPONDENT.

Every item should bear an obvious relationship to one type question or another, but every instrument need not seek every type information. It is more likely that you would have, for example, an instrument with 30 percent Type 2's, 30 percent Type 3's and 40 percent Type 5's, than that you would have 20 percent of each type item. And you are asking for trouble if you include many Type 1's in a print format. The open-ended nature of Type 1 items seeks general problems and areas of need that should already be known to the training professional who is contemplating print surveys.

Print is usually the wrong tool for a fishing expedition. A question like, *"What are the problems your people are confronting with this equipment?"* will go over much better in an interview than it will in a print survey. You need to know about the problem and the situation before you construct a PRINT survey.

For example:

> When faced with preparing a pizza on our new computerized equipment, which of the following creates the **greatest** problems? Mark only one.
> .....a. setting the heat control
> .....b. altering the homeostasis unit for deepdish vs. other
> .....c. order of assembly of the optional garnishes

There are two dozen things that are done in the preparation of a pizza, not just a, b and c. This latter stage questionnaire only focuses on the three problems which earlier TNA stages (examination of extant data and interviews) highlighted. The pizza item is a type 2 question seeking details of a problem about which much is already known. It is likely that it would be followed up with a Type 5 question seeking the cause of the problem or a Type 4 which looks for feelings about the system. Or maybe you will only use print for the Type 2's and 5's, deciding to make phone calls to solicit information on feelings about computerized pizza making and the training to do it better.

In addition to questions which directly relate to the problem or new system, you might want to ask for information about the respondent. You might want to know in which regions he works or how many people she supervises. You might want to know what training she has taken and which job aids he uses to do his job. Or you might want to know if the respondent is male or female. Demography is sought in *Type 6* items.

Why do you want to know? If you have a good reason, like the desire to eventually look at whether sex has an impact on the ability to conduct performance appraisal interviews, or if the extant data is showing some differences in the appraisals based on gender, then by all means go ahead and ask about gender. Don't query about sex, age, years of service, etc., unless you know what you intend to do with the data, unless you have a good reason for the question. Make every question and inch of space count.

Be certain to use the topic and the way it breaks down to cluster your items. **Rather than clustering by purpose (e.g., asking three questions about the causes of the problems), chunk into the natural components of the subject matter or job.** The pizza oven example might involve questions about entering data, closing down, monitoring pizzas and daily maintenance with Type 2's, 3's, and 4's in all four clusters. Use the purposes and typology to generate your items, then be sure to **arrange the questionnaire on the basis of the *content* of the subject or job.**

The Formats for Questions

The two basic question types are **forced choice and open-ended items.** A **forced choice** item will say "which" or "what one of the following" or "rank this list" or "rate these according to . . ." You provide respondents with a fixed set of options from which they must choose. Here is an example:

> Which of these has caused problems when you've made pizza **prior** to installation of the new ovens? Check **all** those that have been a problem.
> ...... maintaining the equipment
> ...... setting up
> ...... temperature control
> ...... judging texture
> ...... doing more than 12 pies at a time
> ...... cleaning the sensors
> ...... cleaning surfaces

An **open-ended item** is just what it sounds like. It in no way narrows the range of possible responses. This is an example of that format:

> In what areas did you experience problems making pizza **before** the computerized ovens were installed?

You may use forced choice and open questions for item types 2-4. Obviously, type 1 questions are best asked in an open format. It is possible to achieve all TNA purposes through either forced or open-ended queries. **However, unless you wish to be driven mad by a flood of written data or by vague and general statements as responses to surveys, I strongly urge you to lean heavily on forced choice items for questionnaires and surveys.**

A compromise format is to combine forced choice and open-ended items. This gives you the benefits of forced questions while still leaving the door open for alternative responses. Constructed after you are pretty sure about the problem, you give the respondents choices **and** allow them to fill in something you may have left out. Here is an example of a **combination** item, an item which gives a list of choices **and** an opportunity for open response.

> Wiring in ovens is causing more problems than ever before. Circle the number which reflects your opinion on the **cause** of the wiring problems. Rate the list below as:
>
>   (2) major contributing factor
>   (1) some factor
>   (0) no factor
>
> 2 1 0 (a) poor quality wires
> 2 1 0 (b) faulty installation
> 2 1 0 (c) ineffective maintenance
> 2 1 0 (d) inappropriate maintenance scheduling
> 2 1 0 (e) if wires don't break, technicians lose jobs
> 2 1 0 (f) other:

Think about the pizza wiring example. Imagine that you had sent out surveys to all 160 store managers. Would you rather contemplate 160 answers to the above item or to the following item, *"What are the causes of the problems you are confronting with the wiring of the new computerized equipment."* Certainly an open-ended version of this example is appropriate for use in *early stages* as you meet with regional groups of managers or as you conduct telephone surveys. But in latter stages of assessment you want to **confirm**. That leaves you with the challenge of knowing enough about the problem to provide realistic choices and to be able to present them in a useful and appropriate format. The combination format leaves you with a way of capturing additional data without confronting 160 written paragraphs.

In **closed or forced questions**, the item constructor has three choices with implications for data analysis:

1. **Nominal** scales name or describe who the respondent is. If there is no order inherent in the categorization, then it is a nominal scale. For example:

Check the one that applies to **you** ......male   ......female

Which best describes the area in which you work? Check only one.
...... sales and marketing
...... personnel and training
...... manufacturing

A question which asks you to check given IQ categories or pay ranges or number of courses that you have taught would *not* be a nominal scale because a *rank order* is perceivable.

2. **Ordinal** scales ask respondents to select a category which reflects some ranking but lacks guaranteed, standard differences between ranks. For example, look at these Type 4 questions:

Which best describes your confidence in your ability to clean the new computerized pizza making equipment?
...... very confident
...... confident
...... somewhat confident
...... not at all confident

"The corporation selected the right computerized pizza makers for our stores." Check only one.

...... strongly agree

...... agree

...... undecided

...... disagree

...... strongly disagree

The problem with these Likert type items is the question about what constitutes the differences between options. Bradburn *et al.* (1979) pointed to how often we create scales like these assuming that everyone will know and share precise meanings for words like *very* and *often* and *above average.* In fact they don't. His research suggests that people vary in their definitions of words like rarely, sometimes and often, and that even individuals will vary in how they **rate** from topic to topic. There is no easy solution to the problem beyond recognition of the *caveats* appropriate to the use of such rating scales.

Training professionals often want sources to **rank not rate** the options. As long as you provide **no more than four choices**, people usually like to do it. For example, here is another ordinal scale, a Type 5:

Our stores are reporting double the number of equipment breakdowns than documented manufacturer's experience with other pizza stores. Why do you think this is happening to our chain? Below is a list of reasons that store managers have suggested. Will you please rank them from 1 to 3 with 1 representing the greatest cause of breakdowns and 3 the least cause, in your opinion?

......a. improperly installed equipment

......b. poor materials in manufacture of units

......c. improper daily maintenance in stores

3. **Interval** scales provide options in which the difference between units is equal and predictable. These are often used to gather demographic data:

How many times have you attended equipment related training in the past five years?

...... 0
...... 1-3
...... 4-6
...... 7-9
...... 10-12
...... more than 13 times

How much money have you spent on equipment repair in the past year?
...... $0-500
...... $501-1000
...... $1001-1500
...... $1501-2000
...... $2001-2500
...... more than $2500

There are several other concerns which relate to effective formats for items. The first is **scale consistency. Avoid switching rating scales and devices in the middle of an instrument unless there is a good reason.** While Zemke and Kramlinger (1982) encourage changing to combat monotony, especially in lengthy instruments, I don't agree. Instead, I would abbreviate the instrument and maintain as much consistency as possible. Respondents want to focus on the content of the questions; the scale type should be almost transparent.

Two other format issues are **highlighting and the use of white space.** I rely heavily on the use of bold letters and underlining to inform sources about what I think is essential in an item. I also will highlight if I think a source might get confused. Here is an example of a Type 3 question which checks up on what respondents actually know:

The pizza dough that is coming out of the ovens is soggy and has been that way **since the evening rush hour**. The temperature meter reads normal for the number of pizzas being baked. Which of the following commands should be entered into the control panel *first*?
......a. REHEAT
......b. REDIRECT
......c. DISPLAY
......d. CONCENTRATE

It is important to produce instruments which look like you know what you are doing. White space contributes to that, as does quality copying, careful font selection and lay-out of items and scales on the page.

The Words for Questions

The characteristics of the population should influence your search for the right words. Select words which are **familiar, without being loaded with controversial meanings.** Phrases like *corporate image, cooperation, and sufficient productivity* have the potential of eliciting an emotional response from one source and confusion about what you mean from another. In an interview you can elaborate, in print you confront denotation *and* connotation. Another issue is the reading grade level of the population. Keep reading grade level down by avoiding poly-syllabic words, lengthy sentences and jargon.

Payne (1951) advocates brief questions, stating that if you need more than 20 words for your question, it is too long. Sometimes, however, I've seen situations where you will want to set up situations in questions which take more than 20 words. The soggy pizza is an example. You can imagine other Types 3's and type 5's which would be **appropriately** lengthy. The key is **appropriateness,** again. Aim for brevity but recognize you may need to establish a question or situation in order to get meaningful responses.

Step 3: Writing Good Directions. It seems like a simple thing. Once you have gotten clear about your purposes and have crafted items **appropriate to those purposes and your audience,** just put in some **directions** which tell respondents how to complete the items. Easy, right? Wrong.

Directions are supposed to clarify things for respondents. Effective directions are crisp, not redundant. Definitions are included when necessary. Directions use words which are appropriate to the audience (see Step 2) and that tell you exactly what you need to know.

What do you need to know?

- what you will be expected to do
- whether we are talking about rating, and if so, what the rating scale is

- whether we are talking about ranking, and if so, what the different numbers signify
- whether you get to fill in your own ideas, as in a combinational item or in a totally open-ended query

In those **rare** instances where you include open-ended questions in surveys, you might choose to provide model answers. Not everyone would even consider this as a possibility. The danger is that you will bias your sample by providing them with a model acceptable answer. The way I address this concern is by offering an example that is on a different topic, but which exemplifies the **level of detail and specificity** that I seek. For example:

> In the questions that follow you will be asked to express your feelings about the pizza making equipment you are now using. Here is the kind of answer that will help us understand how you feel: **"I am very impressed with the performance of my Toyota MR2. It has excellent acceleration and better than 33 miles per gallon,"** or **"That Nagasawa has never worked right. It jerks and heaves when I shift from 1st to 2nd and failed to start up 2 out of 7 days last week."** Please try to provide answers which are as specific as these two automobile reactions.
>
> 1. Will you please describe your feelings about the new computerized pizza ovens?
>
> 2. How do the people on your staff react when you train them to operate this equipment?

Only provide examples when you anticipate inaccurate or inadequate responses to your open questions. Be sure to use an example **from another subject and to illustrate both ways**. I spoke of the excellent features of the MR2; I also exemplified with specific weaknesses of the Nagasawa.

Step 4: Writing Good Cover Letters. This is usually the first thing that the sample sees and it has to be good. What does *good* mean? It has to include the following:

- why they have received this questionnaire

> The Industrial Relations group is sending this survey out to all store managers in the New England area.

- a clear statement of the purpose of the questionnaire

Sales figures and repair costs indicate there are problems with the computerized ovens. We are writing to you to find out what you think about the problem.

- a reason for responding

There are many ways we could solve this problem ranging from removing the ovens to training all store staff in maintenance procedures. Your answers will help us figure out which option to select.

- directions about how and when to respond

An envelope with my address on it is attached to the instrument. Please make sure that you put it in internal mail by the *last* day of *this* month.

- say what you've done before to research the situation

The ideas and choices in this questionnaire are based on repair and sales figures and interviews with 6 regional managers.

- be direct, relying upon words and tone which indicate that a *real person* is concerned with how other *real people* see this issue.

This survey attempts to gather details about your experience using this equipment in the field. Only you and the other store managers can provide us with that kind of information.

- express appreciation for participation

I appreciate the time that you will spend filling out this survey. Thank you in advance for your participation.

Here is a cover letter which was written by Judy Duffield and attached to a needs assessment she distributed to teachers-in-training for a language training program:

> I am studying **second language acquisition** as part of a project for a graduate class at San Diego State. Specifically I am trying to find out *why more prospective teachers aren't interested in learning Spanish*.
>
> I've interviewed several students and teachers, but now I need more detailed information from more people. As someone who is about to become a teacher and who speaks only English, I hope you will give me the information that I need.
>
> The attached questionnaire gives you a chance to express your opinions and feelings about learning a second language. Please remove this cover sheet, answer the questions and return it in the enclosed, stamped envelope by March 15th.
>
> Please give a few moments of your attention to this questionnaire. I intend to look carefully at your responses to see if and how we can make the prospect of learning a second language more desirable and practical for prospective teachers.
>
> Thank you very much for your time and effort.

Note that this example tells what qualifies the individual to be included in the population, the purpose of the survey, and how and when to respond. She obviously needs their responses in order to make important decisions, and she expresses appreciation for their time and effort.

Step 5: Applying the Questionnaire Writer's Checklist. Here is a heuristic which exemplifies the survey writing concepts covered in this chapter. Use this checklist to look at a questionnaire which was developed previously or to help you generate a new one.

The cover
- ☐ Purpose
- ☐ Direct address
- ☐ Appropriate words for audience
- ☐ How selected to receive survey
- ☐ Reason for responding
- ☐ How and when to respond
- ☐ Expression of appreciation

The directions
- ☐ Brief
- ☐ Clear
- ☐ Appropriate to the audience

☐ Defining when necessary

☐ Providing examples when necessary

The items

☐ One purpose per item

☐ Each item linked to an item type

☐ Primarily forced choice items

☐ Reliance upon combinational items to include open ended option

☐ Appropriate use of highlighting, underlining and white space

☐ Consistency in scales and question types

☐ Content clustering by meaningful portions of the job or task

☐ Numbered items and pages

☐ Words and sentences appropriate to reading level and interests

☐ Communication with data processing professional, if appropriate

☐ Sufficient piloting to revise and feel confident

Step 6: Piloting the Questionnaire. Pilot your instrument before you distribute it. What you must decide is how complicated and *real world* you want to get about it. Two variables are involved as you think about piloting: with **how many** will you pilot and from **where** you will get them. It is different to try it out on three training professionals in your office than it is to send it to three store managers.

I encourage both an *intimate* and *expanded* piloting of surveys. An *intimate* pilot uses the opinions of other training professionals and managers to make improvements in the questionnaire. Ask these colleagues to read the questionnaire and give you specific suggestions as to how it might be made more effective. Consider letting them look at the checklist in Step 5 as they scrutinize your work. An *expanded* pilot actually sends the thing out to some store managers or bank tellers, not randomly selected ones or as large a group as will constitute the final sample, but some people who are probably similar to your eventual respondents. If you can, try it on several members of the population from representative locations.

Oppenheimer (1982) describes a pilot of a needs assessment in an article in *Training and Development*. After systematic efforts to derive optimal categories for management behavior, categories which the sample would eventually rate, Oppenheimer piloted the instrument. First he distributed it to seven people from other parts of the company and made revisions. Then he sent it to some managers from across the company. Based on their comments, new and simplified directions were added. After these two cycles of piloting, Oppenheimer was able to confidently distribute his questionnaire across the corporation.

Another Print TNA Tool:
The Delphi

Cass Gentry (1985), in a paper delivered to the Association for Educational Communications and Technology, encouraged the use of a Delphi as a needs assessment survey tool. Though I've never done it, I agree that training professionals can use a Delphi to systematically involve experts in definition of **goals (optimals)** and descriptions of **actual conditions**. I think it would also be useful for gathering a broad range of opinions on the **cause(s)** of performance problems.

During a Delphi, trainers seek information from sources about optimals, actuals and causes through repeated stages of contact based on disseminated, carefully constructed print surveys. The unusual part about the Delphi is that a chosen, elite panel of experts is repeatedly involved in offering their opinions on a narrow topic.

The Delphi involves **recurring submissions** of a series of questions to *selected* individuals who remain unknown to each other. Usually, but not always, the people who receive the questionnaires are considered **expert** in the field. They comprise a panel which is questioned about a particular topic on several different occasions.

There is an initial series of open-ended questions which solicit opinions from respondents. The answers to the original survey are then used to enlighten the construction of the next survey, which once again is sent back to the original panel. This continues over and over again until the person who is sending out the instruments is convinced that some **clear picture or consensus has been achieved**.

Here is how it might be expressed in steps contributing to TNA:

1. Clarify **purposes** for this Delphi. Are you seeking opinions on current performance? what performance ought to be? future directions? causes of impediments to performance or progress? several of these? Generate **items** which will accomplish these purposes.

2. Select a **panel**. Most often this is a panel of **experts**. But not always. I would lean towards a panel of experts if the purpose of the Delphi is to define optimals. If the reason for the surveys is description of current practices or causes, I see no reason to insist that everyone be considered expert in the area. Experience would be sufficient in this case.

3. **Distribute** questionnaires to panel. The Delphis in which I have participated have always involved a lengthy and flattering cover letter which emphasizes the *crackerjack, honored* nature of membership on the panel. Maybe that increases the number of responses. The real reason that I have chosen to respond is that I usually get asked questions about topics that interest me.

4. **Analyze** responses. Cluster content so that trends and disagreements are prominent.

5. Use analyzed data to **develop and refine questionnaires** in light of the purposes established in Step 1.

6. **Distribute again** to the original panel.

7. **Repeat** steps 4-6 until purpose(s) of the Delphi are fulfilled.

A brief example might look like this:

> The McKinley Corporation manufactures and sells advanced electronic equipment throughout the world. They feel that they are, however, not sufficiently using microelectronic technology to enlighten **their own management practices**. They decide that they want to purchase systems appropriate for all management functions and then to train their people to use them. The Vice President for Personnel decides that a Delphi with handpicked external and internal consultants will help her answer these questions:
>
> - What might we be using technology for today, given the functions of middle management throughout the world?

- What hardware and software do we need to anticipate and incorporate in our plans?
- What can we hope that an effective middle manager will be able to do with microelectronic technology in the middle and late 80's? in the early 1990's?

She returned to her experts four times. Each time she went back to them she refined her original instrument and pressed them for more details where there was controversy or a lack of clarity. Her last survey presented detailed results of the first three and focused on technology and international management practices, since opinions and trends in that area was lacking. Fourteen months after she commenced the Delphi, she was pleased that she finally possessed a panel of experts' opinions on optimals for middle management skills relating to high technology here and abroad.

Conclusion

In this chapter we've looked at an important tool in the TNA arsenal: the print survey. We have examined the steps involved in creating and sending out a questionnaire and we have linked that process to the purposes for conducting front end analysis. The numerous examples of items and formats should enable you to generate more effective instruments as well as tastier pizzas.

Resources

Baker, R.L., and Schutz, R.E. (1972). *Instructional Product Research.* New York: Van Nostrand.

Best, J.W. (1970). *Research in Education.* Englewood Cliffs, NJ: Prentice-Hall.

Bradburn, N.M., Sudman, S., and Associates. (1979). *Improving Interview Method and Questionnaire Design.* San Francisco, CA: Jossey Bass.

Gentry, C. (1985). Needs Analysis: Rationale and Technique, paper presented at the Association for Educational Communications and Technology, Anaheim, CA.

Flanagan, J.C. (July 1954). The Critical Incident Technique, *Psychological Bulletin, 51,* 327-358.

Oppenheim, A.N. *Questionnaire Design and Attitude Measurement.* New York: Basic Books, 1966.

Oppenheimer, R.J. (March 1982). An Alternative Approach to Assessing Management Development Needs, *Training and Development*, 72-76.

Payne, S.L. (1951). *The Art of Asking Questions.* Princeton, NJ: Princeton University Press.

Roid, G.H., and Haladyna, T.M. *A Technology for Test Item Writing.* New York: Academic Press.

Zemke, R., and Kramlinger, T. (1982). *Figuring Things Out: A Trainer's Guide to Needs and Task Analysis.* Reading, MA: Addison-Wesley.

Part Four: CONCLUSION

Chapter Twelve: PLANNING TRAINING NEEDS ASSESSMENT

Summary of the Book

This is the beginning of the last part of this book. The purpose of this part of the book is to bring it all together for readers.

In Chapters 1-4 of TNA we looked at familiar phrases: front end analysis; needs assessment; pre-training analysis; needs studies; problem analysis . . . followed by my conceptualization for investigating performance problems and innovations.

In Part Two we examined extant data analysis, needs assessment and subject matter analysis. These analysis techniques are defined and linked to the front end purposes for which they are appropriate.

Part Three of TNA presented the tools we use to carry out these analyses: interviews, observations, group meetings and surveys. Detailed examples illustrate a step-by-step approach to their use.

You've encountered the concepts . . .

- of **purpose-based TNA**, where we are seeking
  - ☐ **optimals**
  - ☐ **actuals**
  - ☐ **feelings**
  - ☐ **cause(s)**
  - ☐ **solutions**
- of **analysis techniques**
  - ☐ **extant data analysis**
  - ☐ **needs assessment**
  - ☐ **subject matter analysis**

- and of **tools** which are used to carry out techniques
  - ☐ **interviews**
  - ☐ **observations**
  - ☐ **group meetings**
  - ☐ **print surveys**
- of **stage of assessment**
  - ☐ of movement from one tool and technique to another and perhaps another to gather information in regard to purposes

The Challenge

The successful TNA is based on clarity about:
- ALL THE POSSIBLE TNA PURPOSES
- YOUR PARTICULAR PURPOSES IN **THIS** SITUATION

At the same time, as a performance analyst or trainer in a real company, with a real boss, and real world constraints, you must conduct the TNA in light of:
- HOW MUCH MONEY YOU HAVE
- HOW MUCH TIME YOU HAVE
- THE POLITICS SURROUNDING THE SITUATION
- WHO WANTS THIS PROBLEM SOLVED AND HOW TO INFORM THEM AS YOU MAKE PROGRESS

Admittedly, this approach assumes decision-making which attempts to balance the quest for information with the economics and politics of the situation. Under ideal circumstances, the front end study or TNA doesn't terminate until you are confident that you know the optimals, actuals, feelings, causes and solutions related to the problem or innovation. Few circumstances, however, are ideal. Money and people quite often impose upon the quest for complete information and opinions.

Purpose-Based TNA Planning

Successful assessments are based on careful planning. That's planning which keeps purposes as the beacon for activities, while at the same time, recognizing the possibilities and constraints of the setting.

A Step-by-Step Approach to Planning TNA

Step 1: Assess the Context

Step 2: Determine Purposes

Step 3: Select Techniques and Tools

Step 4: Develop a TNA Plan

Step 5: Develop Stage Planner(s)

Step 6: Communicate Results

Before moving into the steps in TNA planning, let's have some introductions:

• *The TNA Plan:* that's the document the instructional technologist or trainer develops which lays out a tentative and general plan for the **entire** TNA.

• *The TNA Stage Planner:* that's the document the trainer writes to figure out and carry out exactly what he or she is going to do **at each stage** of the TNA. There's only one TNA Plan, albeit a fluid one. There are as many Stage Planners as there are stages in the TNA.

• *Walt, the insurance man:* Walt is a training specialist for one of America's largest insurance agencies. His corporation decides that sales agents need to use portable personal computers in their interactions with clients. The company is about to make this enormous investment, and they wisely involve Walt right at the beginning. In fact, his boss, having just attended an excellent training seminar, tells him she expects him to do a front end analysis before launching any training programs.

• *Brenda, the fast food woman:* Brenda is a performance analyst for a company that sells fast food. The complaints about quality of french fries doubled in the past quarter. Sales are down. Upper management prides itself on the quality of these fries and fears the effect of lesser fries on total corporate profits. She is charged with developing a program for nationwide consumption that will address this problem. Brenda tells management that she intends to conduct a training needs assessment first. They look blank. "We're interested in crisp fries, not needs assessment. Just do whatever has to be done to fix the problem."

We'll use the challenges that face Walt and Brenda, and a few other professionals in our field, to illustrate the power of a systematic approach to planning front end analysis based on the TNA Plan and the TNA Stage Planner. Now back to the first Step.

Step 1: Assess the Context. Good intentions and eagerness for relevant information are not enough. Without awareness of the corporate or agency context, the performance technologist will blunder into a TNA, creating problems, while attempting to solve them.

Therefore, the first step in planning a TNA is to assess the context. That means taking some time to think about the following questions:

1. **Who wants** this problem solved or this new technology introduced? Why?
2. **Who doesn't?** Is there anyone who prefers for things to stay the same? Why?
3. Is this a solution to a **performance problem or an innovation** which is being introduced? If it is a performance problem, who might fear or attempt to block your efforts to find the **cause(s)** of the situation? If it is a new system, who might not want to support this change?
4. Who are the **sources** of information for this TNA? Will they be accessible? Will you be able to go back to them again and again as you need additional information?
5. What **records** might provide useful information? Will they be accessible? Will you be able to go back to them again and again as you need additional information?
6. How much **support** does this entire project have? Does the TNA also have support or will you have to fight for resources to conduct it? How much time do you have?
7. **Who must be kept abreast of your findings?** Who else might want to know? Who must *not* know—at least at first?

Asking these questions won't solve your problems. What it will do is allow you to anticipate the detailed context for your TNA, converting what you know into resources and constraints. Let's use Walt's situation (he's the insurance man) as an example:

1. **Who wants** this problem solved or this new technology introduced? Why?

Obviously Walt's boss does. He also determines that the enormously powerful Vice-President of Sales and Marketing was eager to move towards computerized sales and that he was the one who wanted to bring the Training group into this early in the process. The managers of the sales staff are particularly supportive because they envision being able to keep track of people, efforts and successes better.

2. **Who doesn't?** Is there anyone who prefers for things to stay the same? Why?

Walt's boss thinks that the heads of two of the product lines were opposed to this move towards computerization. They felt resources could be better spent in the product areas, on rates, and incentive programs, than on hardware and software. The man who heads up the annuity programs, on the other hand, thought computers were a good idea for the sales staff.

3. Is this a **performance problem or an innovation** which is being introduced? If it is a performance problem, who might attempt to block your efforts to find the **cause(s)** of the situation? If it is a new system, who might not support this change?

This is an innovation. No particular problem in sales is being addressed. All sales people will be expected to use computer-assisted sales as a long range strategy to maintain market share.

4. Who are the **sources** of information for this TNA? Will they be accessible? Will you be able to go back to them again and again as you need additional information?

The sources are: insurance sales people; the vendors for the hardware and software; managers of the sales people; and customers.

5. What **records** or documents might provide useful information? Will they be accessible? Will you be able to go
   back to them again and again as you need additional information?

Since this is an innovation, extant data is not particularly relevant. However, vendor information about the use of the program
by other field sales staff from non-competitive companies would
be helpful.

6. How much **support** does the **entire project have**? Does
   the **TNA** have sufficient time and money allocated to
   it or will you have to fight for resources?

The project is a top priority. As Walt thinks about this question, he realizes that only his boss understands why he can't
offer a course tomorrow. He realizes that a top priority problem
or innovation often leads to little support for front end efforts,
just because of the eagerness for solutions. He realizes he is going
to have to educate people in his organization in order to get
sufficient time and money for this TNA.

7. **Who must be kept abreast of your findings?** Who else
   might want to know? Who should not know?

The training manager and the Vice-President for Sales and Marketing must be informed. It might be a good idea to use a TNA
group to inform sales managers from across the nation about this
project and the training which will eventually support the computerized sales effort. The same TNA group could be used to
solicit ideas about field sales staff's feelings about this innovation.
It's important that information about the project be restricted to
in-house employees. Since this is an effort to use an innovation to
increase sales in a competitive market, secrecy is crucial.

The results of step 1 are a clear picture of the context and a detailed listing of the sources (animate and inanimate) who will contribute to this TNA—or stand in its way.

Step 2: Determine Purposes. While the bottom line *raison
d'etre* of every private sector TNA is increased profitability, the
personnel specialist or trainer has to contribute in the best way

he or she can: by getting beyond numbers and into the individual performances and accomplishments which affect these numbers.

Here are the broad, familiar questions central to what we do when we conduct purpose-based TNA:

- **SEEKING OPTIMALS: What is optimal performance?**
- **SEEKING ACTUALS: What are employees currently doing?**
- **SEEKING FEELINGS: How do they feel about the problem or new system?**
- **SEEKING CAUSE(S): What is causing the problem?**
- **SEEKING SOLUTION(S): What solution(s) is preferred?**

During TNA, the training professional seeks answers to these questions. The trainer or industrial relations specialist continues the search for answers from varied sources until confident that he or she knows the answers to the questions. The quest to fulfill the five purposes for training needs assessment are at the heart of planning. **Trainers are only concerned about a purpose until it is fulfilled and the information is available.** Please refer back to Figure 7.4. It reiterates that point.

Let's turn to Brenda's problem with limp fries as an illustration for Step 2 in the planning process. Brenda plans her front end effort by tracking her progress in fulfilling each of the TNA purposes:

☐ Brenda must seek the **cause(s)** of the deteriorating french fries above all other purposes.

☐ She already has a clear picture of **optimals**. A detailed task listing was done when the french fries were introduced years ago, and has been updated to match the new technologies for fry production.

☐ She also has a reasonably good take on the **actuals** through extensive observation reports on file, customer complaints and sales figures.

The problem is sogginess and limpness, which nutritionists say is caused by improper fry timing, relating to steps 7 and 8 in the cook procedure. Presuming the nutritionists' accuracy, then Brenda is still confronting the question of cause of the recent problem with steps 7 and 8 in the cook procedure.

☐ She intends to investigate **feelings** about this problem and about the steps in the cook procedure. This will have significant implications for decisions about the cause(s) of this problem.

Note that Brenda isn't spending time and money on purposes about which she already knows, in this case, optimal fry making and what is actually transpiring. Her interest is in the **cause(s) of the recent problems with limp fries**. She will pursue additional information on feelings and actuals only for the light they shed on the cause(s) of the problem.

As we did in Step 1, we will use questions to guide us through Step 2:

1. Is this a **problem in a familiar job** (what we've been calling a "performance problem") or is it a **new system or technology?** Figure 12.1 illustrates the significance of the answer for determining the purposes of any TNA.

Brenda and the fries are a good example of a problem in a familiar job. Walt, on the other hand, is attempting to facilitate the implementation of a new technology for insurance sales people. Figure 12.1 reiterates the importance of this question to their differing TNA studies.

2. What are my **purposes** for this study? Do I seek information about how they should be performing? how they are performing? how they feel about performance or the system? the cause(s) of the problem? their opinions on solutions?

Brenda wants to know **why** there is a problem with the fries, what specifically is causing the problem with Steps 7 and 8 in the fry cook cycle. Walt will focus on the details of **optimal** use of the computers by sales staff during sales calls and for sales information self-management. If he is to develop effective training, he will also need to know how they **feel** about the technology as a tool for doing their jobs. Cause is, of course, not an issue for Walt. They aren't using the computers because they do not yet have them and nobody has taught them what to do with them.

PURPOSES OF
FRONT END ANALYSIS

SEEKING	NEW SYSTEMS...	PROBLEMS IN FAMILIAR JOBS
• OPTIMALS	X	X
• ACTUALS		X
• FEELINGS	X	X
• CAUSE(S)		X

Figure 12.1

3. Once you've acquired some information, what else do you need to know? Are you confident that you have fulfilled that purpose? Which purposes remain?

Assume that Brenda's sources give her conflicting information about the cause of the problem. The store managers say that the quality of lard is down and that this inferior lard is creating problems with the crispness. Interviews with employees suggest that there have been cut-backs in staff resulting in more pressure on remaining staff to produce more fries. They point to the push to get more fries into the hands of customers quicker. They admit that they shorten step 7 to get the fries to customers quicker. Brenda needs to look into this. She decides to contact corporate purchasing to see if the company is buying a lesser grade of lard. She also takes some lard from a store and asks one of the cooks to follow the task listing, including the criteria for length of time in Step 7, and to produce some fries. She and the store manager agree that these fries are "just fine." The cause of the

problem is not quality of the lard. The cause of the problem may
be supervisory behavior and/or the inability of cooks to produce
more fries in a shorter period of time.

Note that she continues to pursue her TNA purpose, the **cause
of the problem**, until she is certain that she understands what is
going on.

Step 3: Select Techniques and Tools. Look back at the chapters
on TNA techniques and tools. Re-examine Figure 2; it presents
techniques in light of the purposes which they address. Let's
briefly review your options for **TNA techniques**:

Extant data analysis: In Chapter 5 we talked about the effectiveness of this technique for gathering information about what is
actually happening in a performance problem from inferences
based on accomplishments. This is a technique which doesn't cost
much money because the trainer is examining existing results, or
record results of performance. Often, however, there are problems in gaining access to extant data. Why does a trainer want to
look at sales records on a branch by branch basis? Why does an
industrial relations expert want to examine the performance
appraisals that have been filed for the data processing division?

Needs assessment: This is a technique which has the potential
for yielding information on every purpose from a wide variety of
sources. It is, however, a costly way of gathering information.
Since you are seeking a range of opinions and gathering information anew, the effort, though worthy, is labor intensive.

Subject matter analysis and task analysis: These efforts yield
information on optimal knowledge and performance. Based on
scrutiny of documents, references and resources and on interactions with experts, the professional develops a clear statement of
desired skills and knowledge for an employee.

TNA tools are used to carry out TNA techniques. How much
time and money do you have? Is this project controversial or
threatening? Will people reveal what is actually going on without
guarantees of anonymity? Figure 6.3 provides a review of considerations for using interviews and print surveys. Part Three of
this book describes TNA tools in detail. **Here are your options
for TNA tools:**

Interviews: Potentially effective for gathering information related to all purposes, the interview is the most prevalent TNA device. It can be used with all sources and is effective in person or on the telephone. Chapter 8 details the considerations for determining whether to meet in person or to use the telephone for interviews.

Observations: An observation is traditionally used in TNA to gather information about optimal and actual performance. While watching someone perform might enable the astute observer to make inferences about the cause(s) of a problem, observation is not traditionally used for fulfilling that purpose. Observations are the tool most often linked to task analysis.

Group Meetings: This tool might be used to gather information relating to all TNA purposes. When you are seeking information on controversial or threatening topics, however, the interview and the group meeting are less likely to lead to a true picture of actual performance and the accompanying feelings.

Questionnaires: A survey or questionnaire is potentially effective for fulfilling all TNA purposes. In addition to allowing the trainer to query large numbers of people anonymously, effectively constructed surveys lend themselves to rapid analysis of results.

The chapters which describe these techniques and tools include descriptions of how and when to use them. Refer to these chapters as you make your decisions about the techniques and tools to employ in the TNA.

Two important rules of thumb are:

TNA *purposes* influence the *techniques* you select and questions you ask.

The *context* influences the *tools* you employ and sources you contact.

> Walt, for example, needs information on optimal use of computers as a sales tool for insurance agents. He must conduct a subject matter analysis. He also needs information on feelings about this new system for sales. He will turn to needs assessment. Walt is also fortunate in the amount of support he has for his effort. This support enables him to employ interviews with numerous sources including vendors, a group meeting of sales managers, and a print survey of sales managers and agents.

If Walt were under more severe time or political constraints, as Brenda is, he would be limited to examining the documentation, interviewing the vendor and any identified subject matter experts, and calling a manager or two to ask them how their people are going to take to this new idea. The more constrained setting necessitates fewer stages of TNA with fewer sources contacted in each stage.

Step 4: Develop a TNA Plan. Up to now in the planning process, the training professional has been thinking. In Step 1 the training professional pondered the context for the TNA. Step 2 was a consideration of the purposes for **this** TNA effort. In Step 3 the performance specialist reviewed options for TNA techniques and tools in light of this situation. Now it's time to **write** the devices which will enable you to incorporate thoughts on context, purposes, techniques and tools into a general plan for TNA. That is accomplished in Step 4 through the *planner* for the entire front end study.

The *TNA Planner* is:
- **holistic.** It describes the entire front end effort.
- **tentative.** As you learn, you expect to change it.
- based on your speculations about **context and purposes.**
- reflecting the **options** for TNA techniques and tools.
- the **guide** for the plans and activities that follow in TNA.

In Step 4 the training professional does only one thing: fill out a *TNA PLANNER*. This *PLANNER* forces you to write down what you have figured out about context, purposes and information-gathering options. Figure 12.2 is a blank copy of the *TNA PLANNER*.

Let's do one for Walt. Figure 12.3 is one possible *TNA PLANNER* for his project. I constructed this *TNA PLANNER* by going back to the answers I had written down as I contemplated the questions listed in Steps 1 and 2 of Chapter 12. It is also based on the TNA options described in Step 3.

Figure 12.3 presents the plans for TNA activity of a fortunate instructional designer. It is a thorough study of the situation before Walt attempts to introduce computers into the insurance sales environment.

TRAINING NEEDS ASSESSMENT PLANNER

Context		Purposes		
Resources	**Constraints**	**Description**	**Status**	**Sources**

Stages/Techniques   **Tools and Sources**

Figure 12.2

TRAINING NEEDS ASSESSMENT PLANNER

Context		Purposes		
Resources	Constraints	Description	Status	Sources
Mgr. of Training	Two	Optimals	Need Badly!	Vendor, vendor-identified Documentation sales mgrs.
V.P. Sales & Mktg.	prod. mgrs.			
Regional Sales Mgrs.				
Eager Vendors		Actuals	Not applic	
Lots of support for project		Feelings	Need	Sales mgrs. insurance agents
Boss can communicate explaining		Cause(s)		
time frames.		Solutions		

Stages/Techniques	Tools and Sources
1/ Subject Matter Analysis	Review Documentation; interview vendors; interview SMEs.
2/ Needs Assessment	Group Meetings with sales mgrs.
3/ Needs Assessment	Telephone interviews with insurance agents.
4/ Subject Matter Analysis	Interview few agents already using computers in sales.
5/ Needs Assessment	Print Survey 125 randomly selected agents.

Figure 12.3

Let's plan the TNA of a trainer less blessed by external circumstances, Brenda. Management is breathing down her neck for a solution to the limp fries problem. No time for a lengthy TNA involving many sources or stages. See Figure 12.4.

Step 5: DEVELOP STAGE PLANNERS. The *TNA PLANNER* developed in Step 4 presents a holistic picture of tentative plans for investigating the situation. The *STAGE PLANNER*, on the other hand, is the designer's work sheet for planning the details of **each stage of inquiry. A TNA will have one *TNA PLANNER* which might change as you learn more about the situation. This same TNA will have many *STAGE* PLANNERS, each one keyed to a stage of TNA. A stage is an outreach effort to gather additional data to fulfill TNA purposes.**

In Step 5, you produce the detailed plan and instruments to carry out a **particular** stage of TNA. This is done *via* the *STAGE PLANNER*, a device which focuses attention on the stage in which you are **currently** working. A blank *STAGE PLANNER* is presented as Figure 12.5.

If you are at the beginning of a TNA, develop a *STAGE PLANNER* appropriate to Stage 1. Walt's *STAGE PLANNER* for stage 1 is presented next. See Figure 12.6.

After completing Stage 1, you produce a *STAGE PLANNER* appropriate to Stage 2. That is true for Stage 3, 4, and so forth, until you have completed your TNA. It is important to remember to wait until earlier stages are completed before trying to fill out a *STAGE PLANNER* on an advanced stage. **The information gathered in earlier stages serves as the basis for future stages of inquiry.**

We're not finished with Walt yet. Let's continue to use his TNA as an example. We'll presume that the *TNA PLANNER* presented in Figure 12.3 is an accurate representation of the stages of his TNA. Note that his fifth stage is a needs assessment, a technique which has the potential of fulfilling any and all front end purposes. But Walt's fifth stage effort will not gather all types of information. Why?

1. Walt is working on the introduction of an innovation. He will only concern himself with a quest for information about optimals and feelings because of that.

2. In the four stages of assessment that preceded this last stage, he determined the details of optimal use of the

TRAINING NEEDS ASSESSMENT PLANNER

Context		Purposes		
Resources	Constraints	Description	Status	Sources
Branch Mgrs.	time pressure	Optimals	On Hand	Written Task listings + job descriptions
Extant Data Nutrition Dept.	ASAP!!	Actuals	On Hand	Extant Data (sales, letters)
		Feelings	Need	Mgrs., cooks
		Causes	Need Badly	Mgrs. supervisors, cooks, nutritionists
		Solutions	Not Applicable	Determine via cause(s)

Stages/Techniques	Tools and Sources
1/ Needs Assessment	Group Meeting with mgrs. & supervisors
2/ Needs Assessment	Nutritionists
3/ Needs Assessment	Observation of fry cooking

Figure 12.4

TNA STAGE PLANNER

1. SUBJECT OF TNA: STAGE NO.

2. SUMMARY OF WHAT YOU ALREADY KNOW ABOUT THE SUBJECT:
(Describe in light of purposes of TNA.)

3. SUMMARY OF INFORMATION BEING SOUGHT DURING THIS STAGE:
(Describe in light of purposes for TNA.)

4. WHO OR WHAT ARE THE SOURCES OF INFORMATION FOR THIS STAGE?

5. WHAT TNA TOOL(S) WILL BE USED TO CARRY OUT THIS STAGE?

6. IF YOU WILL BE INTERVIEWING OR SURVEYING, WHAT QUESTIONS WILL YOU ASK? IF YOU WILL BE OBSERVING, WHAT WILL YOU BE WATCHING? IF YOU WILL BE USING A GROUP MEETING, WHAT IS YOUR AGENDA?
(If sufficient space is not provided here, attach the instrument or agenda.)

Figure 12.5

TNA STAGE PLANNER

1. SUBJECT OF TNA: Preparing Insurance Agents to Use Computers   STAGE No. 1

2. SUMMARY OF WHAT YOU ALREADY KNOW ABOUT THE SUBJECT:
   (Describe in light of purposes for TNA.)
   This is a Stage 1 plan and little information is currently available.

3. SUMMARY OF INFORMATION BEING SOUGHT DURING THIS STAGE:
   (Describe in light of purposes for TNA.)
   The purpose of this stage of TNA is to determine OPTIMAL use of the technology for selling insurance to customers.

4. WHO OR WHAT ARE THE SOURCES OF INFORMATION FOR THIS STAGE?
   Documentation included in software and hardware; Phil Gonsales, the vendor representative; and Mary Jones and Allan Neilson, the designated SME's. All three know the software and have worked with insurance agents and companies in the use of it.

5. WHAT TNA TOOL(S) WILL BE USED TO CARRY OUT THIS STAGE?
   The trainer will review the literature prior to *interviewing* Phil, Mary and Allan.

6. IF YOU WILL BE INTERVIEWING OR SURVEYING, WHAT QUESTIONS WILL YOU ASK? IF YOU WILL BE OBSERVING, WHAT WILL YOU BE WATCHING? IF YOU WILL BE USING A GROUP MEETING, WHAT IS YOUR AGENDA?
   (If sufficient space is not provided here, attach the instruments or agenda.)
   I think I understand the significant components and functions of the hardware and software. Where I need your help in figuring out the details of how an insurance sales person would use this software in two arenas: 1. to make a sale; and 2. to keep track of sales leads and contacts. First, about the software's capabilities *as the agent sells*:
   1. What exactly is the information to which the agent might want to refer?
   2. Is there other kinds of data about which a customer is likely to ask?
   3. For each of the items on this list, is there a simple listing of how to access it in the system?
   4. Think about the agent who is trying to make a sale. What are the questions which this software answers for him/her while in the customer's home?
   5. Pretend that you are a very competent computer using sales agent. I'll be a customer. Will you please show me exactly how you would use the computer during our interaction?
      Now let's look at the insurance agent's use of the computer to *manage sales contacts* . . . .
   6. Describe the capabilities that this system has for management of files and information.
   7. What I'd like to do is focus on each of the package capabilities you've just described and apply it to the job of an insurance sales agent. Let's start with data entry and go through every aspect of the system . . . .
   8. I know that our agents are going to complain that they have no time to enter all this information. How does the system respond to that concern?
   9. We have some agents who don't possess "keyboard" skills. How does your system accommodate that problem? What are other corporations doing about that?
   10. Imagine a situation where a busy and successful agent is managing his workload through the effective use of this system. What exactly does he do—before calls—after calls—at home—in the office?
   11. What can this computer do for sales agents that they couldn't handle before? How does it stretch sales agent's capabilities?

Figure 12.6

technology in insurance sales. He is confident that he knows exactly what an agent does to enhance sales and file management *via* the computer.

3. He has been getting a mixed picture of the response of the sales staff to the technology. His stage 2 needs assessments with sales managers indicated that their sales staff was generally positive about the use of portable computers. However, phone interviews with sales agents turned up some negativity. Given the lack of anonymity in the use of that tool and the likely unwillingness to express unpopular opinions in ways that can be attributed, Walt thinks there is more doubt and hesitation about the computers than earlier stages indicate.

Therefore Walt decides to conduct a print survey with 125 randomly selected agents. They will be guaranteed anonymity of response and he will be able to make generalizations based on the size of his sample. Figure 12.7 represents Walt's **STAGE PLANNER** for stage 5. In addition to the holistic *TNA PLANNER*, it is based on the material presented in Chapters 6 and 11. Note that the 4 items in # 6 of the **STAGE PLANNER** are Type 4 questions, seeking information on value and confidence surrounding the new system.

Now let's set up a new situation which will take us in a slightly different direction, one which allows me to present another *TNA PLANNER* and its related **STAGE PLANNER:**

A large auto dealership has approximately 75 mechanics doing engine, new car preparation and auto body work six days per week. This fiscal year is different from all others because the percentage of returns and call-backs is up 19 percent over last year. Customers are less satisfied with service on their cars, and they are informing the dealership and expecting the problem to be corrected.

Rex, the owner of the dealership, has invested a great deal of money in computerized diagnostic equipment. He is aware of the direct relationship between service reputation and repeat sales. First, he asks his day sales manager to take a look at the problem. The day sales manager pulls all the files on call-backs, lists the complaints and matches them up with staff. Then he recommends that the boss get rid of 75 percent of the mechanics and one of

TNA STAGE PLANNER

1. SUBJECT OF TNA: Preparing Insurance Agents to Use Computers   STAGE No. 5

2. SUMMARY OF WHAT YOU ALREADY KNOW ABOUT THE SUBJECT:
   (Describe in light of purposes for TNA.)
   Possess satisfactory picture of optimal sales performance using a computer.
   No need to seek other purposes; this is a new technology/system.

3. SUMMARY OF INFORMATION BEING SOUGHT DURING THIS
   STAGE:
   (Describe in light of purposes for TNA.)
   Seeking clear picture of range of sales agent feelings about use of computers in selling insurance and managing sales contacts.

4. WHO OR WHAT ARE THE SOURCES OF INFORMATION FOR THIS
   STAGE?
   Sales agents, the eventual users of the technology, are the sources.

5. WHAT TNA TOOL(S) WILL BE USED TO CARRY OUT THIS STAGE?
   A print survey will be used.

6. IF YOU WILL BE INTERVIEWING OR SURVEYING, WHAT QUESTIONS WILL YOU ASK? IF YOU WILL BE OBSERVING, WHAT WILL YOU BE WATCHING? IF YOU WILL BE USING A GROUP MEETING, WHAT IS YOUR AGENDA?
   (If sufficient space is not provided here, attach the instrument or agenda.)
   1. How good an idea is it to use computers to assist insurance sales people as they work with customers? Check only one.
      ....a. It's a very good idea.
      ....b. The idea has some merit.
      ....c. It's not a good idea.
      ....d. I'm not sure about computers and insurance sales.
   2. Look at the answer you checked in number 1. Why? Write a few sentences to tell us why you feel the way you do about computerized sales.
   3. Which best describes you? Check only one in each category.
      ....a. I'm eager to learn about computers.
      ....b. I'm willing to learn about computers.
      ....c. I'd rather not learn about computers.
      ....d. I'm not sure how I feel.

      ....a. I think I am very talented with "computer-oriented" things.
      ....b. I think I am able to learn about "computer-oriented" things.
      ....c. I anticipate having a hard time learning "computer-oriented" things.
      ....d. I'm not sure how I will do.

      ....a. I support management's move into computerized insurance sales.
      ....b. I am neutral or unsure about computerized insurance sales.
      ....c. I am opposed to computerized insurance sales.
   4. As you know, the corporation will provide every agent with a computer, programs which will make it useful for insurance sales and training on how to use the technology. What are some of the questions that you have as you think about this new sales tool?

Figure 12.7

the service managers. The day sales manager says, "Complaints occur about almost all of the mechanics. So one of their service bosses ought to go too."

The owner of the dealership knows removing so many employees is impossible; there aren't that many good mechanics around to hire. Also, approximately the same staff was working for him when they had fewer problems with service. Turnover hasn't been much of a problem the past few years.

Fortunately, the owner's ex-brother-in-law lives next door to a consultant who calls herself a "performance technologist." The brother-in-law says she worked on a similar problem for a manufacturing plant. While her title amuses the auto dealer, he admits to needing help and will even accept it from someone with a title he considers preposterous. That's how Rex, the auto dealer, met Jan, the performance technologist. Figure 12.8 is the *TNA PLANNER* she constructed to help her figure out all the stages of assessment that she needed to understand the problem. She used it to determine how long the TNA would take; how much money and travel would be involved; and where she would need Rex's assistance in communicating with sources of information.

Rex hires Jan to conduct an analysis of the problem based on a formal presentation of the contents of her *TNA PLANNER*. Once hired she carries out the process and discovers that all sources point to a problem with the staff's ability to use the new computerized diagnostics equipment. The mechanics don't like it. The service managers think the program is strong and try to "stay on them" to use it, but privately wonder if it is strong enough to warrant the hassle. When anonymously surveyed, many mechanics admit to not knowing how to use it in a flexible way during daily rushes or how to feed alternative information into it.

The stage 4 *STAGE PLANNER* presented below is an example of a meeting Jan holds to tell everyone what she thinks is causing the problem, after having completed three stages of assessment (see Figure 12.8, the *TNA Planner* for a description of Stages 1-3). She also intends to solicit their opinions on solutions, another way of seeking their opinions on the cause of the problem. Then Rex will decide how the dealership is going to handle the situation. See Figure 12.9.

TRAINING NEEDS ASSESSMENT PLANNER

Context			Purposes	
Resources	**Constraints**	**Description**	**Status**	**Sources**
Rex, an eager Boss	Mechanics?	Optimals	Known & specified	Mfr. specs & Documentation
Extant Data gathered by day sales mgr.	Service Mgrs.?	Actuals	Inferred from Extant Data	Computerized records, performance appraisal Mechanics, Mgrs.
Computerized Service Order Tracking system → Records		Feelings	Need	Mechanics, Mgr
Clear Documentation from Mfr. specifications		Causes	Need Badly!	Rex, Mgrs., Mechanics
		Solution	As clue to cause(s)	" "

Stages/Technique	Tools and Sources
1/ Extant Data Analysis	Examine Material collected by Day sales mgr.
2/ Needs Assessment	Interview Rex, sales mgrs.
3/ Needs Assessment	Interview selected mechanics
4/ Needs Assessment	Print survey with all mechanics (anonymous)
5/ Needs Assessment	Group Meeting with Rex & his mgrs.

Figure 12.8

TNA STAGE PLANNER

1. SUBJECT OF TNA: Why are Mechanics Failing to Fix Cars?   STAGE No. 4

2. SUMMARY OF WHAT YOU ALREADY KNOW ABOUT THE SUBJECT:
   (Describe in light of purposes for TNA.)
   Know optimals, actuals, and feelings in minds of key characters. Fairly certain that the cause of the problem is discomfort, lack of trust and confusion surrounding the computerized auto diagnostics. Solution(s) are unclear until cause is established.

3. SUMMARY OF INFORMATION BEING SOUGHT DURING THIS STAGE:
   (Describe in light of purposes for TNA.)
   What does Rex and the service managers think is the key cause of the problem? What are they willing to do about it?

4. WHO OR WHAT ARE THE SOURCES OF INFORMATION FOR THIS STAGE?
   Rex and the service managers.

5. WHAT TNA TOOL(S) WILL BE USED TO CARRY OUT THIS STAGE?
   A small group meeting will be used.

6. IF YOU WILL BE INTERVIEWING OR SURVEYING, WHAT QUESTIONS WILL YOU ASK? IF YOU WILL BE OBSERVING, WHAT WILL YOU BE WATCHING? IF YOU WILL BE USING A GROUP MEETING, WHAT IS YOUR AGENDA?
   (If sufficient space is not provided here, attach the instrument or agenda.)

   Agenda

   I. Review of purposes for meeting, including that this is an information-sharing meeting. No decisions will be made at this session. The purpose is to gather ideas on meaning of the data and to speculate on realistic solutions.
   II. Presentation of Jan's findings: what mechanics ought to be doing; what they are doing (based on orders and call-backs with reference to day sales mgrs. earlier work); possible cause(s) of any performance problem.
   III. Recommendations on the cause of this problem based on the data: THIS PROBLEM COMES FROM MECHANIC FEELINGS ABOUT THE COMPUTERIZED DIAGNOSTIC EQUIPMENT. They feel that it gives them incorrect problem identification. They do like the speed with which it gives them readings on individual auto performance elements. Their problem appears to be with the conclusions it draws. In addition, nearly half admit to avoiding the use of the computer as often as they can because they are not always sure how to use it flexibly. Then, because the technology is supposed to save them time, they hasten their own uncomputerized diagnostic procedures.
   IV. What was the reasoning surrounding the initial purchase of the system? Is the computerized auto diagnostics program to blame? Is it weak? Why do vendor-provided figures show it is more effective in other settings? If mechanics could use it better, would it diminish call-backs? Can mechanics be forced to rely more heavily on the computer? Will that help? Do we want them to rely more heavily on this program? Just how committed is management to this system?
   V. What does the dealership want to do to solve the problem? Detail cost(s) of various solutions.

Figure 12.9

Step 6: Communicating Results. There are two kinds of communication related to results: that which occurs **during** the TNA and that which occurs **afterwards.** In this chapter we look briefly at the communication which must happen **as the analyst or trainer is doing the TNA.** Jan is engaged in that kind of activity when she meets with Rex and his managers.

As the training professional moves through the stages detailed on the *TNA PLANNER*, management must be informed about what is being learned about the situation and the implications that information has for solving the problem or introducing the new system or technology. In step 1 of TNA planning, you determined who must be kept abreast of the process. Follow through on those good intentions.   Communication may be through informal meetings or briefings. Here are two examples:

> I am getting a clear picture of how our people might use these computers when they go into homes and offices to sell insurance. The three experts are being very specific and I'm able to convert their ideas directly into goals for the training we'll be doing.

> Rex, do you think the computerized diagnostics system gives the right answers to your mechanics? Will you take a look at that with a mechanic or two whose opinions you trust? Your people are pointing at the computer and we need to know if their complaints about its performance are warranted.

The other option for communication is more formal memos. Note all that it does for the performance technologist and management. Remember that these examples are of communication about results **during** the TNA. The next chapter focuses on post-TNA communications.

> To: Al Higgin, Manager of Training
>
> From: Walt Garbosky, Performance Technologist
>
> Re: Progress on TNA for "Preparing Insurance Agents to Use Computers"

I met with Phil Gonsales, Mary Jones and Allan Neillson from INSUROTECH. After six meetings during the first two weeks of October, I believe I now have a clear picture of exemplary use of INSUROTECH's computer system for our sales agents.

If you want an update on the details of the use of their system for actual customer sales and for sales contact file management, just let me know. I'm eager to brief you.

My next step is two meetings with our own sales managers, the first of which will be October 21st. We'll be talking about the likely responses of agents and managers to a computerized environment. I'll inform you after those meetings.

Conclusion

In this chapter we've addressed the steps involved in using TNA tools and techniques to achieve progress. We've looked at humorous examples and touched on the communication that occurs **during** the stages of TNA. Now we conclude the book with Chapter Thirteen.

Part Four: CONCLUSION

Chapter Thirteen: COMMUNICATING RESULTS OF TNA

Introduction to the Concluding Chapter

While earlier chapters focused on communication to **acquire** TNA information, this final chapter highlights communication which **shares results and makes recommendations**. That kind of communication occurs **during TNA** *and* **at its conclusion**. Here are some examples of situations which involve communication about the results of front end study.

- Leslie has been working on the TNA for introducing a computerized payroll system for installations across the nation. After four stages of assessment, including a needs assessment with nearly 300 employees, she writes a 9 page report which outlines information related to each of the purposes for TNA and includes recommendations and detailed appendices. Her boss tells her that he intends to take her report directly to upper management.

- Orin is asked to do the front end on a sales training program. His boss sort of likes the *Know-Show-Go Approach* which was developed at the Banking Institute specifically for the financial community. While she was impressed when she first heard about it a year ago, she is fuzzy on the details. Orin digs into the literature, interviews experts and gathers a small group of people from the company who are already using *Know-Show-Go*. Then he visits his manager's office to fill her in on the details of the *Know-Show-Go Approach*. She listens to his 5 minute update and thanks him for explaining *Know-Show-Go* and providing the details she'd forgotten. She then asks him to write up a clear picture of the optimals for the new training so they will all have a document which describes the approach and its applications to their financial setting.

- Suzanne, as an initial stage in a TNA, interviewed 12 employees who have recently submitted accident reports after use of the VROOM 2577. She wanted to know why there were so many accidents surrounding that piece of equipment. After the interviews, Suzanne has what she believes is a clear picture of what injured employees think is the cause of the problem with this model VROOM. She writes a detailed memo which presents the cause from the employees' viewpoint and requests permission to enter another stage of TNA to interview engineers and supervisors for their perspective on the cause of the problems with the VROOM 2577.

We'll refer back to Leslie, Orin and Suzanne in this discussion of the briefing, memos and reports which inform sources about the findings attached to TNA stages.

Brief Description

What are you going to do with the results of TNA? This chapter is about the communication that surrounds that question.

What are you finding out? What do employees tell you? supervisors? Do they agree with each other? Do they agree with management's perspective on the situation?

Will the innovation be welcomed? Do employees feel they can master it? What are the subject matter experts saying? the same thing? or are you getting wildly varied descriptions of optimal performance?

What do sources think is causing the problem, if it is a performance problem? Are they clear about how it ought to be? Are they suggesting feasible solutions?

These questions are familiar. They are derived from a purpose-based approach to TNA and serve as the basis for launching and tracking the TNA process. Not surprisingly, purposes and related questions also guide communication about results.

Purposes of Communicating Results

Think back on introductory communications theory. You are the sender. There is a receiver or receivers. In TNA, as we are looking at it in this chapter, the message is about **results and recommendations**.

SENDER ——————— (RESULTS) ————————> RECEIVER

How can you get the most mileage out of this communication? How can a trainer use this communication to accomplish several desirable ends? Let's look at the reasons why we communicate results and recommendations in the TNA process.

1. **To provide information about *results* in relation to optimals, actuals, feelings, causes and solutions.** No one is paying a trainer, analyst or industrial relations specialist to study the situation for the sheer joy of gathering information. Management in corporations and agencies wants answers to questions, and I contend that the questions center on the purposes that have been highlighted in *Training Needs Assessment*. They want to know:

   *** what ought to be happening (optimals)

   *** what is happening (actuals)

   *** how sources feel about the problem or the innovation (feelings)

   *** what is causing the problem (causes)

   *** what sources think might solve the problem (solutions)

Getting this information in a cost-effective fashion is at the heart of the challenge. **The job isn't finished until you have communicated what you know to those who need to know.**

2. **To derive support for the effort.** The *effort* might be the problem you are attempting to understand, the TNA and the project into which it will lead. Often what you learn through TNA provides compelling information that convinces supervisors or managers of something about which they were initially negative, hesitant or ambivalent. This is neatly illustrated through a current project on which I'm working. A Fortune 500 company with 70 percent turnover every five years wants to know the nature and magnitude of the problems in their franchises which could potentially be solved through training programs. Home office management is divided on topics, approaches and technologies. What we learn through TNA, both from its comprehensiveness and its lack of bias, will enlighten training and development decision-making for several years. This isn't unusual. That's why a high quality

presentation of results and recommendations is so important. Oral and written documentation often become the vehicle for justifying corporate and agency actions relating to problems and innovations.

3. **To solicit additional information or to check out a finding.** When you present what you have learned, significant others in the corporation or agency are going to react. That might mean the addition of another stage of TNA or agreement that it is time to conclude the study. Here are some examples of what you might hear:

"Yes, that's what I think is causing that problem too."

"I think you need to talk to Hing Lotakoon and his people in Engineering. They envisioned different applications, I think. I'll let them know you are going to call about how they thought it might be used."

"The people from our region feel differently about this. Let me tell you about it and arrange for you to meet with them."

"I'm glad you sent me this memo. Now I can see why people across the agency are concerned about this. I'm going to ask Will to dig into our files and see if our figures look like this."

"Our people like using computers for these training courses. Then they can work through it at their own pace. If we are going to launch a course on this, maybe the other regions need to try it this way."

4. **To create a history of the TNA effort.** In addition to the TNA Planner and Stage Planners that you use (see Chapter 12), you need a more detailed record of your efforts and findings. This record helps you keep track of where you've been, where you need to go and what it all means. That record guides your introspection on the process. There is also the important and nasty reality of having to respond to statements like:

"How come nobody told me we were moving this thing to a centralized activity? Since when does Industrial Relations make this kind of thing happen? Why wasn't our group consulted?"

"I'm an international expert on Know-Show-Go in financial institutions and I was bypassed when you people put this course together."

"There is no way we can send our people to a course which only reflects the East coast perspective on this thing."

"When are you going to stop talking to people and get on with making the course? What's the point of all this palaver?"

"You got this wrong. That's not how the encryption system works. Who told you this?"

"I can't see how THIS is a priority . . . ."

"What's this KNOW-SHOW-GO APPROACH and how can you expect me to get behind a whole new way of working with the sales staff when I don't know anything about it?"

"Nothing wrong with what we've been doing in the past."

"Did anyone look at our figures on this? No problem here."

It is important to document the sources you have used and the techniques and tools employed to query them. When someone says, "We weren't consulted," you want to be able to show how they were or who was, if they weren't. When somebody says, "No problem here," you want to be able to point to the figures or opinions on which you based your conclusions. When someone says, "You got it wrong," you must be able to cite the authority who said you had it right.

Establish a campaign which informs people in the corporation or agency about the results of your study—as you conduct TNA **and** after you've concluded it. **The essence of TNA is to ask hard questions about performance, accomplishment and responsibility. Absolutely nobody likes surprises about that kind of information.**

Once the entire TNA or a TNA stage has been completed, the analyst or trainer has something about which to communicate. What will be done with the information that has been gathered? The following steps describe the process of communicating what you know to people who need to know it.

Steps in Communicating Results

Step 1. Determine with WHOM you must communicate.

Step 2. Determine WHY you are communicating.

Step 3. Determine HOW to communicate.

Step 4. Answer typical QUESTIONS about results.

Step 5. Use COMPUTERS to facilitate communication.

Step 6. Communicate TACTICALLY.

Step 1. Determine with WHOM You Must Communicate. In Chapter 12, the training specialist is urged to assess context as Step 1 in the planning process. This assessment is also Step 1 in reporting results. The questions listed in Chapter 12, with a few changes, will yield a list of people who need to be informed during and after the TNA.

1. **Who wants** this problem solved or this new technology introduced? Why? Do they want to be informed as you proceed with TNA?

2. **Who doesn't?** Is there anyone who prefers for things to stay the same? Why? Do they know you will be studying the situation? Should you tell them?

3. Is this a solution to a **performance problem or an innovation** which is being introduced? If it is a performance problem, who might fear or attempt to block your efforts to find the **cause(s)** of the situation? If it is a new system, who might not want to support this change?

4. Who are the **sources** of information for this TNA? Will they be accessible? Will you be able to go back to them again and again as you need additional information? Should each one be informed about what you learn from the other? Are **you** the one to be doing the communicating or should it be your superior?

5. How much **support** does this entire project have? Does the TNA also have support or will you have to fight for resources to conduct it? How can you use the briefing and reporting process to garner support?

6. Who **must be kept abreast of your findings during TNA?** Who must *not* know—at least at first? Who needs to be filled in as you conclude? Who gets the **final report?**

Now you've got a list of people with whom you must communicate as you carry out and complete TNA. *You need to think about how they got on the list.* Were they included as supporters, skeptics, subject matter experts, managers, etc.? Are they someone who wants a snappy oral briefing, a pointed memo or a lengthy, documented report? What do they expect? What are you able to give, in light of time restraints?

Step 2. Determine WHY You are Communicating. There are many possible purposes for communicating TNA findings to sources in a corporation or agency. They are described throughout this book and listed as the first purpose for communication in this chapter. Here is a summary of the KINDS of results which might be reported after individual stages or completed TNAs:

☐ information about optimals;

☐ information about actuals;

☐ comparisons of optimals **and** actuals, thereby detailing the exact nature of the problem;

☐ sources' feelings about the problem or innovation;

☐ the cause(s) of the problem;

☐ solutions to the problem or ways of increasing successful introduction of the innovation;

☐ areas of disagreement or controversy surrounding the issue;

☐ reasons for supporting the project and/or TNA;

☐ solicitation of opinions and information from other sources;

☐ historical records of the TNA effort, its sources and its findings;

☐ recommendations and requests for action(s);

Look at the TNA Planner and the Stage Planners that you have constructed for this project. Before you brief or write, it is essential to know **why** you are engaging in this communication.

Step 3. Determine HOW to Communicate. First, let's look at the communications options presented on a continuum with informality to the left and formality on the right:

Oral Communications

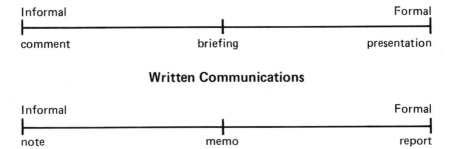

Because these options are not exclusive categories, I've chosen to represent them along continua. There are briefings that are none too brief and presentations which lack detail, complexity and length. So too with memos and reports. The focus here is on length and formality of the communication device. Communication across the entire spectra requires planning. The distinction is also in the fact that the left side is most often used as an ongoing record of what's happening and being discovered. The right side of these continua produces reports which become a more permanent part of corporate history and decision-making. As Joe Arwady of Baker Industries noted, "My brief reports are thought out just as carefully as lengthier reports because I must make my points in a stripped down version when it's only a memo or note." The training professional's challenge is to determine whether to communicate in writing or orally, and then to select an appropriate spot on the continuum. Planning is essential in every case.

What about Leslie's computerized payroll system, Orin's *Know-Show-Go* and Suzanne's Vroom accidents? Where do they fall on these continuua? Leslie (**L**) and Suzanne (**S**) chose written communications. The L and S on the continuum represents the detail and formality of their written efforts.

Written Communications

		S		L
note		memo		report

Orin (**O**) provided a spontaneous, oral briefing to his manager about a sales training program. His place on the continuum is to the left of the midpoint because his communication lacks formality, detail and length. Note that it was, however, effective. Note also that he is expected to follow this briefing with a short written communication.

Oral Communications

	O		
comment		briefing	presentation

Leslie, Suzanne and Orin were all successful because the nature and magnitude of their communications matched two key variables: first, *their purposes and* second, *the expectations of their receivers.* The third factor to consider in choosing a communications device is the *resources, including time*, available for this reporting activity. Let's look at purpose, expectations and resources as they influence the selection of how to communicate results.

Purpose

Findings related to any TNA purpose may be presented through written or oral communications. Straightforward messages lend themselves to the left side of the continua. Here is an example to illustrate this point:

Case: Leah Ann has just finished interviewing first line supervisors in regard to their feelings about the automated tracking system which is about to be introduced. Her findings are that the impression is favorable in all regions; most await the change with eagerness and will support sending their people to training to get up to speed on it.

Recommendation: She has been seeking information related to only one purpose (feelings). Her findings are neither complex nor controversial. She may mention her findings to her supervisor or other interested sources or send a brief memo.

If, however, results relate to several purposes or are particularly complex, lengthy or controversial, then choose the right side of both continua. Also, the more complicated, detailed and controversial are your findings, the more likely it is that you will want some written record of findings and implications, either as the initial means of communication or as a follow-up to oral interaction. An example follows:

Case: Ellie has been asked to do something about the decrease in sales of a formerly successful product line. Management thinks training will return sales to their former status. She examines sales figures from across the nation and interviews sales people and their managers. What she gets is a very mixed bag of performance and opinions. There is no indication at all about a performance problem caused by an absence of skill or knowledge on the part of sales people. Sales staff point at earlier product shortages, inaccessibility of testers, and market concern about compatibility with other business products.

Recommendation: She has been pursuing information related to two purposes (actuals and causes). She acquires information which is complex, controversial and lengthy. In addition, she is beginning to hold an opinion counter to the one that management holds. They want training; her findings uphold her doubts that training will affect the bottom line. Ellie should use the right side of the continua. A detailed and documented oral presentation is one possibility. A substantiated memo or report is the other choice. Perhaps she will prepare a two or three page memo with appendices which support her stance and explain the reasoning for it.

Receiver Expectations

What do your sources expect? What do significant individuals in the hierarchy prefer? What is corporate policy in regard to communicating results during and after front end studies? If you don't know, ask.

Some companies, usually large ones, have forms which must be filled out after each stage in your study; others have specific expectations attached only to the concluding stage of TNA. Most companies leave it up to the individual training or personnel professional. That means an individual assessment of sources and individuals in light of the nature of findings. Most managers with whom I have communicated prefer *less rather than more*. Give them lean statements of findings, with the opportunity for them to dig into substantiation, if they choose.

Resources

A particular manager might prefer detailed reports. The results might be complex and controversial. Indications, then, point towards a formal, written report or documented presentation. Except there is no time in which to do it. If no time has been allocated to plan and produce a professional quality report or presentation, then you won't get to do one. Communication of results, like the rest of TNA, is constrained by economic realities.

Here are some suggestions relating to resources:

1. **Anticipate**. Determine where the TNA might get bogged down and account for it in your planning. If you anticipate complex or controversial results, allocate time and resources to prepare a document or presentation which will *sell and substantiate* your findings. How real is the time pressure? Is management pressing you because they *always* press or because training must be available to accompany a new product or system the moment that it appears in stores?

2. **Use formal devices (right side of continua) sparingly.** Often, the analyst or trainer will want to save lengthy, time consuming communications devices, those on the right, for latter stages of assessment. That's when the complexity of findings are likely to warrant detailed reporting procedures.

3. **Use earlier communications to build support for latter communications.** Earlier reports of findings, although often short, should demonstrate the value of the TNA study for corporate decision-making. Provide snappy and pointed briefings and mention the thorny areas which remain to be studied.

4. **Be prepared to justify the time it takes to prepare and produce formal reports.** All the TNA work that has been done will be to no avail if the results are handled hastily. Make that point and then provide oral and written reports which speak for themselves through their eloquence and significance.

Beyond purposes, receiver expectations and resources loom **individual preference and abilities**. If you think you write well, you will lean towards written communications. If you think you are a fine presenter, you will chose to communicate results through oral means. No problem there.

The problem arises when you **avoid** written formats or oral presentations because of doubts about your ability to write or speak effectively. Honesty is important here. Assess yourself; do a TNA on **you**. Is there a gap between optimal and actual performance in written or oral communication—at any place on either spectrum? If there is, do something about it. While this chapter provides heuristics for thinking about and carrying out effective communication about results, it does not build prerequisite writing or speaking skills. That's up to you.

Step 4. Answer Typical QUESTIONS About Results. These are the questions that are in the minds of the receivers of communications about TNA results:

- *Why* did you carry out this stage of assessment or the entire TNA study?
- *How* did you gather TNA information?
- *What* did you find out?
- What does it *mean* for me? us? the company or agency? advanced stages of TNA? the project?

Let's look at the first question which must be answered:

- *Why* did you carry out this stage of assessment or the entire TNA study?

Answering this question usually involves presentation of background information, introduction of the problem or innovation and statement of TNA purpose(s). Rely on the TNA Stage Planner for this stage or the entire TNA Planner, if this is a final report. Both forms are discussed in detail in Chapter 12.

All statements of results should include a review of the **situation**. The situation often, but not always, begins with information about the target population.

Oppenheimer (1982) reports on the **population** for a multi-staged management development study in *Training and Development*:

The organization in question is a large, multi-plant, urban-based company. The company is a well-established firm experiencing only moderate growth, along with the rest of its industry. Their managerial ranks consist of basically loyal, long-tenured employees who have in-depth knowledge of their company and of their industry . . . .(p. 72)

After presenting the population, it is useful to state the **problem** or **innovation**. A description of the problem would look like this:

The purpose of this study was to find out why there have been so many accidents surrounding the use of the VROOM 2577 model.

A model description for a new system or technology is presented here:

Word processing is gaining acceptance in society and in the corporation. The company has made a major commitment to Compaq computers and WordStar as the word processing system. At this moment, fewer than 20 percent of the staff are competent in this system. The pages that follow describe the study that

Industrial Relations undertook prior to launching training for this system.

In addition to information about the target group, problem or innovation, it is important to describe **what is already known**. That information might have been determined through earlier stages of TNA or provided by management. The WordStar percentage is one example. Orin and Know-Show-Go provides another. Orin might have prefaced his oral briefing with the following:

During the fall meeting, sales managers voiced concern that increased sales skills and sensitivities were needed by their people. You expressed interest in the Know-Show-Go Approach to sales. I've stopped by to fill you in on that Know-Show-Go Approach now that I've taken a close look at how it works in financial institutions.

Finally, the answer to this first question should **briefly** state the **purpose** of the oral or written report or memo. Often, information about the population or innovation includes the purpose. See Orin's introductory statement and the WordStar TNA just above.

Here are two examples of brief purpose statements:

☐ *This report presents what several groups think new employees need to know about our benefits program.*

☐ *This presentation will provide answers to the following questions:*

  • *How can insurance sales people best use portable computers?*

  • *Do our sales people want to learn about computers?*

  • *What do our people currently know about computers?*

  • *How can we best prepare them to use this tool?*

In summary, response to the question, *"***Why** did you carry out **this stage of assessment or entire TNA study?"** should include information about:

☐ population

☐ performance problem, if it is that kind of project

☐ existing information

☐ TNA purposes, expressed in lay language

Another question which must be answered is:

- *How* **did you gather TNA information?**

Who were the sources? How were they contacted? What tools and techniques were used? The challenge is to provide this information in a direct fashion, also without reliance on jargon.

Refer to the TNA Planner and the individual Stage Planner. On those forms you've detailed how you would carry out the front end study. The forms, therefore, are a source of a pithy statement of exactly what you did.

Here are two examples of effective methodology statements, one in the first person, the other in the third person. Christine Parsons reported her TNA to a museum in San Diego:

I gathered data regarding the Museum's needs from three sources:

(1)   the Museum staff
(2)   research and publications on marketing, motivation, and attitude change relating to non-profit organizations
(3)   the target audience

The primary source of information was the Museum. I collected data through personal interviews with the Director and the Education Coordinator. Then I examined marketing surveys, statement of purpose, brochures and exhibits . . .

Diane Ley wrote this for a veteran's group:

Three separate groups were contacted to ascertain what information was needed by patients about to enter 'board and care' facilities. The first group interviewed was residents living in 'board and care' homes. The second groups interviewed was patients being considered for placement in 'board and care' facilities. The third group was social workers who deal with placing patients in 'board and care' facilities or social workers who do follow-up treatment on patients after placement. The patients were interviewed one-to-one. The social workers filled out anonymous questionnaires.

Here is an *ineffective* methodology statement. One instructional designer reported his methods as follows:

An analysis of the instructional problem was conducted during February and March of 1985. Four types of front end analyses were conducted and will be summarized in this section:

1. Needs assessment of learners
2. Needs assessment of clients
3. Subject matter analysis with scientists
4. Extant data analysis of repair reports

This aspiring designer blew it by using jargon and commencing with information about dates. Lead with important information related to methodology and avoid technical or training jargon. Phrases like the list above are appropriate for the TNA PLANNER AND STAGE PLANNERS—**rarely** for reporting TNA results to others. While a training director *might* know what this instructional designer is talking about, nobody else will. It is essential that communications about results of front end analysis be written so that they will communicate to a lay audience. Diane and Christine did that. The last trainer didn't.

While sources are interested in what you did, they are even more interested in what you discovered. That leads us to a third question:

- *What* **did you find out?**

This takes us back to questions about purposes for the stage, stages or entire TNA. Report outcomes in light of purposes. Name and label them. For example, when you are talking about *causes* of the problem, say it. When you have received conflicting information about *feelings* surrounding the new system, describe them. So too for information about *optimals*, what model performers must know and do, *current performance* and *solutions*.

Long and disorganized diatribes on results lack punch and cause confusion. **Use TNA purposes as the organizing theme to present outcomes. Report only information which you judge to be important to the TNA and the project.** Save substantiation, copies of instruments, superfluous but intriguing findings and extant data for the appendices.

Here are key factors in the successful presentation of results:

- ☐ use TNA purposes to organize and present what you learned
- ☐ judiciously select what to include and what to omit.
- ☐ be brief by placing details, elaboration and documentation in the appendix
- ☐ rely on tables and charts when you can

What follows is a slightly edited example of a results section written by Susan Levy and June Dodge. The entire project, carried out for General Dynamics, won the Association for Educational Communications and Technology Division for Instructional Development's Award (1986) in a national competition with other graduate students. Here is a selection from their report of the results of their assessments with supervisors and other potential consumers regarding an AppleWriter word processing course:

The results of the print survey give an indication of the current Apple computer and AppleWriter usage, optimal or desired AppleWriter use, and the feelings of the potential learners surrounding this topic.

LEARNERS' CURRENT ABILITY ON THE COMPUTER: (See questions 1A, 1B, 1C and 1D in Appendix C.) Responses to question 1 indicate that 40 percent of the potential learners have never used a computer before. Forty-four percent have been using a computer for under six months and the remaining 16 percent have been using a computer for more than 1 year. Learners have access to either an Apple II+ (25%) or an Apple IIe (59%). Seventy-three percent of all learners questioned have *not* had General Dynamics' introductory microcomputer class. Of the learners who had taken the course, 86 percent took the Apple course and 14 percent took the IBM course. Of the 60 percent of respondents who were currently computer users, 85 percent felt comfortable with their computers.

LEARNERS' CURRENT ABILITY TO WORD PROCESS: (See questions 2A, 2B, 2C, 2D, 2E and 2F in Appendix C.) Responses to question 2 indicate that 58 percent of the computer users have used various word processing programs (14% on AppleWriter). Seventy-nine percent of respondents have been using word processing for under one year with 68 percent reporting that they feel comfortable with word processing programs. Of those using word processing, 50 percent still consider themselves "novice."

LEARNERS' CURRENT OR ANTICIPATED USE OF WORD PROCESSING: (See questions 3A, 3B, 3C, 4A, 4B, 5A, 5B, 5C in Appendix C). Question 3 was directed towards experienced learners. Responses to it indicate that the learner finds word processing useful (100%), use it daily (80%), and like feature options (editing, columns, equations). Question 4 responses (computer neophytes) indicate that respondents feel that word processing will be beneficial in their jobs (92%) in the areas of speed, editing, updating and sorting. One half of all respondents felt that they would use word processing daily after completing the AppleWriter course. Jobs expected to be completed using AppleWriter included memos, letters, reports and documents.

LEARNERS' OPINIONS ON WAYS OF ACQUIRING SKILLS: (See questions 2D, 3A, 4A, 4C, 4D, 6A, 6B and 7 in Appendix C). New learners believe AppleWriter will be beneficial to learn (92%), solve problems (91%), and be worth the effort to learn (100%). Two four hour training sessions were preferred by 59% of respondents and the majority (89%) liked the idea of one introductory course followed by an advanced one.

This brief results section is effective because it is linked directly to the purposes of the study (detailed information about actuals, optimals, feelings and solutions). It also works because it omits irrelevancies, cites materials in the appendix, and obviously enlightens decisions which need to be made about the course.

The only improvement that I would suggest in this example is support of key percentages with graphic representation. This is especially true if the results were presented orally. Use a computer business graphics program to convert unbroken prose, laden with percentages, into illustrative visuals. (See Figures 13.1 and 13.2.)

Two additional examples demonstrate how tabular representation can effectively present results to readers. Janice Sibley surveyed learners for a self-assessment of current skills in troubleshooting a compound microscope.

Skeptical readers might be wondering about the learners' ability to *self* report actual knowledge of the microscope. Janice Sibley used another stage of assessment to assure herself that she was getting reliable data regarding actual skills. The next table is based on a test that she gave learners during which she asked them to interact with the microscope to demonstrate what they knew and didn't know. Imagine the clumsiness of the report of these findings if this data was offered in prose paragraphs rather than tabular format. See Table 13.1.

Simple percentages and other descriptive statistics are appropriate for representing the vast majority of TNA data. Examples of the use of percentages are provided above. Become familiar with mean, mode, median and standard deviation as concepts which describe what the survey results looked like. Janice Sibley could have talked about the *average score* (the mean). Or she could have talked about the *middle* score, the one that winds up in the middle when all the scores are laid in a line from large to small (the median). Or she could have talked about the most frequently recurring score (the mode). She might also have referred to the

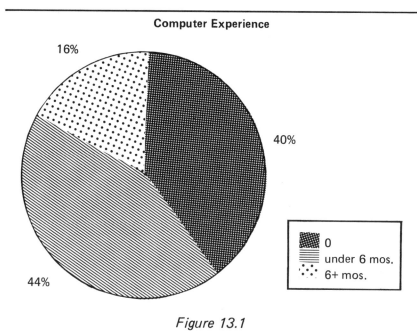

Figure 13.1

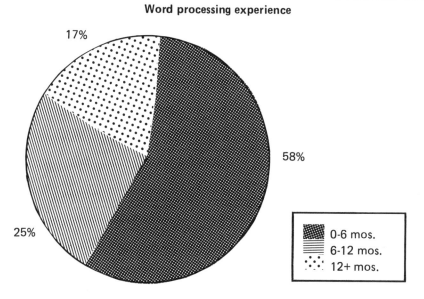

Figure 13.2

Table 13.1: Troubleshooting the Compound Microscope:
Self Report

Competency Statement	Learner Response (%)		
	Yes	Maybe/Sometimes	No
a. I can focus an object under scanning power (4X).	84	14	2
b. I can focus an object under high power (40 or 43X).	63	33	4
c. I know how to adjust my microscope if the field of view is too bright.	90	8	2
d. I know how to adjust my microscope if the object I am viewing is too transparent for me to see.	49	31	20
e. I know how to adjust my microscope if I see two fields of view when I look into it.	57	18	25
f. I know the procedure to follow if I think a lens (objective) is dirty.	67	6	27

Table 13.2: Troubleshooting the Compound Microscope: Observation

Question	% Learners with correct response
a. pointing to a microscope part that might need adjusting if too much light was coming into the field of view	73
b. pointing to a microscope part that might be adjusted if the field of view was too dark or only partially lit	47
c. pointing to a microscope part that might need adjusting if two fields of view were seen in the microscope	41

---

standard deviation of scores in her group, the scatter or spread of scores in a distribution around the mean. Consult an introductory statistics text if these concepts are unfamiliar.

Cross tabulations of two variables were used in a recent needs survey at San Diego State University (Derryberry and Rossett, 1986). Not only did we want to know who our new students were, we wanted to know the career settings to which they aspired. We were also interested in knowing the relationship of gender to preferred career setting. Figure 13.3 presents the two variables after computerized cross tabulation.

Quick perusal suggests that gender turned out to have little to do with their choices. If a training specialist wants to do more than eyeball the data for relationships, a Chi-Square can be used to determine if relationships have occurred by more than chance. This is a statistical test which indicates whether the scores in a table, scores representing the relationship between two characteristics, do in fact bear a *statistically significant relationship to each other*.

In an article in the *Journal of Instructional Development*, Cummings (1985) focuses attention on methods for analyzing needs assessment data to ascertain **priorities** among competing

GENDER AND CAREER ASPIRATIONS
FOR STUDENTS IN EDUCATIONAL TECHNOLOGY

Males	Pub/Priv Educ.	Bus/Ind	Soc Serv	Health	Other	Row Total
	12	14	1	0	2	29/30.2%
Females	32	26	1	2	6	67/69.8%
Column Total	44 45.8%	40 41.7%	2 2.1%	2 2.1%	8 8.3%	96/100%

Figure 13.3

needs. Misanchuk (1982, 1984) and Cummings (1985) propose statistical methods for treating those topics that the employee SHOULD know by weighting the more critical or relevant skill and content areas.

The question is *how do we handle the data that emerges from instruments that capture data along the two familiar dimensions of optimals and actuals.* Here is a playful example of a typical instrument for a needs study on romantic abilities where individuals are asked to circle the number reflecting their current and desired skills.

Content area	Knowledge level that SHOULD exist	Knowledge level that DOES exist
	little extensive	little extensive
1. ability to hug	1 2 3 4 5	1 2 3 4 5
2. ability to kiss	1 2 3 4 5	1 2 3 4 5
3. ability to write love letters	1 2 3 4 5	1 2 3 4 5
4. ability to cook romantic dinners	1 2 3 4 5	1 2 3 4 5
5. ability to listen	1 2 3 4 5	1 2 3 4 5

Typically, data derived from such a survey is summed by category and then divided by the number of responses. Thus a mean for the way it SHOULD be can be compared to the mean for the knowledge level that is ACTUALLY in place, or is reported to be in place by the raters. Simple subtraction of actual from optimal offers a number which lends itself to comparison with other numbers. For example, if the mean knowledge (and skill, of course) for optimal kissing turns out to be rated as 4.75 and the rating for current knowledge is 4.25, the gap is .50. If the gap between what should be known about listening is greater than .50, the presumption is that listening is a higher priority training need than kissing. It would also be possible to prioritize all five training areas by ordering them in ascending or descending order based on the size of the discrepancy. Both Cummings and Misanchuk provide more elaborate means of analyzing needs data to derive a single weighted figure on which to make decisions.

Beyond technical discussion of the various statistical treatments of large survey data, both authors effectively highlight the ratings which must enlighten decisions about training priorities:

- what the employee SHOULD know
- what the employee DOES know
- how RELEVANT or CRITICAL the "should" information is to the job

Why are lists of content areas which are of lesser importance included in a survey to begin with? Since surveys are typically **latter** stages of assessment (see Chapters 6 and 11), then we should already know the degree of criticality or relevance of an area prior to including it in a survey. If you use several stages of assessment in a TNA, including contact with extant data, management and potential trainees, the training professional will have already determined that hugging is *passe*, or that the audience is already champion kissers, and that these content areas, therefore, need not be included in the full blown survey.

The final question in the minds of readers and listeners is:

- **What does it *mean* for me? us? the company or agency? advanced stages of TNA? the project?**

No report of results, oral or written, is complete without some statement of the **implications** of what you've discovered and **recommendations** related to those implications. Here are examples of implications statements linked to suggestions for action.

Implications	Recommendations
☐ We now have a clear picture of how Know-Show-Go could be used in a financial setting.	• Hire Dr. Blast and work with him to develop a customized course.
☐ Trainees have problems with microscopes in very predictable and narrow areas.	• Instead of developing a complete course, produce a brief module and job aids.
☐ The SMEs disagree; I'm not yet confident about the best ways to incorporate lap computers into home insurance sales.	• Scour the company and industry for additional expertise on optimal use.
☐ Absolutely no one that I interviewed perceives our problems with the VROOM 2500 to be caused by lack of information or incompetence. This was confirmed by the employees' ability to answer questions about operation and safety when I queried them, with them achieving a model score of 9 on a test of 10 safety items.	• Go back to the records and supervisors to determine impact of the new productivity expectations. Seek other views on cause(s).

An example from the AppleWriter TNA by Susan Levy and June Dodge follows. Note the inclusion of the **implications** of findings as well as specific **suggestions for next steps**.

> The results of the needs assessment indicate a definite gap between actual performance (as determined by the questionnaire) and optimal performance (as determined by interviews with supervisors).
>
> There is definite demand for AppleWriter training. Future users are well equipped with the proper software and hardware that is necessary for this word processing program. Every respondent agrees that it will be beneficial to learn about word processing.
>
> We recommend a basic AppleWriter course to be developed that will note the differences between editing and printing commands.
>
> A second advanced course should be planned to be given after the first course has been completed and the learners have had an opportunity to practice their skills on the job. This course will serve the graduates of the first class and the employees who are already familiar with word processing.

Step 5. Use COMPUTERS to Facilitate Communication About Results. This section is not about computer-assisted or computer-managed instruction. It is a brief discussion of computer resources for **gathering, organizing, analyzing and presenting data derived from a TNA**. In no way does this section of Chapter 13 claim to be a comprehensive treatment of computers or statistical analysis of survey results. Examine the references at the conclusion of the chapter (e.g., Karweit and Meyers, 1983). Turn to experts who are present in many corporations and universities.

While computers are not yet an integral part of front end activity across the United States, just as they are not yet an integral part of *all* training activity (see *Training* magazine's October 1985 census issue), they have potential for assisting in crunching responses from large samples, serving as a data base which can be easily manipulated, ascertaining patterns and identifying and assuring relationships between variables. This makes the computer particularly appropriate for compiling and analyzing print surveys, usually a latter stage TNA tool, one that is used after the training professional knows enough about the situation to craft targeted, forced-choice questions.

Zemke and Gunkler (1985) reviewed commercial microcomputer software that claims to assist the personnel or training specialist in generating and analyzing questionnaires. The problem with their review, as with any evaluation of computer hardware and software, is that the information becomes outdated because of improvements in existing packages and the emergence of new products. Still it and the listing at the conclusion of this article provide a starting point. Current and popular computer magazines review and advertise the most current products and features.

Zemke and Gunkler stated their preference for generic statistical packages (e.g., SPSS/PC, STATPRO and STATPACK) over those that have been tailored for training professionals. They recommend the use of a word processing program for survey generation followed by traditional social science statistical analysis packages for data analysis.

There are numerous new statistical packages produced for microcomputers. I have used STATWORKS on my Macintosh to crunch numbers, and explore frequencies and cross-tabulations. Other colleagues recommend STATVIEW and STATFAST. Addresses for this software and other programs described in this chapter are provided at the conclusion of the chapter.

Zemke and Gunkler described packages developed specifically for training professionals. The two that I've seen are Karl Albrecht's "A.S.K." (Assessment Survey Kit) and Bauer and Associates "Synthesis." Albrecht's recently updated A.S.K. is useful. It leads a computer novice through generation of a simple survey and then supports data analysis of the survey. It does not, however, help you figure out *what to ask.*

The Bauer materials are intriguing. In addition to supporting file development and management related to surveys, the software makes the life of a survey writer easier by allowing him or her to type in an "L" if the response options for the current question are just the same as for the previous item. While a word processing system would enable the same copy capability, it is an indication that the producers of "Synthesis" understand the unpleasant tasks confronted by survey developers.

At a national conference, I got an opportunity to look at the beginnings of a collection of sample surveys that Bauer says they will be making available to buyers. These models are one way to start, although they will need to be adapted to local purposes and contexts. The Bauer library of surveys might, I fear, encourage the *big bang assessment*: the assumption that one big, long survey is the best way to get information. It isn't. Remember the importance of using multiple, planned stages of assessment to zero in on the problem or new technology.

Neither the Bauer nor the Albrecht materials emphasize question format and analysis. Nor do they address the question of the **substance of survey items**. Chris Parsons (McComb) and I developed CANAID (Computer Assisted Needs Assessment Instrument Design) as a tutorial and job aid for figuring out what questions to ask and for prompting *appropriate* questions for the specific study. If you like the conceptualization presented in this book, then you'll like this short program. Lamentably, CANAID is available only for the Apple II+ and Apple IIe.

Another computer based resource for TNA is THINKTANK by Living Videotext Inc. This is an idea generating and outlining program which can turn the scattered, good ideas of subject matter experts into rational statements of optimals. When attempting to communicate results, it is essential to present clean and clear presentations of ideas in an orderly fashion. The new and jazzier version of THINKTANK is MORE. This program makes movement from ideas to organized ideas to word processor to graphics program even easier. Since we so often want our ideas changed into copy and visuals for reports, MORE is very promising. There are several other idea organization programs available for other computers.

The ods/CONSULTANT^{TM} is another program which aids the training specialist with *computer assisted thinking*. This software for the MacIntosh prompts the user to brainstorm, question, combine and generate scenarios. It teaches about and models rudimentary problem-solving and is probably more appropriate for high school students than for personnel or training professionals. However, if you doubt your creativity and systematic approaches to problem-solving, this program could be useful for you.

Charting and graphing programs are available for every computer. They speed and professionalize your efforts to go from lengthy prose paragraphs full of percentages and numbers to lean visual representations of results in forms like histograms and pie charts. Using such computer-generated graphics to present results is appropriate for supporting written reports and, of course, for enhancing oral presentations.

Here is an example derived from an oral presentation:

We have a problem with our ability to attract and serve minority students. Here are the figures: Just over 6 percent of our students are Hispanic; only 3 percent are black; 5.2 percent are Asian and 1 student in the sample is American Indian. That leaves 82 percent of the students as white, with the vast majority identifying themselves as white females.

How much more potent it would have been to distribute Figure 13.4 and ask the group to study it. You could say:

What immediately gets your attention in this figure? What does it mean to us? What can we do about this?

Step 6. Communicate Tactically. In this chapter we've talked about oral and written communications for the purpose of answering basic questions about the results of front end studies. We've also talked about computer resources for front end study.

The only kind of memo, report, or presentation worth doing is an effective, tactical one. It contributes to the fulfillment of your objectives. It must tell the people who need to know what they need to know—and it must lead them to make the decisions which you are recommending.

Lengthy discussion of effective oral or written skills is beyond the scope of this book. Such skills are prerequisite for our profession; they are tools of the trade on which we depend nearly every hour of every day.

What I am able to do here is to generate a checklist, sort of a simplified heuristic which a trainer can use in thinking about communication about results. Are you planning to communicate about results? Have you just done so? Adjust the following list to your situation.

The Content

☐ Did you explain **why** you are communicating with this source?

☐ Does **everyone** who needs to know now know? Should others hear about these results?

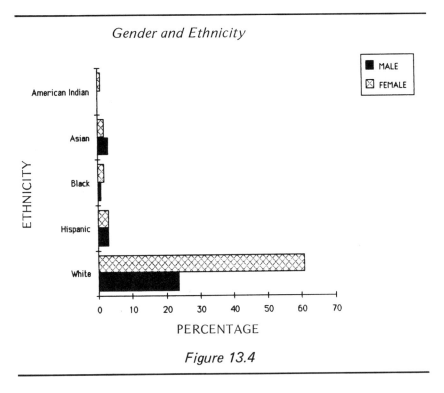

Figure 13.4

☐ Did you answer common and important **questions** about results?

    ☐ 1. *Why* did you carry out this stage of assessment or entire TNA study?

    ☐ 2. *How* did you gather TNA information?

    ☐ 3. *What* did you find out?

    ☐ 4. What does it *mean* for me? us? the company or agency? advanced stages of TNA? the project?

☐ Did you provide an **executive summary** if this is a lengthy report? An executive summary answers these four questions **in only a sentence or two per question.** The emphasis is on *summarizing.*

☐ Did you **support** your findings through appendices and references?

The Format

☐ Did you carefully select an **oral or written** format and its degree of formality and documentation?

☐ Were you as **brief** as you could be, while still answering the questions in the minds of the audience?

☐ Did you give someone who wants to know a little an easy way of doing that? Did you give someone who is very curious and wants lots of details a way of doing that?

☐ Is the **writing** of the **highest quality**? Will it be understood readily?

☐ Was the **presentation** of the **highest quality**? Was it understood readily?

☐ How does or did it **look**? Clear? Clean? Professional? Appropriate?

☐ If the receiver wanted to pass your findings on to higher level management, how much work would have to be done?

☐ Will your recommendations be followed? Why or why not?

☐ How can you do this more effectively next time?

Conclusion

Training and human resources professionals are confronted with several kinds of mandates:

A problem like limp french fries or broken equipment

or

An innovation like a new computer language or policy

or

*A request to **train 'em** on telephone ettiquette just because . . . .*

Trainers, then, with economy of motion and political savvy, must study the situation. That front end study might involve interaction with upper level managers, field supervisors, engineers, telephone operators, hamburger flippers, customers, file clerks, statisticians, computer printouts, personnel assistants, and nutritionists. For specific purposes, we examine, observe, query and survey. And then we cogitate. Do we yet know enough about:

OPTIMALS?

ACTUALS?

FEELINGS?

CAUSE(S)?

SOLUTIONS?

DO WE KNOW WHAT OUR FINDINGS **MEAN**?

It isn't enough *to know*. Training professionals must *use* what they know to act and to make recommendations. Should we train? Will additional education and training make a difference? On what topics? And once we have determined the broad topics, what should be in the course?

This book has been about the tools and techniques which enable us to move from a broad mandate to the use of sources and data to make recommendations. The practice of purpose-based TNA should lead to focused inquiries, sturdier bases for decisions, less training, better training, and happier managers.

Computer Resources

A.S.K.
Albrecht and Associates
P.O. Box 99097
San Diego, CA 92109

THINKTANK
Living Videotext Inc.
2432 Charleston Rd.
Mountain View, CA 94043

SYNTHESIS
Bauer and Associates
210 East Huron
Ann Arbor, Michigan 48104

STATWORKS
Cricket Software
3508 Market
Philadelphia, PA 19104

STATVIEW   STATFAST
Brainpower   2832 East 10th No. 4
24009 Ventura   Tulsa, OK 74104
Calabasas, CA 91302

                                      CANAID
SPSS/PC   3866 Belmont
444 N. Michigan Avenue   San Diego, CA 92116
Chicago, IL 60611

                                      ods/CONSULTANT
STATPAC   ODS Inc.
6500 Nicollet Ave. S.   1011 E. Touhy Ave., Ste 535
Minneapolis, MN 55423   Des Plaines, IL 60018

Resources

Beaudin, B.P., and Dowling, W.D. (1985). Data Collection Methods Used to Determine Training Needs in Business and Industry. *Performance and Instruction*, *24*(8), 28-30.

Cummings, O.W. (1985). Comparison of Three Algorithms for Analyzing Questionnaire-Type Needs Assessment Data to Establish Need Priorities. *Journal of Instructional Development*, *8*(2), 11-16.

Derryberry, A., and Rossett, A. (March 1986). A Survey of Aspiring Educational Technologists. *Educational Technology*, *26*(3), 9-15.

Gordon, J. (1985). Computers in Training. *Training*, *22*(10), 54-66.

Karweit, N., and Meyers, E.D. (1983). Computers in Survey Research. In P.H. Rossi, J.D. Wright, A.B. Anderson (Eds.). *Handbook of Survey Research* (pp. 379-414). Orlando, FL: Academic Press.

Misanchuk, E.R. (1982). *The Analysis of Multi-Component Training Needs Data*. A paper presented at the Annual Meeting of the Association for Educational Communications and Technology, Dallas, Texas.

Misanchuk, E.R. (1984). Analysis of Multi Component Educational and Training Needs. *Journal of Instructional Development*, *7*(1), 28-33.

Oppenheimer, R.J. (1982). An Alternative Approach to Assessing Management Development Needs. *Training and Development, 36*(3), 72-76.

Spitzer, D. (1981). Analyzing Training Needs. *Educational Technology, 21*(11), 36-7.

Zemke, R., and Gunkler, J. (1985). Managing by Micro: A Software Review. *Training, 22*(9), 39-C48.

INDEX

AUTHOR INDEX

293